THE DROPOUT
Causes and Cures

THE DROPOUT
Causes and Cures

by
Lucius F. Cervantes
With the assistance of Grace Platts Husted

Ann Arbor
The University of Michigan Press

To Dr. William C. Loring, Jr.

Contents

Introduction and Rationale

1. THE NEW MINORITY

Give me your tired, your poor,
Your huddled masses yearning to breathe free,
The wretched refuse of your teeming shore,
Send these, the homeless, tempest-tossed, to me:
I lift my lamp beside the golden door.
(Inscription on base of the Statue of Liberty)

For several centuries our country has boasted to other countries: "Give me . . . your poor, Your huddled masses . . . The wretched refuse of your teeming shore." Today the United States is itself creating its own "wretched refuse," its own disadvantaged minority, within the "golden door" of its own "teeming shore." The country which for three centuries welcomed the rejected minorities of foreign shores and provided them with rich opportunities within an affluent and free society is now amassing its own native minority which will have but the slightest chance of integration within the economy of a free society. At the same time that the United States is proving itself the assimilator of racial and ethnic "unassimilables" there appears on the economic horizon the growing figure of a new minority which well may prove unassimilable.

It seems quite plausible that the minority of tomorrow—the high school dropouts—will have more difficulty climbing out of the basement of their poverty than had the minorities of the past. The evidence of the future economic impasse for the educationally deficient youth may be grasped by a casual glance at the want ads section of a daily newspaper. What job is available to the youth without a high-school diploma? There are many positions open for engineers, teachers, social workers, counsellors, opticians, secretaries, skilled labor, technicians of all types; where are the massive ads of previous decades calling for farm hands, assembly-line hands,

1

construction hands, packing hands, wrapping hands, digging hands, railroad-laying hands, elevator-operator hands, the millions of "hands" that were once needed in a pre-automation society? The ads are no more, for frequently the jobs themselves are no more. The ineluctable drive of the age of automation to replace uneducated workers by sophisticated machines is destined to make the uneducated of tomorrow the social pariah and community reject.

More poignant than the want ads are the feature articles that are now appearing with disconcerting frequency. The following is a common enough example of the evidence that points to the social unassimilability of the new minority:

Jobs for Low Skill Workers
Fast Becoming Thing of Past

Climb from Poverty Nearly
Impossible for Those with
Poor Education

"It is harder to climb out of poverty today than at any time in the nation's history. In the modern labor market, an unskilled worker is almost as obsolete as a dinosaur." Charles DeLargy, area manager, Missouri Division of Employment Security.

In the heart of St. Louis's downtown poverty area, a young laborer with a pregnant wife stared dully at an eviction notice.

"I've looked for work, any kind of work, for months now," he said. "But without a high school diploma, nobody will hire me. When we have to leave here, I don't know where we will go. No one wants a family with an unemployed father and four children under school age."

"Automation is steadily wiping out the jobs done by low-skill men who want 'any kind of work,'" Charles DeLargy said. "Ditch diggers, elevator operators, pill packers, street cleaners, and bowling pin setters are rapidly becoming as much of the past as lamplighters. But in former times, men in such occupations could hope to live a decent, frugal life, even raise and educate a family.

"Now employers won't hire anyone they think cannot advance. For instance, an investment firm here wants a mail clerk, but a mail clerk with a college education. Obviously the company is looking forward to the day when a machine may do the work of that clerk. They want someone of junior executive potential." The manager said that a high school education is the minimum educational requirement for almost any steady job today. "For example, here is an opening for a bottle washer at $1.25 an hour," he said, "but only for a high school graduate. Here's another—a factory wants a man to load and unload crates and fill orders for $1.50 an hour. But notice the stipulation, 'Must have high school education and be able to use figures.' "

DeLargy said that even a high school graduate, if without experience or special skills, has few job opportunities these days. He called St. Louis vocational training opportunities "very inadequate."

"The unskilled high school graduate at least can become a clerk, a firemen or a policeman," he said. "But I shiver when I think of the low median educational level between Park and St. Louis Avenues. For someone without a high school diploma the going is very rough indeed, especially for workers over 45." He said that a bright, alert youth without much education could sometimes find employment as a busboy in a drive-in restaurant, but generally only for the summer months. Girls could work as waitresses or domestics. Other seasonal employment was chicken plucking and yard work paying from $1 to $1.25 an hour.

But even for these occupations at least eight years of schooling is needed. The manager explained that about 40,000 functional illiterates within the city limits had practically no chance to get jobs.

DeLargy said that in past slack employment periods, his office used to send unemployed workers to the Missouri Bootheel to chop cotton or pull weeds.

"But the mechanical cotton picker knocked that out," he said. "What's more, now flocks of geese are used for the weeding the humans used to do. You don't have to pay geese anything and you can eat them at the end of the growing season."

The manager said that the mechanical cotton picker and other forms of automation have sent thousands of lowskill agricultural workers to seek jobs in St. Louis.

"That's one reason 40 percent of our jobless are semiskilled and unskilled workers competing for about 6 percent of the total jobs. Professional and technical workers make up only about 4 percent of our job seekers, though almost a quarter of available jobs are in this category," he said.[1]

This annotated case history of the healthy young laborer in the heart of one of our city's downtown poverty areas serves as a paradigm of our unemployed minority of tomorrow. The questions that were pertinent to yesterday's minorities are irrelevant, however, in analyzing why a young, healthy, and alert laborer cannot find a job. Is it a time of depression or of prosperity? It so happens that this is a time of unparalleled prosperity—but the question is not pertinent, for even in a time of peak employment he cannot obtain a job of any kind. Is he Negro or white? It so happens that he is Caucasian but that is of little import. Is he Jew, or Catholic, or Protestant, or religiously unaffiliated? It so happens he is Protestant, but that question is completely without relevance to the situation. Is he Irish, or Russian, or Puerto Rican? It so happens he is English, but his nationality has nothing to do with his inability to obtain a position. The only variable that is of decisive importance is that he is without a high-school education. The invisible mark of Cain is upon this outcast's brow simply because he has not fulfilled certain ill-defined and varying academic and nonacademic qualifications that would have made him eligible for a certain piece of vellum embossed with the approving signature of some unknown high-school principal. Such a signature puts upon each recipient not only a sign of academic accreditation and social approval but a symbol of economic solvency. It is the lack of this accreditation that even today is segregating a segment of our population from full social and economic citizenship. It is our contention that within the decade this slight segment of social outcasts will begin to accumulate to such a proportion that historical parallels will be found only in the Roman Empire, Spartacan slave, and European proletarian conditions of previous eras. It was Professor Norbert Wiener, the reputed father of cybernetics, who darkly prophesied:

> Automation will create an unemployment situation which will make the thirty's seem like a pleasant joke, because the automatic machine is the precise economic equivalent of slave labor.[2]

Early in the 1960's it was already apparent that the dropout of the future would not survive in an automated economy. When James Bryant Conant reported that in our depressed slums as many as 70 percent of the youth who were dropouts were unemployed, he

had read the writing on the wall. They were doomed. The can-
cerous phenomenon of the unemployed hordes of dropouts seemed
destined to spread throughout the body politic. Even the highly
optimistic "Manpower Report of the President" of 1964 grimly
prognosticated "the inadequately educated and ill-trained school
dropouts are likely to form the nuclear of the future hard-core
unemployed." [3] For a decade the unemployment rate had hovered
near the 5 and 6 percent marks. More revealing was the gathering
black cloud that, though there was little or no unemployment
among the well-educated, the poorly educated were having difficulty
holding jobs or even getting them. Throughout the country teen-
age dropouts had the astounding rate of 26 percent unemployment—more than twice the rate of other teen-agers in the labor
market and four or five times as large as that of the general unemployment rate.

Secretary of Labor W. Willard Wirtz stated that the inability
of our economy to absorb the dropout is "one of the most explosive
social problems in the nation's history." We accept the analysis but
before any basic therapy may be initiated we must carefully
diagnose the disease. We would know the genesis of the social pressures and situational inadequacies that produce this autochthonous
new minority known as the "Dropouts."

There are two armies of youth which have recently sprung up
in our society. One is the army of the Peace Corps. The other is the
army of the Dropouts. How can youth with such different destinies
spring from the same soil, the same neighborhoods, and even from
the same families? It is to the second army that we turn our attention.

As of this writing there is no comprehensive work which strives
to present in nontechnical language an original research study sustained by broader scientific findings concerning the origin and des-
tiny of this variant breed of teen-agers. These youth are not confined
to our slums. They interpenetrate the total class structure. Whether
we live on suburban Winchester Drive or on slum area Lincoln
Street, we can say that the dropouts have originated in our own
homes, in our own neighborhoods, in our own schools. They are
among us but, as marginal discards, are becoming less like the rest
of us. What are the perplexing social causes and cures for this rising
army of the coming proletariat?

2 . PREVIOUS RESEARCH

There is a growing library of books, articles, research monographs, and films on the problem of the dropout.[4] The initiative in this drive to understand the situation is being taken by the Federal Government, the National Committee for Children and Youth, the National Committee on Employment of Youth, the Ford Foundation, and various public and private educational institutions, foundations, societies, and boards of education. If one name and one phrase were to be singled out of the thousands of individuals engaged in work on the problem and the millions of words written on the topic, Dr. James B. Conant would be the name and his dramatic phrase "Social Dynamite" would be the words that seem most apt in synthesizing the proportions of the dropout problem.

During the past ten years the present author and Dr. Carle C. Zimmerman of Harvard have been engaged in a study of the influence of the extended family of orientation upon youth's academic achievement. "The Friend-Family System" was the term given to that familial setting usually composed of the ego family and the constellation of three or four close friend-families that "successful" [5] families gathered about themselves to form a homogeneous social system.[6] Our most recent work, *Successful American Families*,[7] reports on a comprehensive survey in six metropolitan areas of high-school graduates' families and their friends. This study of 54,233 families reached the conclusion that "no matter what circumstances—biological, physical, environmental, social—make children run afoul of the laws, good, similar, intimate friend-families around the home . . . help prevent these circumstances from getting out of hand. These friends also help to keep the children interested in life achievement through school and make for better husband-wife relations within the home."

The Zimmerman-Cervantes conclusion was derived from statistical correlations based on questionnaire data. Such statistical correlations, although impressive, are not adequate in assaying the personality and environmental factors which differentiate the dropout from the stayin. The present Cervantes-Husted research is designed to examine, in an explorative fashion, both the sociocultural and psychodynamic factors involved in withdrawal from the academic milieu. The reasons this specific area of research was selected for investigation are: (1) it is in direct line with the emphasis and direction of the Cervantes-Zimmerman research of the past decade, (2) the need for empirical and primary data with respect to early school leavers, (3) the growing national and international concern over the high incidence of withdrawals from the secondary educational process, (4) the direct relationship between rates of school withdrawals and such social disorganization as unemployment and delinquency, (5) the lack of other primary and comprehensive research in the area.

3. PURPOSE AND METHODS OF THIS RESEARCH

The goal of this study is to investigate, analyze, and elaborate upon the social background, "influential others," and personality characteristics of three hundred youths, half of whom continued their education at least to graduation from high school and half of whom dropped out of high school. The final chapter presents a summary of causes and recommended cures.

a) Areas of Investigation

In order to reduce the broad purposes and goals of the study to manageable empirical proportions we have divided the research into six general areas of investigation:

(1) *The Nuclear Family:* This division focuses upon the structure, dynamics, and emotional climate of the family into which the teen-age respondent was born.

(2) *The Friend-Family System:* The nuclear ego family—the family of orientation—gathers about itself a small number of close family friends. This area of investigation ascertains the existence, function, and thrust of the informal social system which serves as the environmental, developmental sac in which the youth was nurtured and brought to term.

(3) *The Peer Group:* This investigation is on the type and influence of the teen-ager's teen-age friends. More specifically we inquire whether the youth's personal friends are parentally approved or disapproved, and, consequently, whether these friends become integrated with or isolated from the ego family's influence. The heterosexual youth culture is examined and analyzed.

(4) *School Experiences:* The respondent's general academic and occupational orientation is investigated.

(5) *Thematic Apperception Test Materials:* A selection of the protocols and the conclusions derived from the administering of the

TAT's to the matched pairs of dropout and stayin youth are presented.

(6) *Recommendations for the Alleviation of the Dropout Situation.*

b)   General Hypotheses

On the basis of previous research and insights of the general literature on the dropout, more than fifty specific hypotheses were drawn up to be tested by the present study. In very general terms they can be stated as follows:

(1) *The Family of the Dropout:* The dropout is reared in a family which has less solidarity, less primary relatedness, and less paternal influence than does the family in which the graduate is reared.

(2) *The Friend-Family System:* The dropout is brought up in a family which has fewer close friends and fewer "problem-free" friends than does the family in which the graduate is brought up.

(3) *The Peer Group:* The dropout's personal friends will be typically not approved by his parents. The resulting "independent youth culture" of the dropout will be in sharp contrast to the youth culture of the graduate whose friends are parentally approved and thus integrated with the adult culture.

(4) *School Experiences:* The dropout was in trouble at school when he terminated his education and was but slightly involved in any school-related activities throughout his academic career.

(5) *Thematic Apperception Test Protocols:* Our hypothesis is that the phantasy life of the dropout as manifested by the TAT is more characterized by unrestrained Id themes and that of the graduate more characterized by restrained superego themes. The youth culture of the dropout will prove to be a culture of revolution, aggression, frustration, and protest; in the words of Conant, it will be found to be "explosive.... It is social dynamite."

c)   Sources of Data: Sampling

In the early stages of the formulation of the research design, it became apparent that a pure random sample was both impractical and undesirable. The heart of the dropout problem is encased in the blue-collar metropolitan area. This area would be our prime target.

In lieu of a random sample, a "matched" sample was developed. The design of the matched sample was that each pair of respondents, one of whom was a dropout and the other a stayin, would be of the same sex, age, I.Q., attend the same school, and have the same general socioeconomic background. Since both the dropout and stayin would be processed with the identical questions, the salient factors of their differential achievement would more likely become evident. This matched sample technique seemed more productive of meaningful results than would have been yielded by a random sample in which every segment of society would have an equal chance of representation. Our relatively small sample could not support a broader spectrum of divergencies as would have been represented had we included the Negro slums and the white suburbs.

d) *Instruments of Research*

The primary research instrument used in the collection of data was an interview schedule (see Appendix I). After several revisions of the questions based on pretest data from high school potential dropouts, the interview was completed and a pilot study was run. A number of weaknesses became apparent and the necessary revisions were made.

A secondary and supplementary instrument was the questionnaire which had been the basis of the research findings of Zimmerman and Cervantes in *Successful American Families*. It was revised and printed in forms applicable in one edition to the graduate and another edition to the nongraduates (see Appendix II).

A third instrument was the Thematic Apperception Test as developed by Dr. Henry A. Murray and the staff of the Harvard Psychological Clinic. This test was administered to the one hundred respondents in New Orleans and Boston, but not to the two hundred respondents in St. Louis, Omaha, Denver, and Los Angeles.

The field work was done by one of the team of three social researchers. Most interviews were prearranged by telephone. The names, addresses, telephone numbers, pertinent background information, and matching had been supplied through the highly cooperative offices of the various school superintendents. It was found through trying experience that the dropouts had to be tracked down individually. They were to be interviewed, if at all, only on their own terms and in their own territory. No matter how many letters, cards, or phone calls were invested asking them to come to some central depot as a school, or university, or library, no true dropouts would make their appearance at any of these places—only those would come who intended to return to school and such respondents could not be termed as either dropouts or stayins. The dropout had to be interviewed in his own locale—either his home or at some community social center. The stayins were commonly interviewed at their school, though some of them, too, were interviewed in their homes or at social centers such as a "Y," or the local "community center." Conditions of privacy were maintained no matter where the interview was conducted. Every interview was tape recorded.

The average interview lasted about thirty-five minutes. It is the considered judgment of the interviewers that good rapport was established in almost every case and there is no substantive reason to question the truthfulness of the responses. In various instances different individuals reported on an identical situation. A parent, a teacher, a counselor, a brother or sister of the respondent might each report on, say, the authority structure within the respondent's home. It might be found that the male respondent had said his father was highly authoritarian or neglectful, while the other gave a slightly different version. Such discrepancies are inevitable and if it were not so we would not be obtaining the information we were primarily interested in: the enveloping social system of the respondent as perceived and internalized by himself. This is a study of the world of emergent youth as reported and seen by themselves. The opportunity to review his life in an orderly, permissive, confidential, and impressive manner (the interviewer's university connections and the use of a tape recorder to take in every golden word for some type of "book" were assurances that this transaction was impressive) provided the respondent with a unique opportunity to "go over it all" in a cathartic experience. Not infrequently the subjects remarked that they had found this "unloading" one of the most enjoyable experiences that they had ever known. Their "unloading" has likewise provided us with an unforgettable experience.

In simple terms the purpose of this study is to investigate the question: Why do American youth drop out of high school?

The research was subsidized by The Warren Benevolent Fund, Boston, Massachusetts.

CHAPTER ONE

The Family of the Dropout

When theorist Sigmund Freud singled out the Oedipal situation as the crucial matrix of human development he was in effect stating that the nuclear family of father-mother-offspring is the matrix and prime determinant of human personality. However much theoreticians would later qualify Freud's ideology and methodology, there is still general agreement in the field that the family orientation is of *prime importance* in the etiology of psychic development and distortion.

It is ironic, however, that in our field of academic achievement there is such a broad discrepancy between the findings of the theorists and the plans of the actionists. The social theorists point out that the family is of maximum importance in the development or lack of development of youth. But the social actionists—chiefly educationists and governmental social engineers—minimize or eliminate from consideration the nuclear family in their plans for the development and direction of the youth they hope will not become dropouts.

1. THE PRIMARY GROUP AS A CONCEPTUAL FRAMEWORK

To reduce to manageable empirical proportions the general hypothesis that the family background of the dropout is in some way different from the family background of the graduate it is necessary to single out some testable variables. And these variables must be capable of incorporation within a theoretical field of reference.

The theoretical field or conceptual scheme that has been adopted in this study is that of the primary group. The reason we adopted the primary group as our conceptual model is that the leaders in the field of the social sciences—from the earlier times of Durkheim, Cooley, LeBon, Figgis, and Brook Adams to the later times of Parsons, Merton, Homans, Festinger, Lazarsfeld, Stouffer,

Newcomb, Sherif, Allport, Broom, and Selznick—have all used it as
a base of operation. By adopting the primary group conceptual
scheme we were able to tap into clearly defined variables that allowed for concise interview questions whose answers could readily
be translated into the understandable language of an existing body
of theory.

Reference group theory, small group theory, communication
theory, organizational analysis, studies in the family, mental health,
stratification, consensus, social disorganization, deviant behavior,
race and ethnic theory, psychiatry, and social psychology do not
move far from the pivotal concept of the primary group. In no small
degree modern behavioral science may be called a dialogue between
the researcher and some concept allied with that of the "primary
group."

The term "primary group" was first used by Charles Horton
Cooley in his 1909 work entitled *Social Organization:*

> By primary groups I mean those characterized by intimate face-
> to-face association and cooperation. They are primary in several
> senses, but chiefly in that they are fundamental in forming the
> social nature and ideas of the individual. The result of intimate
> association, psychologically, is a certain fusion of individualities
> in a common whole, so that one's very self, for many purposes at
> least, is the common life and purpose of the group. Perhaps the
> simplest way of describing this wholeness is by saying that it is a
> "we": it involves the sort of sympathy and mutual identifi-
> cation for which "we" is the natural expression. One lives in the
> feeling of the whole and finds the chief aim of his will in that
> feeling.[1]

It was Cooley who termed the primary group as "the nursery of
human nature." The importance of primary relations lies in the
fact that they give rise to the essentially human experiences so that
human nature may be said to be formed or created in primary
relations.

Three characteristics of the primary group.—Broom and Selznick give us the three testable characteristics of the primary relationship which is the base of the primary group.[2] We have utilized
this division throughout the study. A primary group is characterized
by relationships that are personal, have a depth of intercommunication, give personal satisfactions.

The meaning of these three characteristics will become more

explicit as this report continues but we may give a preliminary guideline analysis of them before embarking on the more descriptive materials:

Personal: Primary relations are personal rather than impersonal. The response in a primary relationship is to a whole person rather than to segments or partial roles of a person. In the primary relation the participants interact as unique and total individuals. The relationship is nontransferrable. The more transferrable the relationship is—as a relationship to a doctor, or lawyer, or salesman, or bus driver—the less can the relationship be called primary. The individual feels accepted as a total person.

Depth of intercommunication: In the ideal, primary group communication is deep and extensive. There are fewer limits placed on both the range and mode of communication. Spontaneity, rapport, and emotional commitments are ready concomitants of this interchange. In such a friendly milieu, similarities of attitudes, values, and behavior tend to develop; there is a sense of "we-ness" —of belonging together and sharing a common identity. Primary relations, though not excluding hostility, cannot subsist on antagonism.

Personal satisfactions: The first two characteristics—acceptance as a person and depth of intercommunication—give rise to the third characteristic—the derivation of personal satisfactions which become paramount. Individuals enter into primary relationships because such relations contribute directly to their happiness, emotional satisfaction, and well-being. Because direct personal satisfactions are gained under a variety of circumstances, the primary relation is not a utilitarian means to further ends but is valued in itself.

These chief characteristics of the primary relation—mutual acceptance as a total person, deep intercommunication, and personal satisfactions—provide us with testable variables when trying to ascertain how the families of the youth who discontinue their high school education differ from the families of the youth who continue their high school education until they receive their diploma.

a)   Acceptance as a Total Person

The first criterion of the primary group to be tested is whether the members accept each other as persons. "To feel accepted," "to be a member of the team," "to feel that you belong" are ways of expressing the resulting psychic state.

Three identical questions were asked of each of the teen-age respondents concerning this first criterion of acceptance of each other. "Would you say that your *whole* family both understands and accepts each other?" tapped the general condition of family understanding and acceptance. The following two questions became more specific as to whether the teen-ager felt that he personally was understood by his family and whether he felt that he understood and accepted them.

CASE HISTORIES

In response to the question: "Would you say that your *whole* family both understands and accepts each other?" the following replies were elicited:

Dropouts

"Very little. Like before you all came. We was having a big argument. My sister keeps dogging me. When I come in she tells me to get out or go to work or something like that. She is stupid. She don't understand me. And my mother doesn't understand me. She just don't have time to understand me. She's got to be worried with my brothers and sisters and I can take care of myself. I can look after myself and make my own decisions and all. . . . My mother doesn't try to understand me. Like when an argument happens. That's the main thing. When an argument happens I think I'm right. The reason why the arguments usually happen is because my brothers start picking on me and I start nagging back and when my mother comes in they tell her what I did and they don't never tell the circumstances and it always builds up a bad argument right there. I just think everybody is against me. . . . No, she doesn't encourage me. In high school I did all my homework and all my lessons by myself. I got mad and said I was going to get an apartment by myself and get a job or go into the service, that's what I was planning on." (Dropout Edward L., # 102, IQ 93, New Orleans)

"No, I don't think my father ever tried to understand me. He always favored my little brother and my middle sister and Mom had to always stick up for me and my older sister." (Dropout Sherry W., # 236, IQ 107, Omaha)

"We don't understand each other. My brother and I don't even talk. I ran away from home and stayed with the family of my girl friend." (Dropout Carlos H., # 304, IQ 102, Denver)

"All of us kids don't like my dad too much because he is disabled and just wants us to hurry up and get out of school. When we brought homework home instead of letting us do it the way we learned he wanted us to do it the way he had learned and we got all confused. . . . I don't think my mother understands me as good as she should but more than my dad does." (Dropout Earl C., # 320, IQ 97, Denver)

"The rest of the family seems to get along well but I'm sort of aft now. I haven't got along with my parents for sometime now. I have left." (Dropout Mike H., # 504, IQ 114, Boston)

"Well, my mother and father are divorced so they must not have understood each other. The kids don't much either. I don't think they understand why I should smoke and that I'm old enough to go to dances. My mother can't understand why I should be out so much with the fellows. I feel I'm giving her thirty dollars a week and that she's getting another thirty bucks from ADC. . . . I'm acting like a man. I help support the family, but they still consider me a child." (Dropout Larry K., # 526, IQ 98, Boston)

"Sometimes. Sometimes, I don't know what they are doing. They just start talking about something and then they change it and it leaves me blank. I know what they are saying, but it don't make no sense." (Dropout Barbara M., # 530, IQ 98, Boston)

"I don't feel close to any of the family. If I could go overseas I sure would." (Dropout Joseph S., # 532, IQ 110, Boston)

Graduates
"They know me to a T, I can see that. But every once in a while we have an argument. But if I think I'm wrong I know enough to apologize." (Graduate Bertha D., # 127, IQ 97, New Orleans)

"All the time." (Graduate Georgene A., # 209, IQ 105, Omaha)

"Yes, my parents understand me even on such things as cars, dates, and the time to get in. They set the time and I think that this is right." (Graduate Dan F., # 235, IQ 98, Omaha)

"Yes, my mother and father both go to work in the morning and my brother and sisters and I have our certain jobs to do in the morning to clean the house up." (Graduate José, Spanish-American, # 303, IQ 111, Denver)

"I think we just about have to. There are seven of us and our mom and dad. We fight a little but I think that's normal." (Graduate Rita, Spanish-American, # 311, IQ 91, Denver)

"I think so. I think maybe they understand me better than I understand myself." (Graduate John Z., # 551, IQ 110, Boston)

"Well, we have a lot of fun during the holidays when everyone is home. Like we'll sit down and razz everyone and everyone has fun. It's all right that way but when something goes wrong everyone gets on you. Like if you stay out and get into a little trouble everyone is on top of your back except your closest brother. My brother Tim —he's actually two years older than I am. He's my friend. We're pretty good pals. And one of my sisters is better than the other one. My sister Mary—if anything breaks she always blames me. And my sister Kate—well, I can just go over to her house and have a good time. Things sometimes go wrong in our family and since I'm the littlest they blame me. Like when the toaster broke they said I pushed it off, and I know I didn't push it off, and then my father said he pushed it off. He woke up in the morning and he twisted it suddenly, and it fell. After everyone calmed down he brought home a new toaster. . . . In my freshman year in high school I had a job and saved up $15.00 and my brother gave me the other $30.00 to buy skates. And I've been skating ever since. And no one else has, except my brother Timmy. I follow him in socializing. He's got a lot of friends. He's a funny kid and I try to be the same way." (Graduate James H., # 559, IQ 98, Boston)

SUMMARY

The responses that the three hundred youths gave to the question "Would you say that your *whole* family both understands and accepts each other?" were scored by the panel of three social scientists on a five-point scale of "understanding and acceptance within the home." The results are presented in Table 1 in percentage distributions.[3]

Our first attempt to ascertain the depth of "primariness" in the families of the dropouts and the graduates was decisive in its results. Of the dropouts, four out of five (43% + 41%) perceive their families as understanding and accepting each other either "very little" or "little." Of the graduates, four out of five (20% + 24% + 38%) perceive their families as understanding and accepting each other "moderate," "much," or "very much." The overwhelming majority of the

Table 1.—Understanding and acceptance within the home
(in percentages)

	Very Little	Little	Moderate	Much	Very Much
Dropouts	43	41	9	5	2
Graduates	3	15	20	24	38 *

* Percentage distributions are rounded after all calculations have been completed. $D = .439$; $X^2(2df) = 130.28$; $p < .001$ (significant beyond the .001 level).

graduates see their families as accepting each other as complete persons; the overwhelming majority of the dropouts see their families as failing to accept each other as complete persons.

"HOW DO YOU FIT INTO THE PICTURE?"

But this question does not adequately test the linkage between the family's pattern of personal acceptance and the teen-ager himself. Is the youth, in replying about the emotional interrelationships that exist within his family, likewise describing the type of relationships that exists between him and his family? When he states that the members of his family accept each other very well, is he implying that they all accept him too? It is quite possible to conceive of cases where all the members of a family understand and accept one another but the teen-ager feels completely misunderstood and rejected. It was for this reason that the question concerning the climates of acceptance among the family members was followed up by the more specific question of "How do you fit into the picture? Would you say that your family both understands and accepts *you?*"

In black-and-white print such a personal and delicate question to a sensitive teen-ager respondent seems brutal. As a matter of fact, within the interview situation there was no hesitation whatsoever on the part of the teen-agers. By the time this question was asked the interview had been operative for about ten minutes and there was now no doubt what the questions were all about. This section dealt with the emotional climate of the family and the young men and women had no doubt as to what was expected of them and they answered this very personal question with all but a sigh of relief that they now had an opportunity to express themselves confidentially on a question which is a tender area in everyone's psyche.

Their tender sensitivities of this question did not prevent them from replying as to whether they really felt "at home" when they were at home.

Rather than take smatterings of various typical responses to this question we can take a rather complete interview which, however situationally atypical, does describe very clearly how a youth can belong to a solid middle class family that is itself an adequate primary group but come to feel that he is neither understood nor accepted by the rest of the family. This case could be categorized under the heading of "Unresolved Oedipal Situation." It records the autobiographical outpourings of an extremely handsome, muscular, granite-faced, chiseled-featured, blonde-haired youth who was interviewed in his cheap basement apartment that he had established several blocks away from the commodious middle class home of his parents. Here he lives withdrawn, pouting in his tent as a modern Achilles, away from but not uninterested in the scene of the emotional battles of his loved ones. The excessive length of his reply is due to the fact that as in so many of the cases he found the interview situation a perfect opportunity to "unload" all of his life's pent-up troubles and frustrations and explanations into the willing ear of the interviewer and the receptive microphone of the ceaseless tape recorder.

My Mother

"My mother was the motherly type but she didn't want to have a lot of people hanging onto her skirt like a lot of people do. She let everybody make up their own mind. I think we were all brought up right but some of us decided to go on to college and some, like me, decided to quit. There was always so much to talk about in the family I think it was better for me to go outside and walk with friends. . . ."

My Dad

"My mother made most of the decisions. My dad is kind of a quiet mouse. He carries them out and if he doesn't like them he may argue a little bit but it doesn't do any good. . . ."

Myself

"I was always shy. I would just get embarrassed and leave the room. I think it comes from home. It's something all kids go through but I just didn't outgrow it. I think in the last few years I have outgrown it a little. I can talk freely with some people and others I can't. I've always had stage fright. It's just lack of self-assurance. I think being between the children in the family had something to do with it."

My Brothers and Sisters

"I think having an older brother and a younger brother ... the younger one and I used to fight all the time and then the big brother used to come over and step in all the time. I'd try to be friends with my big brother and my little brother would come along. It's just that I was left out. It's hard for a mother to make all the kids think that she loves them the same and I just felt pushed aside. I think the real early environment made the difference. I think it makes more difference than people realize and no one can quite pinpoint it. There was a little prejudice in the family against colored people and I kind of always rejected that for some reason. I think I have principle but whether I use it or not is something else. I've been a failure in a lot of things. In school for one thing. It seemed like each one of my brothers and sisters had some kind of talent. Some were good at music or playing an instrument. But I never was good at that or singing. It's not that I couldn't do it. It's just that people told me I couldn't do it and I built up a mental block. Now that I've grown older I've got kind of an attitude that I don't care and then I come to think about it and I do care. I just can't place it. I'm just like a teen-ager: I can't find myself....

"I've had a good life at home. My parents treated me well. In fact I think my mother tried too hard. She has a lot of trouble with her own mind. She is exceptionally intelligent but she had claustrophobia and she is afraid to go out of the building. It's just from nervousness—from bringing up the family and trying so hard. I'm seventeen. I started running around with older people when I was going into my teens and I think that made a lot of difference."

School

"I think the kids my age are a lot better off for they are still in school. It's not that I don't like school. I went back and had a B-plus average but it seems I just quit trying. I had a girl friend and I think a lot of things I do are not because I want to do them but because she wants me to. I just do them for her. I guess I want my cake and eat it too.... I wanted to go into the service a while back because I took the GCT Test and I came out with third year of college. Then I took all kinds of tests and all I would have to do was sign my name and I would have had a high school education but my mother figured that I wasn't grown up enough and with my hot temper—I do have a little bit of a temper—that I would blow up and get mad at one of the sergeants and get a dishonorable discharge or something because I might get mad and reject authority. I'm not blaming my folks, but them and quite a few people have made me reject authority. Instead of talking to you they use the stick and I think that is good for some people. But I think for someone that was as sensitive as I was when I was young it isn't too good an idea."

Work

"I didn't finish school because I was working downtown. It was the worst job I ever had. I started working when I was nine years old. Sweeping a barber shop for forty cents a week. But with that forty cents I could pay my way into shows and I just kind of got independent then. I think it's a good idea for a small kid to make some money. Money isn't everything but it certainly has a lot of bearing on a lot of things. It's not that I wanted a lot of money. It's just as I got older I wanted a little more and a little more and my parents didn't give me any money. So I went out and earned it."

"I Always Felt Left Out"

"I don't think anyone in my family was spoiled except for my little brother. It seems he gets everything he wants and Paul and I had to work for it. I don't think it bothered me that my brother got more than I did; at least it didn't seem to bother me. I think my parents felt I was a little more independent than the others and they just let me go a little more so they could help the others more. I always felt left out. But really, I think I needed the time that the others got. But I don't know. My older brother is nineteen and he doesn't have a job. He doesn't do anything and he doesn't even take a girl out. I think there are too many complexes in the family because of an inexperienced psychologist that tried to do too much. My mother took high school psychology and she thinks she really knew it. She is extremely intelligent but she isn't trained enough. She tried so hard to do everything right and I think she has done a real good job because really I don't think I'm too bad but again I'm pretty terrible at times. . . ."

Beer Episode

"One night after work I decided to get a beer and I got drunk. Then I went to the library and got a book to read; I hadn't done that in a long time. But then I would read the book a little and then drink a little and so on. When I drink I lose my temper easy. Things just seemed to be building up and I just had to let it out some way. I guess I could have gone downstairs and hit the wall or something, or I could have cried. But I gave up crying when I was small. So I came home that night and I was feeling pretty good and my mother and father started to pick on me for everything. My mother was like that. I tried to eat something and they started to pick on me because of the way I was eating. I guess my manners weren't too good that night; so I just got up and left the food and something got into my mother and she threw a plate at me and I didn't know what to think. I got all mixed up and turned toward the door but it was locked so I just busted through it and went downstairs to my room and punched a couple of holes in the plasterboard wall. Then they came down and started yelling at me because of that and I felt like having a nervous breakdown. I probably wouldn't have had, but I was shaking all over. I turned my mother around and made her go upstairs and I locked the door and stayed by myself for a while and cried. I just had to let it out somehow. I guess that's why I did all that; things were just building up. Then my brother came down and I felt ashamed of myself, so I packed a suitcase and went over to my brother-in-law's place. I've done that before when I just have to get away from it for a while. I'll stay with someone a couple of nights or get an apartment for a week. But never more than a week. Anyway, I went back to school for a while and worked one day a week. But I knew my brother-in-law would be getting uneasy having me around all the time and he wanted to go deer hunting so I took off school three days and worked for him so he could go hunting. I knew I would have to earn more so I could pay him or so I could get an apartment for a month or so, but I found out apartments weren't so easy to get. So I kept going back to school and acting like I was coming from home and I got along well with everybody. I took care of myself. I have always been able to take care of my clothes so I would look nice. But I just couldn't keep it up. I couldn't afford to do that and go to school and still have my fun. That's one of my troubles. I guess you would say I have champagne tastes. I wanted to take my girl out but I had to take her in a cab and I had a hard time financially. I went to the principal at school but she just didn't like me and I just quit. . . . I think I'll go back to St. Joachim's because it's the only school that I seem to think I can get along in. I have an awful hard time trying to meet people. When a customer comes in I get along fine with him, but as far as finding my place in school I find it hard. I knew there wouldn't be too many people that knew me anymore because I quit once before and went to North. But I like the Catholic education and I thought it would help me. I couldn't just go to any school and become a bookworm. Also, my girl went there and I would like to graduate from the same school. There are a lot of things I seem to want to go back for that I don't remember."

Money

"I think ours is what you would call an average family. I think our family talks things over the same as any other family. My mother and father had several good friends but with seven children in the family they sometimes didn't have money for enough gas to go anywhere. We always had plenty of clothes and enough food and all the necessities but there was never much left over. I think the kids learned to evaluate money more having to work for it. I think that was hard on mother because she worked hard. My father wanted to take her out but she knew there just wasn't enough money."

Delinquency

"Yes, I've had a lot of trouble. I've been in juvenile hall but that's why I think I have something to be proud of, coming out of that all right and after leaving still doing the right thing all the time. I was running around with older people and they just seemed to be forever getting into trouble, but they were the people I liked. It's not that my parents didn't approve of my friends; it's just that we did so many things behind their back like steal from a store. I think a lot of my friends were just like me—they were sensitive or shy. They were just looking for their place and they just wanted to be somebody."

Teachers

"I didn't have any friends among the teachers because just like a little kid I have the attitude that the teachers weren't there to teach you but that they were there to make you learn. This is the attitude that I really regret because they are there to help you and not make you learn. I think teachers are really great and they will help you but I didn't think so then. I thought of them only as authority and I rejected authority.... I've never been able to find a good friend. I've known a lot of people that I like to run around with but some were in school and some were not. I just don't know where to place my values on friendship.... My brother graduated from high school and he didn't even try. I don't think he is real intelligent and I don't think he could make a go of it in college. Some sort of job would be the best thing for him but he is just so particular that nothing suits him.... I do think he likes girls and he wants to seem rough and he's just nothing but a skinny little runt and he wants to be tough. I think that makes a lot of difference: he just wants to be more than he is. He likes to go out with girls but he says he doesn't and he puts on a front. I think a front runs through the whole family. It's just that I had to cover up something."

"I Have Some Kind of Complex"
"It comes, I think, from my shyness and I have some kind of complex and it has just twisted me up. It's just so deep I can't dig it out. Maybe it's something I'm proud of. I used to be above myself in religion and that's where I have really fallen off. When I was little that was all I lived for. I'm just weaker now.... I'm gullible. I can be influenced awful easily and I'm not really so independent." (Dropout Dan Y., # 324, Age 17, IQ 123, Denver)

That an intelligent, healthy, handsome, young son of a highly respectable middle class family should be able to summarize his childhood by saying: "It's just that I felt left out.... It seems when I was little I was always left out," and then repeat the same feeling of rejection as characteristic of his whole life with his family: "I always felt left out. But really, I think I needed the time that the others got," is a moving thought. But when it is understood that four out of five (79%) of the dropouts had the same feelings of rejection by their families as did Dropout Dan Y. of Denver, we come to realize that his feeling of "not belonging," "not being one of the family... really" is characteristic only of the dropouts, for more than four out of five (84%) of the graduates felt they were understood and accepted by their families.[4]

"And Would You Say That You Both Understand and Accept Them?"

This next question of the interview was in no way meant to be moralistic and instructional to our teen-age youth who were so cooperatively and even eagerly pouring out their life's histories. As all the other questions it was presented to subserve the academic purpose of ascertaining the statics and dynamics of their situation. That the question did, however, serve an instructional and moralistic purpose was obvious from the repeated reactions of so many of the youth. "Oh, I'd never thought of that," they would remark. The question served as a jolt to the standard egocentric belief that it is always the teen-age self that is misunderstood and never misunderstanding. It gave them pause in that it opened up the possibility that parents may be misunderstood and underappreciated by their teen-age children. Relations between parents and children, some seemed to realize for the first time, may be a two-way rather than a one-way street.

The statistical summary of this third question as to whether the teenager on his part felt that he understood and accepted the other members of his family yield identical results as the previous two. Four out of five (79%) of the dropouts judged themselves as understanding and accepting their families "very little" or "little," while four out of five (82%) of the graduates judged themselves as understanding and accepting their families "moderately," "much," or "very much." [5]

"DID YOUR FAMILY ENCOURAGE AND HELP YOU IN YOUR PLANS
FOR A GOOD JOB OR IN YOUR SCHOOL PLANS?"

A person engaged in a social system that is characterized by the "we" feeling of integration and solidarity demanded by the ideal primary group will subordinate to some significant extent his own interests to those of the other members of the group and will in turn feel supported by their encouragement and assistance.

Group integration has been defined in operational terms as "the degree to which units of a social system are oriented toward optimizing rewards for other units of the system." [6]

It was hypothesized that "the graduate will perceive himself as having received more encouragement and help in his educational and occupational plans than will the dropout." This hypothesis was validated,[7] but there were some surprises. Four out of ten of the graduates felt that their family had given them "very little" or "little" encouragement and help in their educational plans. As they saw it, their academic success was due all but completely to their own efforts and not to their family's assistance. Less surprising was the finding that nine times as many dropouts as graduates (18% vs 2%) felt that their parents pushed too much by pressuring and nagging them. When a teen-ager is doing poorly in his school work both he and his parents become sensitized, vulnerable, and adjust to the situation by various defensive and offensive techniques that prove exacerbating to all parties involved.

Thus, our data from the responses of the youth on the first criterion of a primary group—the individual feels accepted as a total person—lead us to the conclusion that four out of five of the dropouts do not feel that they are accepted as such and four out of five of the graduates do.

b) Depth of Intercommunication

When Sigmund Freud's famous patient, Anna O., stated: "Doctor, if you would only let me *talk* to you and if I could tell you how my difficulties started, I think we could do something," she precipitated the "talking cure." More than precipitating the "talking cure" of psychoanalysis and the basis of modern psychiatry she underlined the need that everyone has to discuss with and confide in others. Verbal communication is the psychic battering ram that breaks down the barriers prohibiting an individual's integration with the social system surrounding him.

Solitary confinement—the enforced isolation from communication outlets—is recognized by psychologists and prison authorities as being one of the most traumatic experiences to which an individual can be subjected. Few persons can undergo this form of community-imposed torture without disintegrating mentally and physically. Man is a verbalizing animal and deprivation of verbalization outlets tends to render him more animal than man.

Family members likewise can impose forms of solitary confinement upon each other. And the individuals imprisoned within such emotional isolation chambers tend to disintegrate. Our interviews indicate that where intrafamilial communication ceases and sultry silences grow, the probabilities are high that an emotional detonation is in the count-down stage. Where communication between husband and wife has been impaired or destroyed, divorce, desertion, infidelity or domestic absenteeism are not uncommon. When communication between the late teen-ager and his family has been impaired or destroyed the youth will chafe to extricate himself from the unsupportable confinement of emotional isolation. He first seeks family surrogates within his peer group. Later he seeks full-time employment so that he will not be financially dependent upon his family, and finally, he plans to leave such an emotionally unsupportive disciplinary barrack and concentration camp.

Questioning our respondents concerning their families' verbal communication patterns within their homes proved to be a fruitful source of affect-laden responses that sharply discriminated the perceived milieu of the family of the dropout from that of the graduate.

In lining up the responses of the dropouts to parade the fact that there was little family communication within their homes and by marshalling the responses of the stayins in neat counterposition, there is the danger of conveying the impression that there is a completely dichotomous situation: the dropouts all originate in homes that have defective communication systems and the stayins all originate in homes where the human intercommunication system is ideal. Such is not the case. As with all of our variables, so with that of intrafamilial communication, there is a substantial overlapping. Twenty percent of the graduates experience a notable lack of ease of communication within their homes, and 20 percent of the dropouts report that their homes are characterized by adequate or highly agreeable family communication. As Table 2 indicates, the following cases are typical of the replies of the dropout and graduate:

QUESTION 11:

"Does your family talk things over with each other very often?"

Dropouts [8]

"My stepfather and I don't discuss too much what I do. It's mostly my mom. My stepfather takes care of the bills and things like that but he usually doesn't say anything to me." (Dropout Patricia K., # 6, IQ 107, St. Louis)

"If I had any problems mostly I went to my mother but we never really talked things over that much. I guess it was like most families: they love each other but they just don't say it. We had our arguments but we never really disagreed with too many things. . . . There were quite a few things we didn't discuss but I would talk it over with my buddies. My father helped me with a lot of things but I don't think he really influenced me. If I had a decision to make I made it myself. I think I made my own decisions because I didn't and don't feel there is really anybody that I can talk to. I guess I could talk to my father but we sort of fell apart. And as for my brother, we don't really talk over things that are important. I guess I could. . . .

"When I got in all that trouble I didn't feel they accepted me because I felt like I was the black sheep in the family. But I didn't do it to hurt anybody. Just for kicks. Sometimes when I got into trouble it wasn't my fault. I'd go downtown to a show by myself to stay out of trouble and when I came out of the show somebody would start a fight. Trouble just follows me. Wherever I go I know there will be trouble. Since this has happened my father just picks on me and he doesn't pick on Bill—my older brother. He just rides me more than Billy. And why? I don't know. I guess he could forget about it, but I don't know. . . ." (Dropout Jack F., # 146, IQ 100, New Orleans)

"No. Hardly ever. . . . I was living with my father, and we had an argument—it's one of those things—so, I moved to Mom's and she always accused—first, she always accused Dad of running around with other women—which he never did—and then she accused me of stealing and wrecking her car and everything—which I never did. So I got tired of it and left and now I'm living by myself." (Dropout Harlan S., # 228, IQ 105, Omaha)

"No. Never! We all go on our own ways. It's a family but I can't sit down and talk to my father about what I should do. And my brother and I don't even speak. There is no real companionship." (Dropout Carole H., # 304, IQ 102, Denver)

"No. My mother works about eighteen hours a day and she's never home. She manages a restaurant. . . . If I had a problem, like I did two weeks ago, I would go to my ex-girl-friend's mother. When I was going with this girl, her mother was always real understanding. If we stayed out too late, she would sit down and talk it over with us and she always had a real good answer to my questions. So even though I don't run around with the girl anymore, I do see her when I go over to talk to her mother." (Dropout Chris T., # 402, IQ 102, Los Angeles)

Graduates

"Yes. . . . Lately my father talks with me and tells me why he wants me to go to college—why he and my mother definitely want me to try. And explains how it was for him. He quit when he was young and he works for the city—sanitation department. He had a heart attack about three years ago and now he is a watchman for them and I believe he makes only about $65.00 a week. He says there is no advancement for him. He wants me to get a good job." (Graduate John D., # 103, IQ 93, New Orleans)

"At night, at the supper table, or at Sunday dinner when we are all together, we talk things over. . . . Whenever they get free time they just sit at home and relax because my mother teaches school and my dad is a diesel mechanic. And mother goes to college at nights; she studies logic and philosophy. When she first started I got out her book and tried to explain some of it to Captain F. I'm pretty interested in it myself and if I do go to college I plan to study logic and philosophy." (Graduate Frank R., # 115, IQ 100, New Orleans)

"Oh, yes. I have five sisters and two brothers. I'm the oldest and if they have some kind of problem they talk. . . . If we have free time we usually go on a picnic or we stay home and talk. . . . We all understand and accept each other to a pretty high degree because we all respect each other and we love each other and we talk to each other. . . . When I told my father that I want to go on to college to become a lab technician he said he would help me. He only completed his first or second year of high. And my mother only went to eighth grade but she wants me to go all the way." (Graduate Bertha D., # 127, IQ 97, New Orleans)

"Yes, very much. . . . They really do understand me too. They understand that I have feelings of my own and that I know what I want to do." (Graduate Judith B., # 207, IQ 111, Omaha)

"If there is really anything serious we do. I have two other brothers and we all get together and talk. They both go to college at Omaha U." (Graduate Roger B., # 227, IQ 102, Omaha)

"Usually the family will talk things together if it concerns the whole family." (Graduate Susan T., # 243, IQ 120, Omaha)

"My sister and I talk with my mother when we have problems. My mother and my real dad are separated and my stepfather knows I want to talk to him but it's hard. We don't know what to talk about, I guess. But it's easy with my mother. When I told her about a year ago that Rich and I were going steady, she thought we were going to get married. She told me she wanted me to finish high school and she helped me pick the subjects I should take." (Graduate Virginia M., # 337, IQ 94, Denver)

The differences of family background between the dropout and the graduate in intrafamily communication can be seen in Table 2 from the percentage distribution on a five-point scale.

Table 2.—Communication within the home
(in percentages)

	Very Infrequent	Infrequent	Moderate	Frequent	Very Frequent
Dropouts	43	38	11	6	2
Graduates	3	17	20	24	36 *

*Hypothesis: There is less intrafamily communication in the families of the dropouts than in the families of the graduates. $D = .633$; $X^2(2df) = 87.48$; $p < .001$ (significant beyond the .001 level).

The results of Table 2 are decisive. Eighty-one percent (43% + 38%) of the dropouts receive their life's basic orientation in a nuclear family of inadequate intercommunication and 80 percent (20% + 24% + 36%) of the graduates receive their life's basic orientation in a nuclear family of at least adequate intercommunication.

FAMILY COMMUNICATION AND FORMATION OF COMMON VALUES

The frequency of communication within the family group is important because the expression of feelings and beliefs tends to influence the feelings and beliefs of others. Frequency of communication does not guarantee agreement, but it does facilitate and encourage it. Familial intercommunication tends to develop similarities in attitudes and feelings.[9] Constant intercommunication is a catalyst of value-homophyly. In their study of friendship as a social process, Lazarsfeld and Merton developed the thesis that "it is not easy to have a warm personal attachment where there is an opposition of values. This gives rise to a motivated tendency toward the forma-

tion of common values among fast friends. Not only does intimate
social interaction precipitate a deposit of new common values, but
it also converts originally disparate values into common values." [10]

The bridge between the barren island of the ego and the fertile
mainland of the family primary group is communication. It provides
a transaction link between husband and wife, between brothers and
sisters, and between the conflicting interests of parents and children. That this bridge of family communication is more habitually
traveled in the case of the families of the graduates than of the
dropouts is evidenced by the reports of our youthful family par-
ticipant-observers.

c)   Pleasurable Experiences

Closely allied to the level of verbal intercommunication within a
family is its level of shared recreational activities. Enjoyment of
each other's company in a variety of circumstances is the third
characteristic of the primary group. A family that chooses to spend
its leisure hours in each other's company manifests that antagonism
and tension are not a staple of their relationships, but rather that
harmony and mutual enjoyment are. Pleasant cooperation in common enterprises becomes a habit of all the participants.

FAMILY AND LEISURE

In asking our respondents "If your *whole* family had some free time
how would they usually spend it?" we were not primarily interested
in the type of leisure-time activities in which they indulged. General research has already established such data. We were interested
in the frequency of intrafamilial recreational activities presumably
indicative of the pleasure that the members of a family experience
in being with each other under a variety of circumstances. Here are
some typical replies:

Dropouts

"I don't know. I'm not usually here. I'm usually out going around
with the boys. We just go riding or go to the show or go play some
pool. My brothers and sisters usually go to the show and my mother
goes out. My father doesn't live with us; she had to raise us up."
(Dropout Edward L., # 102, IQ 93, New Orleans)

"Mother just usually stays around the house and takes care of the
kids or watches television or something like that. She never goes
anywhere. My father is either working on the car or watching tele-

vision. If I'm just lost for time completely I'll study or I'll write to friends. I have a boy friend, I think, I hope. He's in Alexandria, Louisiana . . . the Air Force Base. I don't plan to get married as yet, since we just started to go out about two months ago and we better get to know each other before we start thinking of marriage." (Dropout Sandra S., # 138, IQ 92, New Orleans)

"I think it would be spent individually. Each one on their own interest." (Dropout Candida F., # 148, IQ 133, New Orleans)

"We were all never together at one time. . . . My parents left at six in the morning and didn't get home until four. I just played hookey. When I finally told them and they were sick about it but I had already signed myself out." (Dropout Vivian M., # 248, IQ 100, Omaha)

Graduates

"We usually go on picnics, or to the beach for a swim, or we stay home and talk. Sometimes we all have dinner together and then maybe all go for a ride in the afternoon and maybe go to a show that night or go visit some of the relatives." (Graduate John M., # 123, IQ 105, New Orleans)

"Every Friday my parents and my aunt and uncle, who live next door, and my aunt and uncle who live on the other side of town, all get together and play cards." (Graduate John V., # 303, IQ 111, Denver)

"We usually don't spend too much time together. I wish we would." (Graduate Paul B., # 319, IQ 105, Denver)

These responses to the question concerning joint family leisure activities give us the typical replies of our dropout and graduating youth. Not adequately included in these quoted examples are the replies that proved to be more characteristic of the other matched half of the sample. Such replies have been consistently minimized in our quotations so that the typical replies would stand out in bolder relief. This suppression here obscures the fact that almost a quarter of the replies were overlapping. The overall statistical picture, how-ever, is perfectly clear.[11] According to the perceptions of our youth, four out of five of the dropouts' families (79%) "very in-frequently" or "infrequently" participate in leisure activities to-gether. Three out of four of the graduates' families (75%) reportedly

are accustomed to participate in such family activities. It is noteworthy that the inventory of the family climate that is emerging
sustains previous research indicating that the amount of joint activity in families is highly correlated with the amount of communication within the family, the willingness of members to sacrifice for
family goals, and other indicators of family solidarity.[12]

Pleasurable cooperative experiences, the third characteristic of
a primary group, are a regular part of the graduates' family life.
This is not so in the case of the dropouts.

FAMILY MEMBERS AS FRIENDS AND CONFIDANTS

The final question that attempts to test the strength of the bond
that exists between the teen-ager and his family is a question that
was given later in the interview. It concerns the same topic of primary relations but is couched in terms of "friendship." We did not
wish to introduce or define the term "friend" early in the interview;
we wished first to ascertain what the respondent himself thought a
friend was. It was only after he had laid his cards on the table as to
what he thought a friend was that we then clearly defined what we
meant by a friend and asked him if he judged that he had this type
of relationship with individuals in various contexts.

Our definition of a friend was that of an individual with whom
one has a primary relationship. The exact words used in defining a
friend were: "If we said that a close friend was one who (1) really
accepts you as a person, (2) and one that you like to confide in, and
(3) that you enjoy being with under many circumstances. . . ." In
probing about his home life we repeated the definition: "And at
home, how many were there that you could say accept you, and you
like to confide in and you enjoy being with?"

A new emphasis has been introduced in this latter definition. It
is that of depth of intercommunication as implied by the phrase,
"confide in." We had already asked him if the various members of
his family "talked things over" quite regularly. But we had not
asked him to what depth of communication he himself was involved
with any or all of the family members.

ON CONFIDING

Ability and freedom to confide in another seem to be a critical
consideration for the following six reasons: (1) Confiding is one of
the characteristics of a primary relationship. If one has reached the
fullness of communication one confides in another. If one is not free

to confide in another, the door to spontaneous interchange and development has been blocked. (2) A home that does not allow of confidences is a home with but superficial secondary relationships. (3) A teen-ager's development is thwarted and his emotional freedom strangulated without the benign cathartic influence that the confiding experience affords. (4) A confidant is an emotional mooring as well as a strong influence in one's life. Confidants become mutually sympathetic and then mutually similar in their attitudes and values so that they become each other's alter ego and, in a subtle way, "looking-glass self." (5) The confidant acts as a specialized catalytic agent who precipitates formulations and reactions according to his own characteristic "release potentials." In giving the other an opportunity to pour out his inmost thoughts, aspirations, and interests he affords a cathartic outlet for the other in which the confiding person will consciously or unconsciously weave an image of himself which will be in harmony with a pattern that he feels will receive support and approbation from his "bosom friend." In confiding to a gangster one would paint a different picture of oneself than when confiding to a maiden grandaunt. (6) Confidences elicit emotional commitments. If the teen-ager confides in his family, his roots and personality sources will reside in that family. If he cannot confide in his family, his emotional life will be either thwarted or diverted toward other more receptive emotional and value sources outside the family matrix.

The process of "confiding in another" implies the other two processes of primary relationships; a youth who bares his innermost thoughts to another feels accepted as a person and enjoys being with the other under a variety of circumstances. A confidant is another self.

Table 3 serves as a summary of his family's solidarity as seen through the eyes of the teen-ager. No matter what question concerning primary relationships was asked, the responses of the teen-agers were consistent. Whether the question concerned family discussion, leisure time activities, understanding and acceptance or the more personal questions as to whether the respondent himself felt understood, accepted, encouraged, or had confidants within the family circle, the answers consistently reported the same pattern. The emotional temperature of the home out of which the dropout walks is decisively different—cooler—than that of the graduate. This temperature is so congenial to the growth of friendship potentials within the home of the graduates that over half (58%) of these

Table 3.—Confiding in other members of the family
(in percentages)*

	With None of Family	With 25% of Family	With 50% of Family	With 75% of Family	With 100% of Family
Dropouts	35	27	25	10	3
Graduates	7	5	14	16	58

* Distribution by percentages in reply to the question: "And at home, how many were there that you could say accept you, and you like to confide in, and you enjoy being with?" Hypothesis: The dropout has primary relationships with a smaller percentage of his family than does the graduate. $D = .559$; $X^2(2df) = 106.49$; $p < .001$ (significant beyond the .001 level).

students declare that they feel understood by, accepted by, confide in, and enjoy spending their leisure hours with every one of their family members. But the emotional climate is so disagreeable within the home of the dropout that one-third of them report that they feel that there is *not one person* in their home in whom they can confide, with whom they enjoy being during leisure hours and whom they feel understands and accepts them. Those dropouts who say that they can talk in confidential terms to a small percentage of the family almost always have in mind the mother. This means that in the total dropout picture all but a slight percentage (10%) of the teen-agers feel that there is no one in the home who really loves and cares for them except perhaps the mother.

2. HAPPINESS WITHIN THE HOME

As a résumé of the differences between the family backgrounds of the dropout and the graduate we can review all three hundred interviews and evaluate them on the one variable of "happiness."

"Happiness" is an elusive term. Happiness is an elusive condition. Happiness is still more elusive as an empirical item within a research project.

Cartoonist Charles M. Schultz, by means of his "Peanuts" gang, defines happiness through such situational factors as: "Happiness is finding someone you like at the front door." "Happiness is a fuzzy sweater." "Happiness is some black, orange, yellow, white and pink jelly beans, but no green ones." "Happiness is walking in the grass in your bare feet." "Happiness is a warm puppy." "Happiness is a pile of leaves."

There are numerous methodological problems about using Cartoonist Schultz's criteria of happiness. Not the least of these is that a person or family could be in complete possession of all these items and be completely unhappy. Nevertheless, Schultz's criteria seem to have received a more widespread acceptance than those criteria presented by the various social scientists in their studies of family and marital happiness.

The criterion that this study uses to measure happiness within the home is that of primary relationship. Acceptance of each other as total persons, depth of intercommunication and pleasure in being with each other are the three criteria in modern formulations of the ideal primary group. With these criteria already utilized in this chapter, summarizing the degree of happiness within the teen-agers' homes is readily ascertainable.

Table 4.—Happiness within the home *
(in percentages)

	Very Unhappy	Unhappy	Indifferent	Happy	Very Happy
Dropouts	35	27	25	10	3
Graduates	17	5	14	16	48

* D = 4.2; X² = 59.9; p < .001. The hypothesis that the dropout population would report their homes to be less happy than would the student population is validated at the .001 level of confidence.

The typical home of the dropout is reported as unhappy (35% + 27%) and the typical home of the graduate is reported as happy (16% + 48%).

The homes of the youth whom we interviewed were either in similar or identical neighborhoods. Externally the homes appeared identical. Internally, there were on an average the same number of children; the teen-aged respondents were of the same age, the same sex, the same native ability. Yet the different climate of happiness in the homes of the dropouts as contrasted with the graduates is startling. Unhappiness is the characteristic of the one group; happiness that of the other.

SUMMARY OF CHAPTER I

Each of the interview questions that reflected the climate of primary relations within the home distinguished the dropout from the graduate at the highest level of significance (.001). In the semantics of statistical tests this meant that the difference noted between the two groups could not have happened once in a thousand times by chance.

For instance, when asked "Would you say that your *whole* family both understands and accepts each other," more than four out of five of the dropouts implicitly replied "little," or "very little," and more than four out of five of the graduates maintained just the opposite. In the replies to the questions "And how do you fit into the picture? To what degree would you say that your family both understands and accepts you? And would you say that you both understand and accept them?" and likewise, with the replies to the questions "Does your family talk things over with each other very often?" and "If your whole family had some free time, how would they usually spend it?"—the centrifugal force of the dropout families is apparent while that of the graduate families is centripetal. When asked "Did your family encourage and help you in your plans for a good job or in your school plans?" the same pattern of rejection and acceptance was obvious.

There were two summary questions. The one asked "And at home, how many were there that you could say accept you, and you like to confide in, and you enjoy being with?" Since we had listed the number of family members we were able to calculate the percentage of family members with whom the teen-age respondent had primary relations. Three percent of the dropouts had primary relationships with their entire family while 58 percent of the graduates did. The other summary questions concerned happiness within the home. Once again the evidence was conclusive that dropouts are brought up in a different type of family matrix than are the graduates.

THE HOME AND THE "SCHOOL PERSONALITY"

It is being accepted as a truism among both psychologists and sociologists that the "personality type" established in the primary group association is an "enduring core that, though it is adaptable to widely varying social roles, plays an important part in all the interactional processes of the individual with his fellows." [13] That the enduring core of the "school personality" is primarily fashioned within the home as the mirror of the specific domestic subculture existent there is becoming more obvious. The fact that the youth who continues in school has his origins in a family where personal acceptance, communication, and pleasure are staples is particularly noteworthy. The self-confidence that arises from being accepted, the communication skills that are developed in an alert and verbal environment and the pleasure of team-working are the ideal pre-requisites for school life.

Our conclusion from our first chapter is that no matter what other variables are at work, the nuclear family is of critical import in the consideration of the dropout problem. A law of polarization evidenced in the parent-youth world today is that the dropout is the product, generally speaking, of an inadequate family and the graduate is a product of an adequate family. The proletariat of tomorrow springs from the loins of a disintegrate family. The family which nurtured the youth who did not continue his education is of a different calibre than that which produced the teen-ager who continued his education at least into his eighteenth year.

The following chapters will isolate other significant characteristics of these teen-agers who are destined to play such a different role in our society.

CHAPTER TWO

The Dropout and His Family's Friends

1. DROPOUT CASE HISTORY:
ROBERT RAWLINSON

Robert Rawlinson is the meaningless pseudonym we have given this boy, who has just reached his fifteenth birthday. This actuarial fact is not meaningless for he is already an inmate of a state correctional institution. He has been in trouble with the police off and on throughout his short life. When he was thirteen he was convicted of stealing a car and joy riding with an older delinquent and was put on probation. At fourteen he was again convicted of car theft and committed to the state reformatory outside Denver, Colorado. He was not quite fifteen when we interviewed him.

Despite this boy's youth and despite the fact that his origins are in a disintegrate family it is the contention of this chapter that this unlettered lad presents a more realistic picture of family organization in the United States, of the basic issues involved in the dilemma of staying in or dropping out of high school, and of social reorganization than do the majority of textbooks and ivory tower authorities who speak of a vacuum "isolated" American family and a class-bound dropout problem.

This is Robert Rawlinson's story:

"My dad is an airplane mechanic with the Frontier Airlines. But ever since I was fourteen [1] I've been getting into all this trouble. . . . I stole a car. That's when I was thirteen. I was put on probation. This second time some kid wanted to steal some cigarettes out of a car but when we got in we found the keys so we ended up taking the whole car. We went across the state line with the car and then ran out of gas in Wyoming. So we stopped a truck and got a ride into Hot River and turned ourselves over to the police. The last incident was when my friend, Ronnie, was supposed to report because he had violated his parole and he didn't report. So that evening we went downtown and the police were looking for him and they started chasing us. We lost them several times and finally hid down by the railroad tracks. After we were sure they were gone we went over to my sister's house and stole some money and cigarettes and then went out and stole another car. We figured we were in trouble anyway, another car wouldn't make much difference. So we went to Colorado Springs and stole some gasoline and got chased by the police again and we finally gave ourselves up. . . .

"All my buddies wanted to quit school so I went along with them. . . . Myself, I would want to drop out of school but I want to get through with it so I can get a good job. . . . I was still going to school at the time I got in trouble. We ditched school just before it happened. We got caught but then we got straightened out and got back to school. I was doing real good. But then my little brother wanted to ditch school again but I said 'No'; but when I went to get my brother this other kid followed me and we all ended up staying out of school that day. . . . My oldest sister quit school long ago and my younger sister just quit. She was sick and was going to have to repeat the eleventh grade. . . ."

Ego Family

"When we ditched school we did do some drinking. But when I get out of here I'm not going to drink any more. My mother and father were divorced for three years because he drank too much. He's a lot better now and my father has proved himself a lot. He's a lot better man now but he does drink off and on some. Now that I've been in trouble all this time my mom says he hasn't been drinking at all. . . . Yeah, I sure do feel close to my dad but I don't know what decisions he makes around the home. . . . Oh, I guess in a way the whole family understands and accepts each other. My one sister works and helps my mother out with the bills. Ever since my mother has been trying to help my dad after he goes out and drinks the family has been O.K. She didn't used to help him. Most of the problems of our family are between me and my brother and our fighting. Another big problem in our family is my sister's boy friend, Larry. He was the one I got in trouble with the first time and he had quite a record behind him. Now he is in Dakota in a boys' institution and he is finishing school. My sister wants to marry him but my dad doesn't like him since he found out what we did together. It's not really his fault; his parents were split up and weren't much good. He has been living in institutions most of his life.... I understand my brother all right but he kept running around with Ronnie and kept getting in trouble. I quit going around with him after we got in trouble. My mom and dad have helped us and they wanted all of us to stay in school. Neither of my sisters have been in jail but we all four got in trouble at school and my dad can't understand it.... I used to say I was going to run away from home a lot when I got in trouble with my parents. In a way my parents tried to keep me home a lot but I'd tell them I don't want to get in trouble. I try to keep out of it more than anything. The first time I wanted to leave home was when my mom and dad were divorced. We wanted my dad back an awful lot for those three years. In these past few months my family has been staying together. My mom and dad are working together.... I can't understand my dad when he goes out and gets drunk. I don't understand why. I think he gets drunk when me and my brother fight a lot and in that way he doesn't have to listen to it.... We usually fight about any little thing."

My Dad

"Ever since my dad came back he bought new furniture for our home; my mother's father remodeled the house outside and fixed it up inside and had it painted; he's just done everything for us. When my dad first came back we started renting the house from my grandfather but we bought it back from him. We were in pretty bad shape for a while ... while my dad was gone and my grandfather took over the house payments. My mother consults a lot with my dad now and the whole family sits down and talks about what has happened. My mom used to tell us that my father would just have to go because he was always drinking. My dad was a pretty nervous wreck and I think a lot of it is us kids' fault. If I would have done what I was told to do and not done what I wanted, none of this would have happened. And if my sister would have done what she was told to do and not leave home things would have been better. Now everything seems to be going better. My sister said she wanted to leave but now she says she never wants to leave home and wants to help with my father and my mom and us. She said she feels our family can be brung back together. That's what us kids want to see more than anything in this world—to see the whole family back together."

Friend Families

"Both my mother and father have a lot of friends. One of our friends, Mr. and Mrs. Brown—they're Christians and do a lot of church work. Mr. Brown used to talk to me a lot after I got in trouble and he never acted as if I was any different from anyone else because I did get in trouble. I was never friendly with any teachers. The only guy I was close to was Mr. Brown. Me and my brother and his boys used to go bowling every Saturday night.... I met him through Juvenile Hall at a Sunday meeting; he talked to me. After I got out my second time I looked him up and we got together—his family and mine—and me and David started doing stuff with him and his boys. I always thought he was a nice guy. ... My dad's friends are mostly from bars. But they're good people. All my parents' friends has always liked us kids. Another bad thing in our family is that my dad's mom never did like my mom. My mom didn't see them for about eight years and then my grandfather died and she felt real bad. Now she sees my dad's mom every chance she gets.... Three people tried to help me most. One is my probation officer—he has tried to help me a lot by showing me the right way. Then there is Mr. Jones—he has worked with me a lot. Another one is my cousin. He's an Arvada Police Officer. Another one is my dad and my mom; they tried to help me a lot. My aunt and uncle have helped and they told me if I ever got in trouble to come out to their house. But I feel I let all of them down because I got in trouble.... If I needed help and advice to make a big decision I think I'd go to my cousin. He could help me. Or I would go to my parents first."

Personal Friends

"I had a paper route but I never got to my job because I always messed around with the kids.... I was going with a pretty rough crowd for a while. They got kicked out of school once in a while and said they wouldn't go back. Like Ronnie. He has the nicest mother there ever was. She's just wonderful. She gives him everything he needs. But when she asks him to empty the trash he beats around the bush and they fight a lot. He has a stepdad and he hates his stepdad and he says he hopes his mother divorces him. He says this right in front of his stepdad. The only time that family got in a fight was one night when his mom threw a butcher knife at his dad

and cut his arm. I stayed with Ronnie that night to help him clean
up all the mess—clean up the blood and to help with his dad. Mrs.
Black is awful nice. She wants to build a place in her basement so
we won't be on the streets. She will ask Ronnie if he wants to give a
party and he says 'No.' Then the next minute he has a party and
she gets all mixed up. There is a lot of conflict. Ronnie hates his
older sister because when Ronnie was about nine years old he was
sent to the state reformatory at Bailey and he thinks it was because
of his sister and he hates her. Otherwise, he's O.K.; he always treated
me real nice. My dad doesn't mind him. He wants him to come over
to the house but he doesn't want me to run around on the streets
with any kids that have been in trouble. I only ditched school about
six times and got by with it most of the time. I don't know why I
ditched, sir. Just to be doing something big. I liked school."

Peer Group: Approved and Otherwise

"My parents tried to pick the good friends out for me. They wanted
me to run around with the better kids. But I don't see nothing
wrong with kids that have been in trouble and proved themselves.
And when they would oppose my choice of friends I'd get mad and
argue with them and say I wouldn't stop running around with
them. But later, after something happens, I do find out that my
parents were right and I was wrong. And with Ronnie, my parents
told me if I run around with kids that get in trouble I would too.
They said he could come over to the house but I couldn't go out
with him. They didn't want me on the streets with Ronnie. I wasn't
going out on the streets too much with Ronnie but after Ronnie got
kicked out of his home, after we ditched, his parents said they
would have us both put in Juvenile Hall because we wrecked their
home pretty much. But we never; it turned out that none of this
damage was really true. Ronnie ran away from home for about
three days and he didn't have any place to go. He walked around
most of the nights so I gave Ronnie some blankets and told him to
go down in our basement and sleep. I couldn't see a kid kicked out
of his own home with no place to go so I let him stay with me a
couple of nights. Finally we took him out to Arvada—he has friends
out there and he was going to stay there. Then his parents wanted
to know where he was. Ronnie told me he was going to stay out
there just that day and go to his parents that night but instead he
got mixed up with a gang and he got picked up and got sent home

that night. I said to him, 'Aren't you glad I told your parents where you were?' And he said, 'No.' And I said, 'Yes, you are.' And he said, 'Yes.' Ronnie doesn't mean any harm. He's just mixed up.

"I've never failed a grade. But a couple of my friends have. But it wasn't their fault. Don Dickie, he don't drink or smoke or anything and he tells his mother everything but in third grade he failed because of his eyesight. And another friend failed first grade because he missed a lot of school because he was pretty sick. But he done the grade over. If I had stayed with these two guys I would have been better off. I wouldn't have been in any of this trouble. I'd still be out with them and could join in the football and basketball games. . . ."

Plans for the Future

"My parents' friends want their children to be educated just like my parents do. I could of made something of my life if I had kept going. The way it is, when I get out of here I want to go home and the family is going to move to Phoenix, so my dad can stay with Frontier. We want to get a fresh start and make new friends. My mom has often talked about it. Us kids, in a way, we don't want to move because of all the kids we know; but we know it will be a lot better for us to move for there would be people in the block that don't want their kids to run around with me because I've been in trouble and in a way, if we start over, I can meet new kids and the past could be forgotten and we could start for the future and just forget the past." (Robert Rawlinson—Golden Reformatory—IQ 111, Interview # 328)

INTRODUCTION

Fourteen-year-old Robert Rawlinson's strong and sensitive story provides a point of entry into a treatment of the second band of influentials in a child's life—the close friends that frequent his family's home. The Rawlinson home is relatively functionless and isolated. The purpose of this chapter is to test whether the dropout and graduate homes are similarly functionless and isolated.

Home, to Robert Rawlinson, could almost be defined as a place where nobody is and nothing happens. Had he been born into a rural civilization, home could almost have been defined as a place where everybody is and everything happens. Between these two extremes we find the substance of our present chapter.

Chicago University's Louis Wirth stressed, as Marx, Engels, Durkheim, Simmel, Toennies, and Mannheim before him, that the urban family was losing its social significance:

> The distinctive features of the urban mode of life have often been described sociologically as consisting of the substitution of secondary for primary contact, the weakening of the bonds of kinship, and the declining social significance of the family, the disappearance of the neighborhood, and the undermining of the traditional basis of social solidarity.[2]

Burgess and Locke in their classic, *The Family: From Institution to Companionship,* take for granted the demise of the institutionalized form of monogamy and espouse a very ancient form of mating known as the "companionate" which they judge to recommend itself to American society because of its "adaptability to a rapid tempo of social change." [3]

The common analysis of the modern urban family would have us believe that not only is it relatively functionless but likewise "isolated." We are told that it "may be stated as a fact that the family of procreation, and in particular the marriage pair, are in a 'structurally unsupported' situation. Neither party has any other adult kin on whom they have a right to 'lean for support.' . . ." [4]

2. KINSHIP PATTERNS

KINSHIP ASSISTANCE IN EMERGENCY SITUATIONS

The youth whom we interviewed seem to tell a different story. Their answers seemed to infer that relatives and close friends had played a very important part in the lives of their families. Even the kin of the culturally disadvantaged Rawlinson family rally to aid when the father becomes an alcoholic and absents himself for several years. As our young informant describes the situation: "Ever since my dad came back he bought new furniture for our home; my mother's father remodeled the house outside and fixed it up inside and had it painted. We were in a pretty bad shape for a while . . . while my dad was gone and my grandfather took over the house payments."

Quarantelli has reviewed over fifty different reports of disasters and summarizes: "The extended family is the major source to which disaster victims turned for help—and the smaller the scope of the community disaster the more probable is the kin group the major source of help." [5]

That this help during the time of stress is not limited only to parental assistance to their children but of the group as a system is apparent from the same study:

Disaster studies lend little support to the general proposition that the protective function has been basically relinquished and that the extended family is of little importance in mass societies. The kin group is the preferred, sought, and major source of short and long-run help in time of such crises. In this sense at least the protective function is clearly still a major function of the extended family.[6]

KINSHIP ASSISTANCE IN NONEMERGENCY SITUATIONS

In an emergency the nuclear family looks primarily to the kinship group for assistance. More subtle and more important is the interdependence of the kinship group in nonemergency situations.

As with the Rawlinson family so with the other families of both dropouts and stayins; we find that relatives were constantly interwoven in the life histories of the respondents: "Our closest friends are my aunt and uncle because they live upstairs from us and we get together a lot." (Dropout Gene O., # 226, Omaha)

"No, our family does not get together with relatives on holidays. There are over one hunded relatives in the Omaha area alone and it would be too difficult to get together with them over the holidays. There is sort of a family agreement that the holidays are spent with your own family and other Sundays are for visiting relatives." (Stayin Susan T., # 243, Omaha)

"Most of the neighbors and our relations live close to us. My grandmother and my two aunts come in quite frequently. Both my parents work and they don't have too much time to entertain." (Stayin Gary M., # 327, Denver)

"When we are all together we usually have a group discussion— political discussions or something in the news or the future, or if somebody in the family has a problem we talk this over.... I feel I can discuss everything with my aunt and uncle just as I can with my mother and father; we are very close." (Stayin Bill S., # 501, Boston)

"Up until about a month ago all my aunts and uncles used to come over every Friday night. We have a stereo and they used to bring their records. Lately they haven't been coming over but we used to have a gathering here every Friday night." (Stayin Thomas M., # 513, Boston)

"Well, I was going with this boy once. My Aunt Alice didn't like him at all. She's not prejudiced, but she said Portuguese boys and Italian boys are more determined than the rest of the races. She said there's good and bad in every race but they are more so. So when I was going with him he asked me to marry him, I was only sixteen, so she said it was silly. I was all for it; I thought I was a big wheel. She really made up my mind. She talked to him and she broke us up and we parted as friends and everything. But if she hadn't talked to me I would probably be married with a couple of children. I'm glad she did it." (Dropout Betty Ann W., # 520, Boston)

"My aunt from Columbia Street comes over very often.... I sold papers with the kid, her son." (Dropout Lawrence K., # 526, Boston)

"All the relatives are close." (Dropout Loretta W., # 536, Boston)

"Before I quit school I talked it over with my aunts and uncles; they wanted me to stay in too. My uncle told me I'd be better off if I stayed in but I couldn't leave my mother home in the position she was in and the kids wouldn't stay with her and she had enough problems already." (Dropout Shirley B., # 542, Boston)

"The closest friend my mother has is her sister; she lives upstairs. Whenever there is an argument my mother will always go to my aunt and she will comfort her and tell her what to do." (Dropout JoAnne C., # 544, Boston)

A SURVEY OF THE LITERATURE

There is a growing belief among family sociologists that the concepts of the "isolated" nuclear family is misleading when used to typify the contemporary urban family in the United States.

In a comprehensive article on the kin family network in modern urban society, Sussman and Burchinal refer to the lag between apparently antiquated family theory and empirical reality as an "academic cultural lag." [7] They point out that the still dominant family theory "stresses the social isolation and social mobility of the nuclear family while findings from empirical studies reveal an existing and functioning extended kin family system closely integrated within a network of relationships and mutual assistance along bilateral kinship lines and encompassing several generations." [8]

We may cite four ideal types of family structure and functioning that emerge from the current literature on the family: [9]

(1) *The extended kinship family.* This traditional "classic" type
of family grouping is characterized by geographical propinquity, occupational integration, strict authority over the nuclear family, and emphasis upon the extended rather than the
nuclear family relations.

(2) *The nuclear family.* A group "composed of a man and a woman
joined in a socially recognized union and their children." [10]
Prominent social theorists in characterizing the family in the
United States commonly speak of it in terms of the "relatively
functionless," "isolated," and "structurally unsupported" nuclear family.[11]

(3) *The modified extended kinship family.* "Unlike the classic
(extended kinship family) type, the modified extended family
does not demand geographical closeness, occupational integration, or strict authority relations. Nor does the concept of
the modified extended family replace that of the nuclear family. In the modified extended family system each nuclear family
is one of a series of such families bound together on an egalitar-
ian basis and providing significant aid to one another." [12]

Earlier analyses of industrial society had stated that the traditional extended kinship family had been replaced by the relatively
isolated nuclear family. More recent research has suggested that this
formulation may have been applicable to an earlier period when
immigrants and immigrant groups were coming into the city to
work during the period of urbanization in Western society, but that
it is an inadequate notion when applied to contemporary urban
society. Warner and Lunt,[13] Greer,[14] Hill,[15] Fellin,[16] Litwak,[17]
Reiss,[18] Sussman,[19] and Burchinal have found that the contemporary urban family is by no means isolated from its kin.
The contemporary kinship groupings are found to be without the
characteristic requirements of the traditional extended kinship systems: strict authoritarian control (as in patriarchal systems), geographical propinquity, occupational nepotism, and broad social
integration. The modified extended family is seen as a more optional social system composed of neolocal, nuclear families in a
bilateral kin or generational relationship. These voluntary group-

ings serve as a kin family network of help, service, emotional support, and common identification.

(4) *The Family Friend System.* The family friend system differs
    from the modified extended kinship system only in that non-
    kin elements may be admitted into the chosen circle of friend
    families. But even under this circumstance the kinship model
    remains; the children are usually bid to call their parents' close
    friends "Aunt" and "Uncle." The basis of sociometric choice
    is not primarily kinship but friendship.

VOLUNTARY AND SELECTIVE NATURE OF
CONTEMPORARY KINDRED INTERACTION

The fact that the modern kinship groupings are no longer obligatory but optional is of capital import. It has meant that only those relatives are kept within the family circle who are "easy to get along with." It has likewise meant that nonkin elements are introduced into the extended family circle and that these nonrelatives are considered relatives. Frequently children are not certain whether "Uncle George" or "Aunt Helen" are "really" relatives. Analogously, a relative who is not on a friendship basis with the respondent's family is either unknown or not listed among related persons.

Modern friendship groupings are found to be within such family friend systems which include both kindred and nonkindred. It is within the conceptual framework of this informal grouping of the family friend system that the present data of our research is considered.

3. CHARACTERISTICS OF THE DROPOUT'S FAMILY FRIEND SYSTEM
a) Less Extensive

The first characteristic that became apparent was that dropout families had fewer friends. The 150 dropouts recorded data on 260 family friends; the 150 graduates recorded data on 516 family friends.[20] The mean number of friends of the dropouts' families (1.7) was one half that of the graduates' families (3.4)

The question of the number of friends is such a critical feature of our study that we would broaden the view by placing it within the comprehensive context of other studies of friend families conducted by the St. Louis University Family Research Center. In a

study of 12,549 college and university students living in the same six
cities as our dropout sample it was found that the college students'
families had 47,413 close friend families or an average of 3.8 close
friend families. At the other end of the socioeducational scale we
obtained a sample of those families who are providing no education
for their children in that they had placed their children out for
adoption. Among this group we found that the number of close
friends had averaged less than one: 0.4.[21]

There is a positive correlation between number of friends and
educational adequacy. Those families that were able to see their
children into college had the most close friends (3.8). Those families that were able to see their children at least through high school
have somewhat fewer close friends (3.4). Those families whose children were high school dropouts have half as many friends as the
educationally adequate families (1.7). Those families who were
either incapable or unwilling to give their children even a basic
education and placed their children in foster homes or public institutions generally have no close family friends (0.4).[22]

If we were to ask "Are there isolated families in our comtempo-
rary culture?" the answer from these considerations would be
"Yes." There are a great number of isolated families without any
close friends but these families are fringe members of society un-
integrated with their community and their society's goals.

b) The Family Friend System of the Dropout's Family
is Less Intensive than That of the Student's Family

"Rootedness in the life of a community is essential for the proper
development not only of an individual but also of families" is a
conclusion of Simone Weil's study of societal living.[23] As the number of friends that one has in a community is an apt index of the
degree to which one has "sunk roots" into that community, so the
intensity of the friendship pattern is an apt index of the vitality of
these roots. That the families of the dropouts have one half the
number of such "roots" has already been established in the survey
of the "extent" of their family friendships. The data of our study
are just as definitive in indicating that the vitality of these roots, in
both structure and vital flow, is similarly underdeveloped in comparison with the vitality of the family friend systems of the student
respondents.

Four criteria of intensity were used to compare the extended family friendship systems of the dropout families with those of the graduate families: the length of time that the family friendships had continued; the meaning that the families attached to the term "close friend"; the proportion of kindred in the friendship groups; and the frequency of interaction with these kindred. Each of these indices showed that the nature of the friendship groupings differed significantly in comparing our two groups.

The friend system of the graduates' families is not one that is composed of casual acquaintances. In the cities of older settlement—Boston, New Orleans, and St. Louis—half of the friends had been visiting the students' homes throughout the youths' lifetimes. The Boston graduates' families had been on close terms with all but 17 percent of their family friends for at least ten years. The longitudinal reinforcement of life-long and long-time friends is much less marked, however, in the case of the dropouts. Whereas 44 percent of the family friends of the stayins' families had been known for 15 or more years, only 28 percent of the dropouts' family friends had been close friends for this length of time.

The second index of friendship intensity utilized was the youths' replies to the question: "What would your family mean by a close friend?" Their replies were scored on a five point scale that ranged from a purely hedonistic reply to one that included the perfection of a primary relationship. The following examples will make the scale more understandable:
1. Hedonistic: "A friend is one you can get a lot of fun out of."
2. Utilitarian: "A friend is one who will help you." 3. Reciprocal: "Friends are people who help each other." 4. Empathic: "Friends are people who understand each other." 5. Perfective: "Friends accept each other as persons; they confide in each other; they enjoy being with each other."

There is a statistically significant tendency [24] of the families of the dropouts to consider friendship in terms of the hedonistic and the utilitarian and of the families of the high school graduates to consider friendship in terms of mutual understanding, depth of communication, and pleasure in being in each other's company.

The presence of kindred in one's circle of close friends—the third index of intensity—tends to add a degree of stability to the organizational structure since kindred are long-term friends of well-known background and expectations. In our present predominately blue-collar sample it was found that 50 percent of both the dropouts' and the graduates' family friends were related either by blood or marriage.[25] Since the graduates' families had twice as many friends this meant that twice as many relatives were in the close circle of family friends surrounding the graduate throughout his lifetime. It may be noted that in every city except one (Los Angeles) the families' kindred take precedence in nearness of friendship. First friends contain more kindred than second friends, second friends contain more kindred than third friends, and so on in order of closeness. The upwardly mobile middle class, however, tend to shuck off their relatives as they ascend the golden stairs ... especially those relatives on the outer fringe of their friendship circles.

The fourth index of friendship intensity was that obtained in reply to the question: "Does your family get together with the relatives on big holidays?" Though there was great overlapping in the replies, by central tendency the dropouts replied "Never" or "Rarely" and the graduates "Frequently" or "Very Frequently." [26]

Our evidence unmistakably indicates that the family friend system of the dropouts' families is not only less extensive but likewise less intensive than that of the graduates' families.

c) Less Homogeneous

Pavlov is said to have dramatized the deleterious effects of value conflicts and environmental discontinuities by producing a neurosis in a dog. He did it by conditioning the dog to respond positively to a great circle of light thrown on a screen. The same dog was conditioned to respond negatively to a great ellipse of light thrown on the same screen at another time. Then when the great experimenter changed the light from a circle and an ellipse to a midway type of figure, the dog did not know what to do, and broke down in a fit of trembling. A somewhat similar dysfunctional effect is produced in individuals who are intensively subjected to conflicting values and social discontinuities.[27]

The homogeneity theme stresses the need for harmonious values in the socializing process. Our previous study of 54,233 families who formed the family friendship circles of 9,253 high school graduates underlined this core need. Value conflicts are evident in interfaith marriages. The dramatically higher incidence of divorce and delinquency in families in which the father and mother have different religious persuasions than in those families in which the principals have the identical religious belief was evident from the fact that both Protestants and Catholics who engaged in interfaith marriages had twice the incidence of divorce between the parents and twice the incidence of delinquency among their children while the Jews who participated in an interfaith marriage had five times the amount of divorce and delinquency than those who married a person of their own faith.[28]

In measuring the homogeneity of the informal family friendship pattern we used four indices in the present study: same socioeconomic status, same region of origin, same religion, and same educational aspirations. On each of these indices the friend families of the dropouts proved less homogeneous with the parental families than was the case of our graduate sample. Most critical was the difference in educational aspirations: the dropout saw little conformity (33.3%) between the aspirations of his parents' friends and his own family while the graduate in nine out of ten cases judged that his family's close friends agreed with his parents as to the desirable amount of education for a youth.[29]

That the dropouts are brought up in a social system of friend families which is less homogeneous than that in which the graduate is enmeshed is clear from our sample.

d)   Less Careful in Avoiding "Problem Unit" Friend Families

Jackson Toby in his study "The Differential Impact of Family Disorganization" concluded:

> The family not only transmits socially acceptable values to the new generation; it also seeks to prevent the child from being influenced by deviant patterns. The better integrated the family, the more successful it is as a bulwark against anti-social influences emanating from the neighborhood of the peer group.[30]

This conclusion is harmonious with the "differential association" analysis derived from studies in deviant behavior:

> In our American society the definitions of the legal codes as to or not to be obeyed is always mixed and therefore we have a culture conflict. A person becomes delinquent because of an excess of definitions favorable to violation of law. This is the principle of differential association. It refers to both criminal and anti-criminal associations and has to do with counteracting forces. When persons become criminal, they do so be-

cause of contacts with criminal patterns and also because of isolation from anti-criminal patterns.[31]

To concretize in terms of our Rawlinson case history: A family friend by the name of Ronnie was a teen-age gangster. The Rawlinsons admitted him into their home so that he might be with their son Robert. Because of his dubious character, neither Ronnie nor Robert was admitted into the homes of his neighbors. Insofar as the neighbors were more careful about the type of persons allowed into their homes, insofar as they excluded such problem units from interacting with their own children, so argues our hypothesis, these neighbors would be more successful in seeing their children through at least high school.

For our purposes "problem unit" families were those in which any of the children were either dropouts or delinquents and in which either of the parents had been divorced, deserted, or remarried. Originally we had postulated that the widowed were likewise "problem units" but since widows in this study proved more able than nonwidows to get their children through school we had to drop them from the less than flattering category of "problem unit."

As was hypothesized the following patterns became clearly evident:

(1) There is a higher incidence of divorce, desertion, delinquency, and dropouts among the families of the dropouts.

(2) There is a higher incidence of divorce, desertion, delinquency, and dropouts among dropouts' family friends.

(3) Families of graduates are more careful about excluding or demoting problem units in their family friend systems.

(4) The homogeneity principle is realized insofar as the more the friend circles have in common the more successful they seem to be in avoiding rupturing their marital and parental relationships and in seeing that their children avoid rupturing their relationships with the police and the school system.

It is not enough, however, to point out that there are roughly double [32] the number of "problem units" in the friend circles of the dropouts as there are in the friend circles of the graduates. Merely to list the doubled incidence of social pathologies in the respective friendship groupings is to miss the dynamic of the small group system. It is much more than "birds of a feather flock together." A bluebird will remain a bluebird even if he should start to travel with blackbirds. But this is not the case when humans interact within primary groups. Friends either find each other alike or make each other alike. Values are involved. Shading and change of values are involved in the flocking phenomenon among humans. Paul Lazarsfeld and Robert Merton in their revealing article on "Friendship as a Social Process: A Substantive and Methodological Analysis" develop in some detail the way a continued friendship all but inevitably changes formerly disparate values into homogeneous values:

> It is not easy to have a warm personal attachment where there is an opposition of values. This gives rise to a motivated tendency toward the formation of common values among fast friends. Not only does intimate social interaction precipitate a deposit of new common values, but it also converts originally disparate values into common values. As a result of these two processes, we should expect value-heterophily to decrease among any given aggregate of friendships observed over an extended period of time.[33]

George Homans expands this same principle of interaction producing value-homophyly into a broader social principle which he calls the "mode of standardization." From his study of the "Bank Wiring" group and other social systems he concluded with reference to the present point:

> The more frequently persons interact with one another, the more alike in some respects both their activities and their sentiments tend to become.[34]

MEANING OF THE FAMILY-FRIEND SYSTEM

Our subtopical expedition into the land of the friend families leads us to this conclusion: "No matter what circumstances—biological, physical, environmental, or social—make children run afoul of the law, good, similar, intimate friend-families around the home, deter it, prevent it, and help it from getting out of hand. At the same time these friends help to keep the children more interested in life achievement through the school system and make for better husband-wife relations within the home." [35] These two sentences put the main practical results of our investigation of the friend-family systems in a nutshell. They likewise indicate that these friends reinforce the nuclear family's functions, reinforce the nuclear family, and integrate both with society's aspirations.

The kin and client system of antiquity is not dead; it has risen again in the civilization-adequate families of our modern society. Of old, the kin provided the bridge between the nuclear family and the broader society and served as a shield against its hostile forces; the clients were those nonkinship members of the extended family who had assumed the obligations and privileges of kindred. The modern friend families, who assist members of the nuclear family to make occupational and social contacts, who babysit and act as godparents, who discuss and advise on personal and intimate family matters, who are known to the children as "uncle" and "aunt," form a part of the modern synthetic extended kinship system. Though there is a lack of direct, functional relationships between such a family friend system and other societal subsystems, there are informal and latent functions which it performs. It provides a status and security on a wider basis than that of the nuclear family and possesses a latent function of personality stabilization. In doing so, it assists the nuclear family, which, although functioning in the same area, can by its very nature provide a status and security based only on a very small number of individuals. Thus the friend-family system represents a larger unit with more personal and material resources which functions as a second line support system for the nuclear family in the performance of its principal functions.[36]

The meaning of the slight family-friend system of the dropout's family was that there was little reinforcement of the nuclear family's functions by extended family personnel, few common interests between parent and child, little family cohesion, and most markedly a lack of male companionship and leadership. As the teen-age boy and girl become mature in their adolescent vigor and seek to be complemented by and identified with adult males they are driven outside the family circle to obtain this male image. Hereby hangs another story. It is that of the teen-ager's identity crisis.

4. TEEN-AGER'S IDENTITY CRISIS

Robert Rawlinson was scarcely fifteen years of age. As he poured out his story, the drama of his life seemed to resolve itself to the question of identity: What kind of person did he want to be? What kind of people did he want to identify with? With whom should he cast his life's chances—the type of people that his parents wanted, or the type that he had previously wanted?

It is noteworthy that he reviewed his life not in terms of institutional goals—educational, occupational, criminal, political, religious, or familial—but in terms of people who appealed to him. He recounted his educational history not in terms of whether he could make his studies or not—he could and did make them; not in terms of whether it was necessary to finish school to get a good job—he knew this; but in terms of the conflict of his parents' wishes and his buddies' wishes. His parents wanted him to go on, he wanted to go on, but his buddies wanted him to follow a way of life in which school had no part and so that was what he did. It was a choice between parentally approved "squares" and parentally nonapproved "buddies"; a choice between the dull and the exciting, the conventional and the exhilarating, the ins and the outs, the priggishly righteous and the sympathetically deviant.

In the course of the interview Robert boasted loyally of the criminal records of his delinquent friends, rationalized their deviations, then expressed feelings of personal guilt and remorse, and a determination to break completely with his deviant past and return to his father's house. To accomplish this break with the past he judged it necessary that the whole family move to a different city, form new family (and family-approved) personal friends, get into a new social system, and start all over with the dead past burying its dead. His resolve—though extreme—lies within the meaning of the data in this chapter: The family friendship system is a critical reinforcing buttress of nuclear family values and a vital bridge between this social group and the broader society.

It may be of help in visualizing the elements of a teen-ager's identity crisis to single out the chief characters in the drama of Robert's life, suggest sequence articulation points, and add pertinent, descriptive comments as given by our protagonist, Robert Rawlinson.

DRAMATIS PERSONAE

Family members

Robert Rawlinson: A handsome, outgoing, juvenile delinquent and dropout. He is scarcely fifteen years of age. Above average in IQ, social skills, and general vitality, his unconscious theme seems to be the unresolved identity crisis as centered in conflicting love-hate feelings toward his father.

Mr. Rawlinson: Robert's ineffective, undependable, presently unemployed, inebriate, loved father. About him, Robert stated: "I do want to take airplane mechanics; my father had to take four years of it before he knew everything. . . . The first time I wanted to leave home was when my mom and dad were divorced. We wanted my dad back an awful lot for those three years. . . . I understand him some of the time but I don't understand him when he goes out and gets drunk; I don't understand why."

Mrs. Rawlinson: Cold, colorless, stand-offish, hard-working mother.

Diana, Doris, David Rawlinson: Two older sisters and younger brother of Robert. The best that Robert had to say about his siblings was: "Mom and dad wanted all of us to stay in school. Neither of my sisters has been in jail but we all four got in trouble at school and my dad can't understand it."

Family friends

Maternal grandfather: Saw family through hardships while Mr. Rawlinson separated from Mrs. Rawlinson for three years.

Uncle and aunt: Told Robert that if he got in trouble again he could come and live with them in another city.

Cousin: A suburban policeman who tried to help Robert.

Mr. and Mrs. Brown: "One of our friends, Mr. and Mrs. Brown, they're Christians and do a lot of church work. Mr. Brown used to talk to me a lot after I got in trouble and he never acted as if I was any different from anyone else because I did get in trouble."

Mr. Jones: Bland individual who tried to help when Robert "got in trouble."

Probation Officer: Became auxiliary friend of the family.

Mr. Rawlinson's shadowy bar friends: Never seen in the home, "but they're good people."

"I've never been influenced to do anything bad by my family friends. . . . All my parents' friends has always liked us kids. . . . They want their children to be educated just like my parents do."

Parentally Approved "Friends"

Don, Dickie, Jack, and various other sickly, dull schoolmates who "don't smoke or drink and who go to school regularly and tell their mothers everything."

Bill and Matthew Brown: Sons of the court-appointed church workers. "Me and my brother and his boys used to go bowling every Saturday night."

"My parents tried to pick the good friends out for me. They wanted me to run around with the better kids. But I don't see noth-

ing wrong with kids that have been in trouble and have proved
themselves. . . . I'd get mad and argue with them and say I wouldn't
stop running around with them. But later, after something happens, I do find out my parents were right and I was wrong. . . .
Don Dickie, he don't drink or smoke or anything and he tells his
mother everything but in third grade he failed because of his eyesight. And another friend, Jack, failed first grade because he missed
a lot of school because he was pretty sick. But he done that grade
over. If I had stayed with these two guys I would have been a lot
better off. I wouldn't have been in any of this trouble. I'd still be
out with them and could join in the football and basketball
games. . . ."

Parentally Nonapproved "Buddies"

Ronnie: An older, hardened delinquent who has at some level
    seemingly been a father-substitute for Robert's fantasy life and
    self-image. Ronnie blatantly defies his stepfather and hates his
    sister and refuses to cooperate with his mother, but "he always
    treated me nice." "Ronnie doesn't mean any harm. He's just mixed
    up."
Ronnie's mother: "Nicest mother that ever was"—knifed her hus-
    band—"I stayed with Ronnie that night to help him clean up
    all the mess—clean up the blood and to help with his dad. His
    mother is awful nice."
Larry: "He was the one I got in trouble with the first time and he
    had quite a record behind him. . . . My sister wants to marry him
    but my dad doesn't like him since he found out what we did to-
    gether. It's not really his fault. His parents were split up and
    weren't much good. He has been living in institutions most of his
    life."
Ricky, Len, David, etc., etc.: "I was going with quite a rough crowd."

THE DRAMA

THE DELINQUENT DROPOUT

Act I

Robert and His Broken Family

Scenes
  i. A vigorous, intelligent lad seeks appreciation, identification,
     excitement.

ii. His home is empty, his father gone, his mother stoic and un-loving. Family friends try to help keep home together.

iii. Robert finds appreciation, excitement, and identification with various delinquent youth. Anti-academic orientation.

iv. Truancy, dropout, police-conflict, probation, finally committed to reformatory.

Act II

The Reformatory

i. The reformatory psychologist, Dr. W. T. Adams, summarized Robert's early adjustment: "It would appear that due to his very outgoing nature and his very good social skills that Bob will probably be able to get along well in the school situation. He does not seem to have the defiance, hostility, nor the en-trenched feelings of cynicism that exist in many of the boys. ... He is operating with some of the difficulty in the family setting and is reacting to it. Basically, he seems to be above average in intelligence and also in social skills. He wants very much to be in a counseling situation so he can work through some of these difficulties. He finds himself generally very capable in the peer relations although he seems to be somewhat afraid of the older, more hardened delinquent children. He seems to feel he may have some difficulty with them. It would appear that he probably needs a good deal of support at this time and also some counseling to help him through his very difficult confusions and ambivalence toward his parent figures." (Text in toto in Appendix.)

ii. Agonizing reappraisal: Identity crisis
   A. Should he identify with parentally-approved "squares" who don't drink, smoke, or truant, and who "tell mother every-thing"?
   B. Or, should he identify with parentally nonapproved "bud-dies" who do drink, smoke, "hooky," drop out of school, have police records, and who don't "tell mother everything"?

iii. Recognition that the resolution of the crisis involves a choice of two different ways of life:
   A. The first alternative means returning to school, forming new study habits, seeking new friends, trying out for football and

basketball, being accepted by family, neighbors, uninteresting classmates, and becoming an airplane mechanic so he can "make something out of my life."

B. The second alternative involves a continued undisciplined existence without the need of returning to school and abandoning his habits of drinking, smoking, and not "telling mother everything." It means more new experiences and thrills, acceptance by and identification with his delinquent friends. He can still strive to satisfy his craving to "be doing something big."

iv. Feelings of guilt: "My mom used to tell us that my father would just have to go because he was always drinking. My dad was a pretty nervous wreck and I think a lot of it is us kids' fault. If I would have done what I was told to do and not done what I wanted, none of this would have happened."

v. Decides on the first alternative because "That's what us kids want to see more than anything in the world: to see the whole family back together."

vi. To implement his decision of personal and family reformation he foresees a radical step: Get rid of present personal and family friends by moving to a new area and make new friendship groupings: "My family's friends want their children to be educated just like my parents do. I could of made something of my life if I had kept going. The way it is, when I get out of here I want to go home and the family is going to move to Phoenix, so my dad can stay with Frontier. We want to get a fresh start and make new friends. My mom has often talked about it. Us kids, in a way, don't want to move because of all the kids we know. But we know it will be a lot better for us to move. [If we stayed] there would be people in the block that don't want their kids to run around with me because I've been in trouble and in a way, if we start over, I can meet new kids and the past could be forgotten and we could start for the future and just forget the past."

Act III
The Future

This act has not yet been written by Robert but there are two basic alternatives:

i. Returns to the sphere of influence of his nuclear family which includes school, parentally-approved friends, occupational orientation, and good citizenship.

ii. Returns to the sphere of influence of the parentally nonapproved friends with its fourfold bias against family authority, school authority, police authority, and occupational authority.

We submit that Robert Rawlinson, for all of his youth and undisciplined ways, analyzed the situation correctly. His problem, and the common problem of most dropouts, is primarily a question of affiliation with people—the family people or the antifamily people. Their dilemma is whether to identify inside or outside the sphere of influence of the friendship-extended nuclear family system.

POSTSCRIPT

In the popular text, *The Family: From Institution to Companionship,* Burgess and Locke stated:

> The basic thesis of this book is that the family has been in transition from an institution, with family behavior controlled by the mores, public opinion, and law, to a companionship, with behavior arising from the mutual affection, equality, and consensus of its members. The companionship form of the family is not to be conceived as having been realized but as emerging.
>
> The ideal construct of two contrasting types of families—the institutional and the companionship—is employed as the central concept for the understanding and study of the family in this text. Our use of ideal constructs includes in addition the following:

Authoritarian and democratic
Familism and individualism
Stable and unstable
Sacred and secular
Rural and urban
Continuity and mobility
Conflict and accommodation
Prudential and romantic.[37]

Granted that Burgess and Locke were using Max Weber's "ideal" typology with its identification, isolation, and accentuation of the logical extreme of a selected attribute,[38] their analysis is inadequate and seemingly misleading. Insofar as they prognosticate that the nonauthoritarian, individualistic, unstable, secular, urban, mobile, "gutless" (accommodation), and romantic family is the family of the future, our research indicates quite the contrary. The family of the future is the family which is educated—and these families are more "institutional" (in the Burgess-Locke sense) than "companionship" families. It is the dropout family which is laissez faire or nonauthoritarian, individualistic, unstable, secular, urban, mobile, gutless, and romantic. And the dropout family is not the family of the future. We would agree with the evaluation of Miller and Swanson of the prediction that the "companionship" family is the family of the future:

> It is our impression that the companionship family described by Burgess and Locke represents, not the growing wave of the family's future, but one of those sudden surges of history that are swallowed up in even mightier currents. We, like Burgess and Locke, see the new trends documented best among the middle classes, those parts of the population which we believe were the first to experience these new social conditions. The companionship family is the end product of the entrepreneurial society. The bureaucratic order makes different demands on husbands and wives, and on parents and children.[39]

Our study of the friendship systems of the high school graduates' and dropouts' families shows that the graduates' families are responding to the challenge of the twentieth century with a restatement and strengthening of their familial and societal environment. The graduate's family has selectively introduced into its home similar families and thus installed a sort of social filter which admits to the children who live within its environs only healthy educational and achievement aspirations. This new system of social filtering is an old family device similar to the groupings of kindred and friends in earlier periods. It has worked to reduce withdrawal from the educational processes, delinquency, and family breakage. By making the family groups viable and creative it has enabled these children to seek and achieve newer goals in the educational system.

A minority of American families has not utilized the social filter system of friendship selection and out of their deficiency has come a polarization of families in the country. The growing majority are producing the civilization-adequate education children; the minority are producing a troublesome harvest. The next two generations will see a widening of this polarization and an increased difference between the "successful" families and the disturbed minority.

The new requirements of modern life are better met not by a fictionally functionless, isolated, nuclear family but by the nuclear family reinforced by similarly creative family friends. "Institution" and "companionship" families, if the terms are to be used, are more polar types representative of the educationally adequate and educationally inadequate families of the United States.

CHAPTER THREE

School Experiences of the Dropout

The typical American public high school is a large and comprehensive one which teaches all things to all boys and girls. A small town will have only one high school; it is a common idea that a school is completely democratic because "everybody" is mixing together. The facts are quite different.

First, about half of the adolescents will quit school before receiving a diploma, and this half will come almost entirely from the lower classes. Once withdrawn, these teen-agers have very little contact with those who stay in. Second, most of the upper and some of the upper-middle-class children will be sent to private schools, and many of the Catholics to parochial institutions. Third, there is separation within the public school according to curriculums (in Massachusetts, for instance, there are four distinct courses of study: college preparatory, commercial, general, and trade). There is a substantial correlation between prestige class and curriculum chosen, and this separation carries over into recreational cliques. Fourth, even within curriculums boys and girls separate into groups according to family background.

It is true that the mere presence of all sorts of adolescents in a school makes it *possible* for a person to make contacts with others who come from a class different from his own—and in fact, most mobile students make a specific effort to do just that. But it is also true that *on the average* students separate themselves into cliques that are relatively homogeneous in their prestige-class composition. This is even truer in large cities with many high schools, for the schools in middle-class neighborhoods are very different from those in lower-class neighborhoods.

A high-school boy whom I interviewed described the groupings in his public school in New England in the following terms:

Q: What about the good students, what kind of people are they?
A: The really good ones are fruits—you wouldn't want to associate

with them. When you get lower you get in cliques—your marks get lower—they don't seem to know any better. I don't know, if they would stop and figure it out and realize what they are doing in playing around and having a good time.

Q: You think it is mainly the ones with the lower grades that get in gangs?

A: Yes, definitely.

Q: What sort of things do they do?

A: Oh, well they just go around and they stand on street corners and they are always in a crowd and they never can be alone— always their crowd.... They don't want to be told anything; they know it all.[1]

1. PRE-DATA CONCLUSIONS

We can better follow the drift of this chapter on school experiences by looking at some of the conclusions before reviewing the data:

(1) Class theory has led us to believe that continuation in school is only a function of class. Our findings indicate that there is a polarization within class groups that is independent of class. These polarization pools serve as presocialization centers for entry into a lower or higher class. This conclusion in no way denies that the lower class subculture is highly conducive to the dropout situation.

(2) Economic theory has led us to believe that withdrawal from high school is only a question of lack of funds. Our data indicates that lack of funds is all but irrelevant in the immediate situation. Perhaps 5 percent of the youth withdraw from high school because of an inability to pay for their education. A greater percentage of those who withdraw from high school have cars than do those who continue in the identical high school.

(3) Educational theory has led us to believe that continuation in high school is a matter of IQ. Our research in metropolitan areas has led us to the conclusion that there is a vast over-lapping of IQ's among dropouts and stayins and it is not the critical feature. With adequate parental direction or school counseling there is a school and a curriculum for practically every youth already in high school, no matter how high or how low his inherent ability.

(4) Psychoanalytical theory would have us stress the mother-child relationship in understanding the problem of the dropout. Our study would indicate that the mother-child relationship is more taken for granted; greater stress is needed on the father-child relationship as the problematic one in the home-school transaction.

(5) Sociological theory has tended to consider the home and the school as independent and isolated social systems. The patterns apparent from our research are that these two social systems tend to be isolated and independent in the case of the dropout but tend to be interpenetrating with the school acting as an agent of the family in the case of the graduate.

(6) Social work literature has tended to indicate that it is the environment of the dropout that presents all but insuperable difficulties for his continuation in high school. Our sample indicates that there is practically no difference with our matched sample in the magnitude of the difficulties that both the dropout and the stayin must cope with. Orientation and motivation are the critical factors rather than physical environment.

(7) Reading ability vs. reading inability; retardation vs. nonretardation; satisfaction vs. dissatisfaction; school participation vs. school nonparticipation; parental interest vs. parental noninterest; friends at school vs. no friends at school—these are the basics in the calculus of early school withdrawal. This finding is quite at odds with the emphasis given by leading educators to the question of finances, federal aid, curricula offerings, size of school, etc.

(8) There are core values and peripheral values in the high school educational experience. The youth who has latched onto core values will more probably continue through college; the youth who has latched onto peripheral values, however, is just as likely to finish high school. The more basic consideration is how to get the youth interested in any values connected with the high school experience.

(9) The characteristics of the dropout are apparent by the first year of high school if, indeed, not by the first grade of elementary school.

(10) Participants—be they football captain, beauty queen, water boy, or time keeper—do not drop out of school. Their intra-psychic and interpersonal role definition has been established; they feel they belong.

(11) There are two broad categories of youth—those who are inter-ested and those who are not. Those who have no interest tend to drop out of high school by their own dead weight. Those who are interested can be subcategorized into those whose inter-ests are according to the institutionalized family norms and those whose interests are according to group norms antithetical to their families' norms. The former continue their education; the latter drop out.

(12) The problem of the dropout is less an academic problem than a disciplinary problem. The problem of discipline is a problem of peers and positive interests.

(13) The academic dropout could just as well be called the academic "pushout."

(14) Positive interests are directly related to continuation in high school.

(15) Despite the fact that our respondents lived in the same neigh-borhoods, those who continued their education felt that the large majority in their neighborhood were continuing and those who dropped out felt that the large majority were dropping out. Their differential perception of the objective situation was based upon their different reference groups.

(16) In an academic institution, academic values should be the prestige values. The fact that in most high schools the out-standing student is considered a "grind" or academic "rate buster" and the football captain and beauty queen are con-sidered the campus heroes is an indictment of the adminis-tration.

(17) The dropout's self-image, role expectation, and occupational orientation are markedly deficient.

(18) Considering the length of time that the teachers spend with the students, their influence, from the youth's perception, is neg-ligible.

2 . INTERVIEW WITH A LOS ANGELES YOUTH COUNSELOR

So much for our varied conclusions. Our data are basically that given by our teen-age respondents. Beside the interviews with the youth, however, there were any number of other supplementary interviews with parents, counselors, teachers, administrators, psychiatrists, employers, labor leaders, clergymen, police, and other resource persons. One of these interviews presents a vivid overview of the dropout problem especially with reference to our chapter's topic of school experiences. This is an extensive interview that was conducted by the senior author, by Dr. Carle C. Zimmerman of Harvard, and Dr. Joseph Ford, Director of the Department of Sociology of the San Fernando State College on the outskirts of Los Angeles. Our dynamic and knowledgeable interviewee is Maurice J. Colwell who has been working with the dropout problem for a decade. His service is sponsored by the local Rotary Club and is located at the Hollywood YMCA.

A DELINQUENCY PROJECT BECOMES A DROPOUT PROJECT

"We did a study which started in 1958 that was brought about because of a delinquency problem which was brought to the attention of the Court Council by the Juvenile Police. In investigating this delinquency problem we came upon the age-old problem of the dropout.... There was no money put up so we had to carry on with our own personal interest. There was our own little group and we all gave our own time to it. A volunteer came from the police department as well. This officer is extremely helpful and is the probation officer in this area. The Probation Department loaned us a secretary. We carried the ball along with the Welfare Attendance Supervisor. The Attendance Supervisor was the key in the whole thing because we had no other way to get into the schools in the area and when we had called the school before about dropouts we got the standard reply to the effect 'Dropouts are a problem in the Negro and Mexican areas. We don't have that trouble in Hollywood.' But we knew differently. We had seen the dropouts accumulating on the street corners. They start to gather in clusters. For instance, right now in a western part of the city—part of Hollywood —there is a group of dropouts. Just two or three start the ball rolling and now there are a dozen. This clustering would occur —now here, now there. Boys from fourteen years of age right on up to late teen-agers. We knew the dropout problem was there and we wanted to do something about it but we knew we couldn't do anything about it until we proved that there is a dropout problem in the area."

Locating the Dropout

"In the spring of 1959, we isolated out of perhaps 1000, 57 dropouts. In the following semester our welfare and attendance supervisor isolated another sixty-one or sixty-two. We had trouble with a few of them. These were boys who were dropouts, who were excluded from school for various reasons—some of them illegal. Some of them had been excluded too young, some of them had been excluded without parental consent. These were 'pushouts' rather than 'dropouts.' From the information that I receive from people in this area most 'dropouts' are 'pushouts.' They can't go back even if they want to. The school authorities say that they can go back but since the rules say that the youth may come back if he goes to another school and proves himself—he is sent to another school and somehow or other he never gets back. I suppose on a very rare occasion some boy will go to some other school and get good grades and come back. But I've never heard of the situation. I am speaking, of course, of how things are in high school...."

Other Loopholes

"There is also a medical exclusion. Theoretically, a boy has to go to school until he is eighteen. There is no way out unless he has a medical exclusion, or is in some state institution. Even with girls who are married, they should be taking four hours a week until they are eighteen. Marriage and being ruled an adult mellows the compulsory school attendance law but even then they should be attending until they are eighteen. That's what the law says. But it is not enforced. Many of these boys who drop out have work permits. You have to have a work permit according to state law. If you have to have a work permit you must get it through the school. The school in turn is supposed to enforce the four-hour-a-week regime. But they can't enforce it. Or, at least, they don't."

Seeming Hypocrisy of Some School Administrators

"Some of our school administrators, despite the fact that out in the open they have the do-good attitude and always seem willing to help, behind the scenes are just pushing the youth out. In every case that I have seen it is this way. Unless you get a vice principal who is exceptional. We did have an exceptional one once. He made a special effort to place dropouts with their peers and help them with a program. It seems when the kids get to be fourteen or fifteen they have problems and act out their problems. They start to get aggressive in school. They start to make themselves felt and start to smoke in school and start to cheat a little. Now the vice principal has to put up with it. There is nothing he can do except just keep moving them around until the parents get a little fed up and put him in one of these little private schools where he doesn't have to attend at all—he can just do as he pleases. Actually, in these private schools they don't have to attend and they will still get credit. We found many of these schools in the Hollywood area. Little theatrical schools. There are two in particular. These are two schools that are schools in quotes. By that I mean they are schools in that they have teachers and books and they give credit. But they are actually cesspools where students can go and get credit without being required to attend. As long as they pay their money they advance through school. But strangely enough in highly exceptional cases I've had some of these boys who have gone to a little school—never attend —get credit for it, go away—perhaps in the armed service—then come back, go to college and do just beautifully. It sometimes makes me wonder: Is high school just a ritual?"

Burying the Dropout

"What we did then was to go into the junior high school to follow up our leads. This is really where our concern was—in the junior high. It was pretty evident that these cases would arrive at senior high school and would get kicked out or be lost somewhere between junior and senior high. Supposedly the welfare and attendance department is handling these cases and some kind of referral or placement is worked out but we lost all kinds of children in the process and we had no way of finding them. We couldn't follow it through any further but we found that the biggest problem was with the fourteen-and-a-half- and fifteen-year-old boy. He was now actively aggressing against the school and the school had to put up with him. The thing that disturbed us was that they never did anything about it in a positive way. At least not that we could find out about, except that they would switch the problem cases around within the schools ... and lose them. We have coined a term of our own here. We call it 'burying the dropout.' The dropout somehow doesn't fit into the accepted patterns of doing things. Both at home and at school they are looking for acceptance. If they can't find acceptance at home they can find it in some kind of a peer group, their own little clusters. They get acceptance and recognition and they in turn must live up to certain standards such as dress and behavior and so on. Then when the boy gets in trouble with the police and is taken home, the parents say, 'It's those boys he goes with.' But that peer group itself is the product of their previous rejection."

Peer Leadership

"The peer group itself is what bothers me. Some of these peer groups will stay in school and some will drop out. We have an example here now in one junior high school: a Japanese-American boy. Everyone else in his family had dropped out—his two sisters, his brother-in-law, and his brother. But he is sticking because the group he is involved with is sticking. I can't say why they are sticking. This group is unique. The oldest boy is not quite sixteen and he is doing very well academically but he is hostile. The youngest boy is twelve and a half. They have a wonderful opportunity here at the 'Y' although this service is not of the 'Y.' And so do we, because we are right with the boys. I like to go into the community where they are. I did do a lot of visiting with groups.... The leader of these groups, I find in many instances, has access to more sex knowledge and has access to a car. A car is extremely important in this area. Here a car is god to these people. If I get football tickets, say to a Pro game, a championship game to which kids in some eastern city would kill to go, I could call up ten or fifteen boys and they wouldn't want to go. They'd say, 'Forget it.' But if I went to a drag strip or something to do with automobiles, I could get hundreds to go. In other studies in this area we have found that the delinquency often starts with a car. The youth need gas and start stealing for that, then tires, and then something a little bigger and they are gone."

Jobs for Dropouts

"What kind of jobs do the dropouts get? First of all they are looking for one job—work in a gas station. They want to work in a gas station; they want to work around cars. I've both seen why they want to work in gas stations and I've got some hunches. I've gotten boys jobs in these gas stations. In gas stations there are older men that give these kids complete acceptance. The mechanic will say, 'Hey, Bill, get that for me.' 'Hey, Bill, get that for me.' 'Hey, Bill, pull off that wheel for me.' Actually he is taking advantage of the dropouts for they'll work all hours—they will break every law in the Labor Code. This is one of the places that we try to place these boys if they are placeable. Some of them drift from job to job. There is something about gas stations, though, that doesn't gratify what they are looking for and they'll move from job to job, and we do a lot of service placement when they get up to that seventeenth birthday. We get them into the services so we can clear their records. Of course they are not all on probation, they are not all in trouble and if they are, frequently it's just curfew—staying out after ten. One thing I feel about dropouts is their inability to accept authority. This community is different from the communities around it. Further east there is a more stable community. A community that is not in such a state of upheaval as this community. This area has a high rate of apartment starts—building apartments—and they are building ahead of the demand. There are vacancy signs all over but they continue to build. We have another attraction here—Hollywood Boulevard. This is 'Prostitute Row.' For homosexuals. There is a neurotic undercurrent in this town that is really something. You can't conceive of boys twelve and eleven who are really hep on homosexuals—how you operate them, how you thumb them to get rides from them and work them for whatever you can. This is with these youth all the way from fifth or sixth grade right through how many years they may stay in high school."

"Box Boys"

"Hollywood, in the last twenty or thirty years, has gone on a complete transformation. What was formerly a good residential area is now an area of cliff-dwellers. The only good residential areas that are left are now up in the hills. Some of the apartments are very fancy but the typical family here is an apartment family with few if any children. People eat out a lot. Restaurants, entertainment spots, and the bars do a good business along with a few department stores. We have huge markets in this area and the competition kills the smaller markets. These large stores are at key corners. They hire a great number of 'box boys.' The retail clerks have organized all these box boys within the Retail Clerks' Union. The box boys' jobs now fall into the category of the highly paid with a lot of fringe benefits. These are premium jobs and the dropouts get into these jobs. We have found that they do stick there because the monetary gain is so great, compared to the other jobs they can get. They start out at about $1.37 an hour. With overtime a boy can make a considerable amount of money. He can make fifty or sixty dollars a week. In the East I understand that chain stores are less and less hiring anyone without a high school education. Not so here. They'll hire anyone that looks good for the job irrespective of how much education he has. The chain stores generally pay such low wages here and they hire so few males that we have had very little call for such jobs from our young people. But because the supermarket is union scale and is a premium job without educational requirements, the dropouts point toward these jobs. How the boys work it is: one boy gets in and gets to know the manager and mentions to him that his friend who has dropped out of school is just hanging around and has nothing to do. He will then get him in part-time and work him up to full-time. One big market will hire twenty or thirty box boys and some of them are open from eight o'clock in the morning until twelve o'clock at night. Up till ten o'clock at night they are able to hire these young kids. This has absorbed a great number of dropouts. Five or six years ago this employment possibility did not exist for the dropouts."

The "Japanese Gardener" Stereotype

"Another area that presents employment opportunities to the dropout is that of being a gardener. But the dropouts don't buy it. Here in Hollywood there are a lot of yard jobs because the yards have to be taken care of all year round. But it is difficult to find anyone who will do the job. The dropouts won't. They can make ten dollars in a day—clear; there are no taxes. Nothing is demanded of them except that you go in and do the job and get paid at the end of the day. The dropout doesn't want these gardener jobs. It's physical work and to be seen working in a yard is out. The 'Japanese' gardener is a stereotype here and his status is low. . . ."

Peer Group Rites and Trappings

"Peer groups are characteristically rigid. The Hollywood boy of today has a certain style of dress in this category. He must wear khaki pants, French-toed shoes, a certain shirt, a specific type of haircut, and use a certain type of cigarette. The type of haircut is a semi-exaggerated long hairdo; about two years ago it was extreme.

"It is very interesting that all the schools in my area have ruled against the specific things that these children do—as the way they wear their hair. Boys don't like to wear belts; the school will say you can't come to school unless you wear belts. The schools will forever come up to meet the situation with a rule against it. It is not done centrally by the superintendent's office but seems to be spontaneous by the particular school administration."

Mexican-American Fad

"The French-toed shoe—flat toe and high shine—came from the Mexican-American boys and it has spread over into this part of town. I feel that they copy many things of the Mexican-American boys just as they took over their hairdo. I've had Mexican-American boys who live in the community come over here and say, 'Gee, this is weird. I come over here and I'm a "bean." That makes me a big attraction. I have kids following me around. They act like me. They think I have all kinds of hidden talents.' These boys become leaders in the community. There are certain hangouts where Mexican-American boys really make out. The girls are wild about them. These 'beans,' as they're called, have all kinds of favors done for them by the others, they get invited to all the good parties. It is rather amusing that in the Jewish community there is a place called the 'Kosher Puppy.' The kids that hang around there are almost all Jewish. They go to Jewish schools, Jewish community centers, and you will find far more Mexicans hanging out around there than live in the community. Perhaps as many as 10 percent of the habitués of the 'Kosher Puppy' are Mexicans because they find that they are so well accepted there. But the school will meet any of these new fads and styles with a rule. The boys who go to school will have to have their hair cut; if it isn't they are sent home to have it cut. Many of the youth, though, provoke the administration on purpose to stimulate some excitement around the school. But it seems that there isn't too much difference in the attitude of the boy who wants to drop out and the school who would just as soon push him out. Believe me, they are helping him all the way without knowing it. The problem is that the boy knows at fifteen or fourteen-and-a-half that they can't kick him out. Sure, they'll threaten him, expel him for three or four days, send him home to his parents, and this goes on and on and on."

Catholic Schools

"There is a variation between the public and the Catholic schools. You see the Catholic schools don't have to keep these children and we find that to get into a Catholic school, especially in this area, is a privilege. A lot of parents would like to have their children go but the schools are overcrowded and you have to wait to get in and they have no time for problem children. If a girl gets in trouble she is out. I get a considerable number of boys from Catholic schools who have not made the grade and I find when they take them out it is a little different. It isn't so much your behavior but rather you're not making the grades. 'Why don't you just go somewhere else and do a little work so you can catch up? Because we have no time, you have to do it on your own.' Of course they have their pushouts too. 'Get out of here' is quite effective. There is a crucial difference in the legal situation. The Catholic school is not under the restraint of the state law to keep them. It is a common thing for me in placement to have non-Catholic parents come in here and say—for an example, I have one mother who works in a restaurant from eight until midnight or sometimes until two in the morning, gets good tips and good money but it probably involves a little hustling on the side with the richer customers—prostitution. The boy is left alone and has his friends up to the house and they goof around and break into the liquor closet. Now she says this boy is bringing her trouble so she is sending him to a Catholic school because 'the Catholic schools know how to handle these situations; Catholic schools are more rigid; Catholic schools teach them the three R's better.' What she really wants to do is keep on doing what she is doing. As in this case, so in the majority of the others, the father is absent. This one has been absent for a long time and there have been several little interim affairs or 'marriages' that have had no stabilizing effect."

The School Counselor

"I can cite any number of my cases from my file right here on my desk. No names; so no one can identify them. My cases are a little weird because I get a lot of disturbed people. [Fingering through file on desk] This boy is fifteen years old and has been expelled from school for lighting fires in trash cans. He hates the school and he hates all the people there. He went into the counselor—and I better explain that term. A counselor is someone that is an ordinary teacher who has taken a few extra units of courses in education about counseling; this presumably qualifies him as a counselor and gets him thirty to forty dollars more a month. He really does grade counseling. Like this: 'Well, Bill, why don't you get along with Mr. Jones in your math class? Well, we will switch you to this class.' There is never anything done with the problem the boy has. Anyway, this firebug is a dancer. He has been taking dancing lessons for about eight years. He is a Catholic boy; has been to a Catholic school. He has lived at times with his stepfather and natural mother and at times with his natural father. He has been handed back and forth but he now lives with his father. He is completely withdrawn. He is now going to junior high because he is living with his father and his father says, 'You go to school or I'll beat the daylights out of you.' When he comes to see me he is not allowed to hang out with any of his buddies. When he goes to school he is physically there but the first chance he gets, he runs away. He is fifteen and his whole problem started two years ago. I find that thirteen and fourteen, especially fourteen, is the real crucial time and the problems explode then. And this is where we have no counteracting forces to meet the problem. In senior high school we have a tendency to put the blame on the junior high school, especially the administrators. But back in junior high where it gets its start it is just kind of nursed along. One of the common things in junior high—if a boy doesn't get along in your class, you bring him down to the office and he can sit in the office that period. It is not uncommon to go to the office and see ten to fifteen boys sitting outside the office for different periods. There is a certain home-room teacher at one of the schools who is extremely difficult. The vice principal says, 'I don't understand it. None of the boys can get along with that man.' But yet the dropouts have been excluded from school because of the problems they had trying to get along with that one man."

Military School

"Here is a case of a mother who wants me to place her boy. He is a dropout from a junior high because of his truancy. She has another boy who had the same trouble but we finally got him in the army. She wants me to place this boy who is thirteen in a Catholic boarding school or in a military school. I would rather place him in a Catholic school where the discipline is good and they learn their stuff. But there are all kinds of military schools for the very young. And they are cheap. When the parents find out what they cost they are shocked. You can go for $135 to $175 a month plus uniforms. Some of them cost less and this includes room and board. Many of them have the boy come home on Friday and go back on Sunday night so the parent has to take care of them on the weekend. We do a tremendous business with these military schools and the results are terrible. Some of the things that go on in the military schools, as we hear from the boys later when they return, are wild—homosexuality and all kinds of weird things. We have found that military schools are targets for homosexuals—working in them, coaching, etc."

The Law and the Underage Dropout

"Here is another case of homosexuality. There are two boys in this family. One boy was twelve years old and the other two years older. Both dropouts. Both having a difficult time and the mother works as a waitress. They called the grandmother in from New York to try to stabilize the situation. They are a Catholic family and they tried to get them back in a Catholic school but the boys refused. They have been transferred all over and finally the parents have decided to leave the community. There was no father there though she has had three husbands. The twelve-year-old hides out and refuses to attend school. He was sent to a child guidance clinic but wouldn't accept it. The mother has no control over the boy. I go into the home and the boy screams and cries. He does what he pleases and the mother can't control him. Then she breaks down and there we go.

"The boy is truant. After three days he is legally a truant. After he is gone three days, he is legally truant and some action is supposed to be taken. But the mechanics for taking action is so involved that no one wants to start it. It is a court action. It means that the vice principal and the welfare and attendance officer must fill out a petition. The petition then goes down to a supervisor in charge of these welfare and attendance people. They check it over and then it goes downtown to one man who is supposed to take care of the whole Los Angeles system's truants. He reviews it and checks it for corrections. They are very concerned about the wording of these things because when it goes into court the school wants it to appear that they have done everything that they could to help the situation. The case is then sent back to the junior high school vice principal. He OK's it and sends it to the probation department. This whole process takes weeks and weeks and in the meantime many of these boys are waiting for a filing—this is called an 'I' filing. It takes from six to eight weeks to get this thing into court. So they almost never do it. I've even heard a man who is the head of the Los Angeles School System and his assistant tell the committee sent down here by the government to investigate delinquency, dropouts, and the whole problem, that they had made no more than 46 filings in one year from a school district where they have about 300,000 children! Something is very strange about this and the children know it. They know that there isn't going to be any follow-through. Still if the boy is picked up away from school he is threatened: 'If you don't go to school, you'll go to court.' So the kid says 'OK.' And some of his buddies say, 'Forget it. They aren't going to send you anywhere.' I have had boys who agitate them for months and that filing never comes. Each of the administrations tries to get someone else to make the filing. So what they finally do is to get the police department to go to the family and ask the parent to file against the boy stating that they can no longer control the boy. This saves face for the school. They are afraid of publicity and they would just as soon pass the buck. I have strong feelings about the way they handle it. . . ."

Vandalism

"The middle of last week we had a group of boys picked up. There were about twelve boys. Someone turned them in by writing a letter. All these boys were dropouts. All of them were hanging around with nothing to do. Several of them had little part-time jobs. They started out by breaking into schools. They went to the junior high that most of them had attended. They went into the rooms and they were starting to swipe things in there—typewriters —and they would throw things around and just mess it up in general. Then from there they learned to get in from roofs and they would go into places and scare the daylights out of somebody, like a costume shop—there are a lot of little unique businesses in Hollywood. They got in the habit of stealing parts—what we call 'midnight auto supply'—taking carburetors off cars, and one of them took a door. This was most interesting to the police department. They took the door off a car that was sitting right out on the street. They get bolder and bolder and they start doing things. This one has been an epidemic: They get seltzer bottles and drive down streets and when they see people waiting for a bus they lean out the window with the seltzer bottle and let the people have it. This really spread. . . .

"We get patterns in vandalism. Certain things will occur like this squirting with the seltzer bottles. It just happens once or twice and if it works well and people get a lot of kicks out of it, then it spreads like wildfire. You must remember if you went down Hollywood Boulevard on a Saturday night, for a mile and a half it would be one solid car—car to car. They go up and down, looking at each other, screaming at each other and making remarks. The sidewalks are packed with them. They come from all over the city to Hollywood Boulevard. It's a great place for fights and for kids to get together and have arguments and so on. . . ."

Marriage Patterns

"I have followed their marriage careers long enough to see the pattern. In fact I have a deal with some of the ministers in town concerning these marriages. I am referring specifically to the dropouts' marriages. These kids marry at a very early age. They marry a girl who is maybe in the first or second year of high school. The typical dropout is working in a gas station or perhaps by this time he has gone into the service. He gets married; immediate pregnancy; in debt; terrific financial problems; tremendous arguments; the boy going out to be back with his group, with his guys. There is almost the feeling that the girl is marrying this guy for some kind of security. I don't know what kind of security they can get from him. It is common for some of these boys to go over and visit so-and-so who is married. Marriage seems to be the badge of maturity. Forced marriages are common. We have had very good luck in the community. A service club will put up the money to have a wedding for them—buy a cake, and I've gone out in the car and gathered some of the boys together to make it look legal. The basis for marriage is pretty unstable in that the boy can't give himself completely to the home. He simply can't give himself completely to the home."

The Car Culture

"Here in Hollywood we have the car industry. The remodeling of cars is a big business and it is not done by large places. It is done in small shops. Now there is one shop in Hollywood and we could go over there right now and drive in and I'm willing to bet that we would find that the owner is a dropout and that four of five of his employees are dropouts and the fellow who owns the place has sort of chosen these guys because he thinks they can do better than the rest and they learn by being there. My brother-in-law is the perfect example. He has become an expert in fixing special-built cars and he has learned it from the time he was fourteen years old. He can fix any kind of special-built car, especially with glass involved. On several of our streets in Hollywood you'll find maybe fifteen or twenty of these establishments within half a mile. The rebuilding of cars is the thing that is unique to California. It started here. Most of the companies who make special parts for rebuilding hot rods are

local. The magazines come out of this area. If you were to go to
some of the parking lots at the schools you would see some of the
cars. There are certain types of cars that are premium. They are
called 'stud cars' or 'hound.' And the cars that are not 'hound' are
the 'reg' cars like Hudsons, Plymouths, Nash. These are considered
nowhere. If his parents have one of these cars he wouldn't be seen
riding in it because it has no appeal. They want certain models—
'51 Mercury, '51 Fords, '40 Fords, '32 Fords. Foreign cars are considered pretty rank. The important thing is that it must have immediate thrust, tremendous horsepower. They don't like sports cars
because they have their own transmissions that do build up speed
but they don't care how fast the car will roll in third. They're
interested in how fast the car will go from one light to the next
light. You'll find in our police stations here that one of the major
problems is dragging. One boy will have a driver's license and a few
bucks and he will involve five or six of these kids. He will allow
them to hang around his house and he will send them on errands.
You ask them, 'What are you doing today?' and they say, 'We're
building a car.' And they got an old Ford in the bake. For example,
there is this famous dance team, the X's. They bought a big home
over in the west part of town. The father walked out on them and
left them with four children. The oldest boy made it through school
but the second boy dropped out. He refused to go to school. He was
involved in this gas sniffing incident. They took him down and
they tried to make an example of him. They took him downtown
and put him in Juvenile Hall and tried to prove to the other boys
in the area what will happen to you. So he was in Juvenile Hall for
five or six days and came out of Juvenile Hall and went back in the
community. As a consequence, we had all kinds of boys who wanted
to go to Juvenile Hall. He had this experience and he had the
badge and he was one of the boys now. Today this boy's house is a
hangout. They have a big back area, a patio, and at all times there
are about three or four cars being taken apart or put together and a
couple of motorcycles. I would say at this point that probably
twenty-five or thirty boys have contact with that backyard within a
week. When the police are looking for someone, they will go—there
are about four or five of these homes—they will automatically go to
one of these homes. The parents will call me up and complain:
'Why do they always come here?' The police know that where you
have a lot of dropouts working on cars you have youth who have
stolen spare parts from junk yards and who have been getting their

training to take parts off cars on the streets. The ultimate in a car would be a Corvette with a four-speed transmission, a full race engine, and a blower on it. If you would ask any boy on the street he would say that was the ultimate."

Organized Competitive Sports

"Any organized sport like baseball, football, and so on—these are out. They just don't figure in at all. These boys don't want to be involved in group activities where they might be shown up for not being able to do it as good as everyone else. When I first came here I tried everything. This one boy, Sandy, I took him out in the back and taught him how to throw a football. Once he got the hang of throwing that football, and he could throw it pretty far, he would go around to all the playground areas. When he got into the game all he wanted to do was get the ball and throw it. The others would then all see how well he could throw. When you go to the park and see a group of boys playing certain games you can see on the out-skirts the dropouts. Dropouts on the whole are not geared for com-petitive sports. These imply control, discipline, team play. But they're pretty good at fighting and other aggressive activities. I guess I could get them involved in a game of football or baseball if there were just a few and no one would see them and I did all the planning and providing. Being at a certain place, at a certain time, in a certain costume, with definite equipment, to abide by rules in strict team play, and where you can still come off the loser—no, no thanks; that's not for the dropout. . . ."

THE NEGATIVE POLE

Youth counselor Colwell's picture of the more dramatic aspects of the dropout culture in Hollywood is authentic and brilliant. This spontaneous report of the Los Angeles situation may seem extreme to those of the more conservative portion of the United States but his sketch of the dropout subculture in the California metropolis may well be considered the negative pole of our hypothetical law of polarization that separates the dropout subculture from the student subculture. It seems to be the polar direction to which the indepen-dent youth culture is leading in other metropolitan centers of the country. What one does not get from the interviews of the dropouts themselves is the tremendous energy and sharp vitality which Mr. Colwell imparted to the dropout picture. This will become im-mediately apparent from the replies that we received from our respondents to the questions concerning their likes and dislikes while attending school.

3. YOUTH IN SCHOOL: LIKES AND DISLIKES

"WHAT DID YOU LIKE IN PARTICULAR ABOUT GOING TO SCHOOL?"

"What did you like in particular about going to school?" was the simple question that began our series of questions concerning the school experiences of our graduating and dropout respondents. A representative sampling of their replies is the following.

Dropouts

"I didn't mind anything about school at all really. The only thing I thought was hard about school was waking up in the morning to go." (Dropout Marshall M., # 100, New Orleans)

"It gives you something to do. That's about the only thing I liked about going to school." (Dropout Albert S., # 108, New Orleans)

"Nothing, I didn't like nothing about it." (Dropout Kathleen S. M., # 136, New Orleans)

"Meeting new people and making new friends and I pretty well liked my teachers and it was fun going because staying home all day at the house was no fun because all your friends went to school. You didn't really enjoy yourself at home because you had no one your age to talk to or to be with." (Dropout Mrs. Shirley B., # 140, New Orleans)

"I liked Tech best because they had auto mechanics." (Dropout Larry B., # 204, Omaha)

"There wasn't a whole lot. I liked the football games and the fun that went along with it." (Dropout Robert M., # 222, Omaha)

Graduates

"I like it because I want to learn more things about growing up and all that type of thing. I like being with people. If I stay home for any reason at all I don't like it. The fact that you can do a lot of things and have a lot of fun. It's not work, really." (Graduate Sherry H., # 9, St. Louis)

"Everything. I love Notre Dame. And I want to go on. I think I want to be a nurse, but I'm not sure yet." (Graduate Marilyn R., # 27, St. Louis)

"I like the atmosphere around here. It's not like other schools. In other schools they act like you are somebody low but in here everybody is equal. I'm glad I came here." (Graduate Russel M., # 101, New Orleans)

"I could say nothing but that wouldn't be right. I like English and math. I always liked to read. You don't have to work. But I would rather work and have money coming in and spend it.... I'd like to be an oceanographer. I don't know whether biological or mathematical." (Graduate John Mc., # 123, New Orleans)

"Friends and clubs and teachers." (Graduate Margaret D., # 221, Omaha)

"The thing I like is that you are forever learning new things." (Graduate Leroy G., # 335, Denver)

THE TALLY

In reply to the question "What did you like in particular about going to school?" the dropouts were understandably defensive and obviously not accustomed to conceptualize their reactions within this frame of reference. By numerical count of items liked it was found that the graduating group listed 4.4 and the dropouts mentioned 2.4.[2] More important, the replies to this question give us an idea of the texture of the reactions of the youth who are subjected to the educational process. We shall try to evaluate this differential texture after we present the negative counterpart to this same question:

"WAS THERE ANYTHING IN PARTICULAR THAT YOU DISLIKED ABOUT GOING TO SCHOOL?"

Dropouts

"Oh, there's nothing in particular that I disliked, except getting up in the morning." (Dropout Roy S., # 18, St. Louis)

"Sometimes the teachers got under my skin." (Dropout Jimmy D., # 22, St. Louis)

"Some of the teachers I didn't like but I loved going to Mercy High. It's a very good school." (Dropout Trina L., # 24, St. Louis)

"Everything. I didn't like to go." (Dropout Lorry W., # 44, St. Louis)

"Sometimes I got too much homework. Naturally I got a little bored." (Dropout Charlene T., # 128, New Orleans)

"The whole thing. I just couldn't get interested in it. Just the whole thing." (Dropout Elaine D., # 132, New Orleans)

"Geography and some of the teachers could be more helpful. Some of them, it seems, are just there for the money. The kids like a teacher who kids around with you a little bit." (Dropout Vivian M., # 248, Omaha)

"There was a feeling that you couldn't really do what you wanted to do." (Dropout John C., # 404, Los Angeles)

"Politics. I don't know. For some reason the schools in Downey—I went to Downey Senior High School—it seems . . . I shouldn't say this frankly . . . but as far as I'm concerned there is nothing there for any kids because the teachers want to tell you their problems. There is nothing to interest you. The politics end is from the teachers, and the people who are in the attendance office. All they want to do is, if they don't like you, they'll run you out on a rail. Throw you out, blackball you out of town and that's ridiculous. If a kid is run out and he is sort of a difficult person, they should work right along with him. Instead, if you haven't got money you're out of the door. But if you got money, O.K., they're real friends with you and you get along all right. That is the way it is in Downey. The schools aren't what they should be." (Dropout Ronald C., # 406, Los Angeles)

"Nothing particular. It's just a drag. You have to walk up so many stairs. You couldn't use the elevators. Just the teachers could and that's what I didn't like. Four floors! I started on the second, went down to the first, then up to the third, went to the fourth, went down to the first again and then went back up to the fourth. You get tired." (Dropout George W., # 516, Boston)

"One thing I didn't like at Rindge was the way they marked your homework assignments. You might work two or three hours on an assignment and when you turn it in they just check your name. And if you don't have it you don't get a check. They don't look to see what you have done. None of the teachers had any interest in the students. I was just like a regular job to them. They just work eight hours a day. The only reason they teach is because they get paid for it. I think some of them are there because it's an easy job. They don't do no studying when they go home, which they should to keep ahead of their students. I disliked having just twenty minutes for lunch. But I really liked school. I learned a lot at Rindge but I could have learned more if the teachers were more interested.... I didn't have no spending money because I just had my mother. I just had enough money to go to school and come back. In a way that's good because you couldn't go to shows. But even on weekends I didn't have no spending money. I quit and went back and I quit and went back. When I quit I was behind in school but when I went back I was doing good if you consider the marks I was getting. I did flunk one subject—that was Algebra II. But then I started talking to Carol and I never had any money to take my girl out.... Another thing about school—they ought to be harder on the kids in truancy. Instead of just giving them detention they call their mothers up every time, instead of throwing them out—the ones that are really goofing off. Even if they do it once I would call their parents up about it and if they don't want to do anything about it I would just throw them out." (Dropout Tom D., # 546, Boston)

Graduates

"No, I have always liked school." (Graduate Sherry X., # 9, St. Louis)

"No. The teachers I had were wonderful. Most of the kids I had classes with were really swell. I really miss them. But then again there are always rotten apples in every bushel. For them I am glad to get out of school. Other than that I will miss it very much." (Graduate Peggy K., # 17, St. Louis)

"It seems to me that you run across kids of your own age and your same grade and they think they are better than you or they think they have more than you and they are really equal to you and it is kind of hard to make friends with them. But you have to adjust yourself to them and to the different dislikes that they have. Then there is always the feeling that you are not liked in school and I think you overcome this in high school because you feel you are more free and you can do what you want. In grammar school they have to be more strict but in high school you have a feeling of independence." (Graduate Patty S., # 137, New Orleans)

"Classmates. . . . I couldn't say that I liked every one of them. . . . but I realized that everybody isn't perfect but there are some things that I don't like about some people." (Graduate Virginia B., # 145, New Orleans)

"No. Except this year I have too many outside activities and it keeps me pretty busy." (Graduate Margaret D., # 221, Omaha)

"The short lunch hour. I like to socialize." (Graduate Rita V., # 311, Denver)

"I disliked our principals. For the first two years we used to have a real mean old grouchy thing. She used to come at me and say that if I didn't get all straight 'A's she would throw me out of school. No, she wasn't fooling. She really embarrassed me in front of the assembly when she passed out the report cards. She said next time she wanted to see nothing but straight 'A's." (Graduate Frank K., # 317, Denver)

"The Monsignor was set on kicking certain kids out and last year he said anyone caught ditching would be kicked out and wouldn't be able to return. But he let the ones who were out for sports back in because he said he needed the guys back in school for sports to keep the school going. It didn't seem quite fair to the other ones that got kicked out." (Graduate Augie L., # 345, Denver)

"The 'drives'—it's a constant 'push,' 'push.' " (Graduate Bob J., # 429, Los Angeles)

SUMMARY

As was to be expected on the American scene, the dropouts voiced more than twice as many items that they found less than gratifying during their school histories than did the graduates. They averaged 3.3 complaints and the graduates averaged 1.2.[3]

THE TEXTURE OF ACADEMIC APPRECIATION AND PROTEST

Little is learned from the mere counting of the bouquets or brick-bats launched by the teen-agers into the general target area of the school. The type of encomium or criticism must be considered. A core criticism is of greater weight than a fringe criticism. We had hypothesized that the dropout would be more critical of the core of the educational process—the curriculum—than would the graduate. Consequently we had our panel of judges sort the replies of each respondent into a rank-value scale as follows:

(Take maximum value of each respondent)

(1) *Nothing noteworthy* liked.

(2) *Noncurricular* (Personal, nonschool related): e.g., "I liked school because it gave me something to do." "I liked school because as long as I went to school I didn't have to work."

(3) *Extracurricular:* Nonschool activities but school related, e.g., comradeship with fellow students; nonschool sponsored social activities; status symbol of attending school; "Need diploma for job" (with implication that skills and knowledge obtained in school process not a factor).

(4) *Cocurricular:* School-sponsored activities—dramatics, debate, band, dances, sports, etc.

(5) *Supracurricular:* Administration, teachers, staff.

(6) *Curricular:* Studies themselves as integrated with higher academic and developmental or occupational goals, e.g., "I liked the studies." "You learned something there." "I liked everything about school." "I wanted to make something of myself."

"LIKES" AND "DISLIKES" IN DEPTH

A new dimension emerged. All that was known before this sorting into types of likes and dislikes was that the dropouts had voiced one-half as many things that they liked about their academic career and almost three times as many things that they disliked. But now a polarization in depth became apparent. The dropouts typically (70%) found fault with anything that had to do with the curriculum, the staff, and the school activities. The graduates' "gripes" in more than seven out of ten cases were of a nonconsequential type such as "I have too many outside activities and it keeps me pretty busy" or "I couldn't say that I liked every one of my classmates . . . but I realized that everybody isn't perfect." [4]

The same polarization emerged in the types of "likes" expressed by the dropouts and the graduates. The dropouts (60%) liked either nothing about school, or something that was extracurricular; while the graduates (79%) expressed their likes in terms of the curriculum, the staff, the school-sponsored activities.[5]

These polarizations would seem to make a consistent pattern

only if the dropout was not identified with the school and its activities and the graduate was.

The critical point of these differences remains that our sample consists of youth of similar or identical native abilities as well as of similar or identical socio-economic backgrounds. The matched sample insures us of meaningful results.

REASONS FOR DROPPING OUT

Educational and sociological literature is without a systematic report in the dropouts' own words as to why they terminated their education. Neither is there any study available that investigates whether graduates have had comparable or even greater difficulties to overcome in order to continue their education.

It is this intriguing question of the comparable difficulties encountered in the continuance of education that we now took up.

The method of eliciting the youths' responses to this question was extremely simple. Since the youth had just been questioned in detail as to what they had disliked about their school experiences we now asked them to look back upon those reasons and select the reason that either did or would have ranked first "in your decision to leave school."

"WHAT REASON RANKED FIRST IN YOUR DECISION TO LEAVE SCHOOL?"

Dropouts

"I stomped a kid's head in. I didn't mean to, but I did it. Turned loose and started fighting 'cause he was a lot taller than I am. He was about six-one. I just knocked him down and started kicking him. The principal told me to stop. I stopped and he took me to the office and started talking to me. He said either I get out or I get kicked out. So I got out. This was my last year. Right now I go to Hadley. But I haven't went but one day. I was going to go to O'Fallon. Hadley's all colored except for maybe twenty white kids." (Dropout Dennis D., # 000, St. Louis)

"I was taking a secretary course and I wanted to be one until I got [pregnant and got] married and then I didn't want to be much of anything." (Dropout Mrs. Joan H., # 8, St. Louis)

"Well, when I quit Southwest I was flunking out and I couldn't get along with the teachers. They set too high standards for me so I dropped out." (Dropout Billy L., # 42, St. Louis)

"I got sick of it and I didn't want to go no more. I'm planning on finishing it in the service—you can do that. I figure if I can finish high school in two months why should I go two years." (Dropout Edward L., # 102, New Orleans)

"I just couldn't stand it any longer." (Dropout Errol C., # 106, New Orleans)

"Some of the teachers. They plugged you too much. I shouldn't say that. But some teachers just push you too hard and I just can't take it." (Dropout Roland L., # 124, New Orleans)

"I had a car and had insurance and car payments to keep up with. I didn't want my parents to pay for everything so I got a job and went to night school for a while . . . I was having trouble with my school work." (Dropout Larry B., # 204, Omaha)

"I was kind of interested in school for a while but after a while I figured I was sixteen and I was going to quit. I had that in my mind too. Any ordinary person has this in their mind too: 'When I reach sixteen I'm going to quit.' They don't have to bother getting up in the morning. I can sleep all day and just do nothing. . . .'" (Dropout Walter J., # 502, Boston)

"I dropped out when I was in ninth grade the day after my sixteenth birthday. Most people stay for a couple of weeks after they are sixteen but they know they are going to quit. But I thought to myself, 'Why stay in the couple of extra weeks—you could go out looking for a job in those weeks.' So I just dropped out the day after . . . I've been looking for a job but not very hard." (Dropout George W., # 516, Boston)

"So I didn't pass English or something and I said: 'I'm not going back and face the kids.' I talked to ma. She could kick herself for not having finished high school but I figure she needs the money and pretty soon she says 'O.K.' and I quit." (Dropout Donna G., # 524, Boston)

THE GRADUATE REPLIES

"Did you ever think seriously of dropping out of school?" "What reason would have ranked first if you had decided to drop out?" "What finally made you decide to continue your education?"

In presenting this triad of questions to the graduating respondents the trio of interviewers generally received the same type of

answers—"I wouldn't think of dropping out." And probing generally met with resistance. The graduates seemed to feel that they
would be betraying their hard-won ideals if they even discussed the
possibility of their withdrawing from school. And those who did
reply in detail to this question were usually those who had actually
entertained and then wrestled with the prospect of dropping out of
school. Of particular interest are the replies of those teen-agers
whose friends dropped out or who belonged to families in which
other siblings had withdrawn prematurely from school.

Graduates

"Yes. Being bored or getting into an argument with the family,
something like that. The only time I figured I should drop out was
when I got mad. My mother and father were divorced when I was
ten and the family split up and I live with my mother and the rest
of the children live with my father and we all get in arguments and
then sometimes I want to quit. But I like sports and since I was
elected co-captain of the football team I feel I sort of have something to live up to." (Graduate Jerry J., # 105, New Orleans)

"I hate to admit it, but I didn't like school at all. Maybe it was
because I couldn't take part in the activities at school because I had
to work to pay my way through school. I think I would have enjoyed it more if I could have taken part in the activities. Not just
going to school and hurrying up at three o'clock and you had to be
at work at a certain time. Then you get off of work at nine and have
to come home and study. I just didn't like school and I almost quit.
But I wouldn't because I wanted my education. I wanted to go to
college but I couldn't afford to in the first place. But where there is
a will there is a way and I figured I could get in one of them. It was
O.K., but if I could have taken part in all the activities I would
have liked it; I know it...." (Graduate Patricia C., # 131, New
Orleans)

"No, If I would have left it would have been for a boy friend—
getting married. I had two steady boy friends and the first one—he
was in school and he never did tempt me to leave school. But the
second one—he quit school and he wanted me to marry him and I
told him I couldn't because I wanted to finish my education. I told
him that my parents had asked one thing of me: they asked me to
complete my education, at least high school. I told him that would
be the least I could do for them in return, and that still wouldn't

measure up to what they had done for me. He didn't like that too much and we started arguing constantly and we started breaking up and making up and finally we broke up in October for good; and he asked me to start dating him again, but I wouldn't. So he got married January 7—to spite me, he said. I guess he figured I'd never be able to live without him and it did hurt at first; but I figured you got to be adult and mature about the whole thing. I knew that I really wanted to finish my education and nothing would stand in the way.

"My best friend did leave school and I talked to her. We were both born on the same day, the same age, we were both in majorettes and we were both the same type ... but she wanted to get married ... she told me that she would finish school after she was married and I told her I knew better, that she wouldn't and she didn't ... there was no influencing her at all." (Graduate Patricia S., # 137, New Orleans)

"Yes. When I was a freshman. My father, like I said, when he gets mad he'll hit you. He always hit my mother and he used to hit me sometimes. I'd rather get hit when I do something wrong than just get talked to; but I'd rather have my mother hit me because she didn't hit so hard. When my dad hits you it's just like he was hitting another man. I ran away from home a lot of times because I couldn't get along with him. When I ran away from home I never knew where to go and they always say you should go to your priest so I did but they didn't seem to help because I had to go back home or to Juvenile Hall. The last time I ran away from home I went to Juvenile Hall and stayed there for a while and then went home. I guess I'll have to wait until I'm eighteen. I stayed last time in Juvenile Hall two weeks. I didn't mind it except for the other girls. They are the ones that make it bad. Otherwise it's all right. They feed you good. The other girls talk and brag about what they had done and if you hadn't done anything like that you're just a little square or something like that. My mother said I should tell no one. No one knows except my girl friend. My dad talked with me for a long time after that. He always said if any of us got in jail he would be embarrassed and wouldn't come and get us out, but he came. There were times when my little sisters did something wrong ... you know, little boys will call them up or something, and he will say it's because of me ... that they are following in my footsteps. He says I'm not as good as I should be, but I am. What he thinks doesn't really matter to me.... My dad doesn't like visitors. He says they are not minding their own business. My mom thinks differently but it doesn't do her any good to say anything because my dad doesn't like it; so we don't have anyone come over. But she's happy anyway; she loves my dad." (Graduate Olivia C., # 315, Denver)

"They sort of ran the class at the speed of the lowest member. I was bored. Rather than the track system I think they put the cards in alphabetical order and deal them around to the home rooms. I wasn't learning a thing." (Graduate Allan F., # 403, Los Angeles)

"No. Because I don't have a job where I make enough money. My brothers have influenced me, especially my oldest brother because he quit school and he has gone through the experience of having to find a job. He tells me it is better to go." (Graduate Ken A., # 407, Los Angeles)

"Yes. My father died last August; but it was my dad. There are nine kids. We own an ice cream shop and I work there about twenty hours during school and I work at a gas station on the weekends and sometimes during school. I'm second oldest." (Graduate William E., # 431, Los Angeles)

RECAPITULATION

After reviewing the critical incidents which precipitated the premature withdrawal of the dropout from high school and the critical incidents which would have precipitated the premature withdrawal of the graduates had there not been the as-of-now unknown intervening variable or variables, we are now in a position to compare the obstacles that both the dropout and the graduate had to surmount in order to continue their education.

When we speak of "obstacles" that the teen-agers had to surmount in order to continue their education we are not speaking of subjective states of mind as the psychologist would be prone to, but we are alluding to objective environmental obstacles as the sociologist is prone to speak of. A father's death, for instance, is a serious loss to any teen-ager. However, one youth may be stirred on to greater educational achievements while another is determined to abandon his scholastic orientation. But it is the fact of the father's death that we take into account and for both youths of the lower class, we count this a "serious obstacle" to continuation in high school.

But before we assay the obstacles that objectively presented themselves in the lives of the respondents let us recapitulate the steps that have led us to this point.

(1) Our immediate sample consists of 150 dropouts and 150 high school graduates in six metropolitan areas who have been matched in pairs according to sex, age, and IQ.

(2) They originate in families which have likewise been matched in general socio-economic backgrounds: seven out of ten of the dropouts' fathers were blue collar workers and seven out of ten of the graduates' fathers were blue collar workers (unskilled, semiskilled, and skilled). The average family income was a little less than $5,000 per year for both groups. Both groups averaged four children per family.

(3) But despite this similarity of personal and familial character-istics, 50 percent of the youth had dropped out of high school and 50 percent had graduated.

(4) Earlier in this chapter we have seen that in reviewing their academic histories the dropouts recalled almost three times as many things that they disliked about their school experiences as did the graduates and the graduates recalled twice as many things that they liked about their school experiences as did the dropouts. Qualitatively, the things disliked by the dropouts and liked by the graduates tended toward the core or curricular interests; the things liked by the dropouts and disliked by the graduates clustered about the noncurricular. To put this phe-nomenon in another form: In a total summary of this chapter to this point we find that six out of ten dropouts (62%) report their school experiences to have been either "very unfavorable" or "unfavorable"; while three out of four graduates (76%) found their educational experiences to have been either "favorable" or "very favorable." [6]

(5) Our next step was to ask the dropout to describe why he left school and to ask the graduate to describe why he would have left school.

(6) It is at this juncture that we take the total life histories of both dropout and graduate and attempt to evaluate objectively the comparative seriousness of the obstacles that were in their paths toward high school graduation. The panel of three interviewers

went over the 300 interviews and evaluated each of them on the following five-point scale:

OBSTACLE COURSE

(1) *No obstacle:* From the life history of the individual under consideration there did not seem to be any noteworthy obstacle to his continuation in school, e.g., lack of finances, health, parental encouragement, pleasant school surroundings, etc.

(2) *Ordinary obstacles:* This is the type that practically all students must undergo as a condition of educational and human existence, e.g., boring classes, homework, tests, getting up in the morning; being just ordinary in academic, social, and athletic competition.

(3) *Serious obstacle:* That beyond which most students must tolerate to continue school, e.g., death of either parent, racial antipathy, a serious misunderstanding of one's character by the faculty.

(4) *Very serious obstacle:* That under which the panel judged 85 percent of the students would buckle, e.g., practical social ostracism from one's fellow students because of the accouterments of poverty; serious and continued "scape-goatism," etc.

(5) *Impossible obstacle:* Where the situation seemed practically hopeless for the individual to continue his high school education. By definition the graduate did not have to and could not cope with an "impossible obstacle."

4. OBSTACLES TO COMPLETION OF HIGH SCHOOL: DROPOUT AND STAYIN

In reviewing the life histories of the youth we find objective obstacles to the completion of their high school careers (see Table 5).

The immediate conclusion that we can draw from Table 5 is that in our sample there is no significant difference in the objective magnitude of the obstacles that confronted the youth who graduated and the youth who did not. It is only in the category of "impossible obstacles" that we find a notable difference.

In fairness to the graduate it must be stated that if the same situations that occasionally were overcome by the graduate had occurred in the lives of the dropouts they well might have been put in

Table 5.—Obstacles to completion of high school

	No Obstacles	Ordinary Obstacles	Serious Obstacles	Very Serious Obstacles	Impossible Obstacles
Dropouts	5	55	25	6	9
Graduates	12	56	22	10	0 *

* Testing the hypothesis that the nongraduates encountered greater objective obstacles to the completion of their education we find that $D = .080$; $X^2 = 1.92$. Not significant at the .05 level.

the "impossible obstacles" category but because the graduate did overcome the objective difficulty it could not be termed impossible. For instance, the case of Graduate Olivia C., # 315, Denver (*supra* pp. 91–92): her father beat her, she ran away from home and lived at the Juvenile Hall on various occasions; she seemingly had a blameless history but was completely misunderstood by the only loved ones she had, and was not allowed to have friends. Or, the case of Graduate William E., # 431, Los Angeles (*supra*, p. 92): one of nine children, his father died, and he held down two jobs while trying to carry on his school work. These seemingly impossible situations the graduates overcame. The only cases of "impossible obstacles" that the dropouts had were those of premarital pregnancies. But these illegitimate pregnancies were presumably of their own making and consequently might be considered less objective obstacles, as we scored them, than prevenient subjective ones.

The equality of objective obstacles in our samples' lives makes us conclude that the nongraduates' fault seems less in their stars than in themselves that they are dropout underlings.

DO ALL YOUTH HAVE IDENTICAL LIFE CHANCES?

In denying that in our sample the "objective obstacles" hindered youths' progression to graduation are we saying that in the United States it makes no difference if one has an IQ of 50 or of 150, is the son of a millionaire or a pauper, comes from a rural or a metropolitan area, or originates in the upper or lower class, as far as chances of graduation from high school are concerned?

The answer to this question is obviously a resounding "No!" High school graduation is not random. It does make a great deal of difference whether one has the intelligence of a moron or a genius,

whether one comes from a rich or a poor family, from the slums or
the suburbs, whether one is white or black, male or female, Jew or
Gentile, from the North or the South, is a participant or nonpar-
ticipant in school activities, is taking a college preparatory or vocational course, has a father who is a nuclear physicist or a garbage
collector, etc.

Any conclusions drawn directly from the data of our present
research must be taken within the limits of our sample. Our sample
was a matched sample of working class youth. So conclusions may be
drawn from this material only about the working class youth and
not, for instance, about upper class teen-agers. We may, of course,
answer from our matched sample if the economic inadequacies
were, at this particular level, the major reason why our working
class youth withdrew from school.

THE DROPOUT: VICTIM OF FINANCES?

There are two common assumptions about the cause of inadequate
education. The first is more common among those who accent environmental conditions; the second more common among those who
accent heredity. The first assumption is, "The dropout is a victim of
inadequate finances." The second is, "The dropout is a victim of a
low IQ."

When we address ourselves to the question whether a youth
drops out of school because of a lack of money we are faced with an
apparent contradiction of evidence. Poverty is the condition of the
dropout, but inability to pay for his education *is not* the reason why
the dropout withdraws. Only one out of fifty of the very wealthy
class do not finish high school and one out of two of the very poor
class do not finish. Yet when we investigate the reason for the very
poor dropping out of school we find that it is not because there was
not enough money to continue but because of other less tangible
reasons.

This is a phenomenon that deserves further corroboration. In
the United States poverty is the milieu but not the cause of premature withdrawal from high school.

POVERTY: MILIEU OF THE DROPOUT

Every study that has considered the question of finances and education has recognized the class relationship between lower income
class and lower academic achievement. When Hollingshead made
his extensive study of the impact of social class on adolescents in a

midwestern town a quarter of a century ago the results were pre-
dictively decisive.[7] Class position was calculated by the income of
the family, its style of life, its possessions, the amount of education
of the father and the mother, the family's standing in the community, and its participation in community activities. Hollingshead
found that all of the youth of high school age of the upper classes
were in school. By far the largest proportion of the dropouts, eight
out of nine, came from the lowest social class. A very small proportion of Class III (the middle social class) dropped out of high
school, but 64 percent of Class IV and 75 percent of Class V (the
lowest social class) had dropped out of school *before* they were sixteen years of age.

In a more recent study of sixteen- and seventeen-year-old dropouts we find the same broad results. Dividing his universe into six
classes based primarily on economic factors James C. Davie found
that the percentage of dropouts increases sharply with each downward step on the socio-economic ladder. On the top rung (the upper-
upper class) one out of fifty youth failed to finish high school; on the
second rung (the lower-upper class) one out of ten failed to finish;
on the third rung (the upper-middle) one out of six failed to finish;
on the fourth and fifth rungs (the lower-middle and upper-lower)
one out of four failed to finish; on the lowest rung one out of two of
the youth failed to complete high school. The families of the upper
two classes took it for granted that their children would attend
college and they frequently made sure of this goal by sending their
youngsters to private secondary schools where they would receive
special tutelage and the group support of similarly minded peers.
Middle class families (Classes III and IV) were likewise insistent
upon their children finishing high school and wanted their children
to go on to college "if the family could afford it." In the two lowest
classes (V and VI) families felt that high school should prepare
their children for "good" jobs as semiskilled workers and they emphasized the importance of "practical" courses. Class V families
were generally able to provide their offspring with adequate clothing and some spending money, but they considered high school as
the end of formal education. The attitudes of Class VI (lower-
lower) families toward education, and the conditions which contribute to their value judgments, are described by Davie as follows:

> The parents of the children had generally received less than a
> high school education. Both parents worked in semiskilled and

unskilled capacities to earn enough to pay the rent for their cold-water flat and to keep the family fed. When the children weren't "needed" at home, they often left school anyhow in quest of a job and "some spending money in the jeans" which the parents could not provide. The one positive influence keeping them in school was the knowledge that more and more employers were asking for high school diplomas. However, the attraction of earning one's own money was often too great.[8]

Even more dramatic and persuasive of the thesis that inadequate income is all but the sole reason for dropping out of school is an array of figures such as the following. Table 6 deals only with youth whose IQ's are between the extremely high levels of 117 and 146.

Table 6.   Income and education

Parental Income	Percentage of Children in College
$8,000 and over	100
$5,000–$7,999	92
$3,000–$4,999	72
$2,000–$2,999	44
$1,000–$1,999	29

Source: Kurt Mayer, *Class and Society* (New York: Random House, 1961), p. 36.

NOT ONE IN TWENTY DROPS OUT BECAUSE OF ECONOMIC NEEDS

Yet, strangely enough, when the economically disadvantaged youths are interviewed, or when an objective appraisal is made of the reasons for dropping out, lack of finances is extremely rarely found to be the reason.

In the year that this survey was conducted (1961) the mean family income in the United States was $7,020. The mean family income of our sample was slightly less than $5,000. With an average of four children in each family there could be little doubt that our sample was firmly implanted in the lower economic classes. Yet not 5 percent of our dropouts could be judged to have withdrawn from school because they could not afford to continue their education.

In a study of 22,000 school leavers in seven communities, the Unites States Department of Labor concluded concerning

> *Economic need.* This did not seem to be a major reason for dropping out, if that phrase is interpreted to mean that the family of the dropout could not supply him with the necessities for school attendance. The statements of the dropouts themselves and their school records as well, attest that real economic hardship was present in few instances.[9]

Dr. George Mowrer, Director of Guidance of the St. Louis Public School System, was studying the dropout problem in the municipal area of St. Louis at the same time that the present study was being pursued. With the aid of his research assistants he evaluated the reasons for withdrawal of every dropout from the public school system between September, 1960, and September, 1961. He found that of the 2,579 youths who dropped out only 3 out of 100 withdrew because of financial need or because they were needed at home. Though the youth might state on a questionnaire or checklist that financial difficulty was the reason they were leaving school, the interview situation would reveal in the majority of cases that general lack of interest and academic difficulties, along with the pregnancy problem, were the real reasons.

THE "SLUMS AND SUBURB" ANALYSIS

The "slum and suburb" analysis of the dropout problem is misleading. Insofar as it suggests that the poor in general and the slum dweller in particular drop out of school because of inadequate funds and that the cure of the dropout problem lies in finances the analysis is at odds with careful research. Statements that "dropping out of school is essentially a function of the lower class" [10] are likewise misleading insofar as they suggest that finances are the crucial factor in academic achievement.

The United States is a highly mobile society. If lower class membership were as binding as a cement mold or Egyptian winding cloth then America would be a static caste society rather than the highly mobile class society that it is.

Granted that the vast majority of dropouts come from the milieu of poverty it is still true that "only 5 percent give clear evidence of having to leave school for financial reasons." [11]

Those who cite poverty and blue collar class membership as the cause of the dropout situation might consider the fact that from this identical situs originate most of the school teachers in the United States! [12]

One out of three professionals and one out of two college graduates come from the lower economic classes of our society.[13] Of itself membership in the lower economic class is not a determinant of academic achievement.

With more specific reference to the teenagers, we find that more than twice as many dropouts as stayins of any particular school have cars. More than twice as many stayins as dropouts have jobs while in school.[14] Neither of these facts harmonize with the "economic deficiency" analysis of the dropout situation.

THE G.I. BILL OF RIGHTS

That money is not the critical issue in the question of premature withdrawal from school can be deduced from the history of the G.I. Bill of Rights. Youth who were in the armed service were afforded a unique opportunity to further their formal education. If they had not finished their high school before entry into service they could obtain high school credits through an "equivalence" examination. By the time they left service they could have both the academic and financial requisites to continue their educational career in college and beyond; such were the provisions of the Bill. This was a singular opportunity for all American youth without bar of color or creed or code or class of origination. Yet it was found that this vast program did not substantially change the slight attendance at institutions of higher learning of the lower classes who had been presumed to be the potential prime beneficiaries of such economic assistance.[15]

To further underline the fact that scholastic opportunity and youth's acceptance of this opportunity are by no means identical is the phenomenon in the United States that only one in six dollars available for scholarships is utilized.[16] In one research study, Harvard University found that practically all of the youth who had applied for scholarships and had been refused had attended another university anyway.[17]

The economic interpretation of the dropout situation seems singularly inadequate. We would suggest that the evidence upholds Wolfbein's conclusion: "The financial reason for dropping out is apparently less important than is commonly supposed.... The lesser importance of the economic reason for dropping out is apparently confirmed by some of the ongoing studies of the Office of Education." [18]

THE DROPOUT: VICTIM OF A LOW IQ?

The second facile "analysis" of the dropout problem is to assume that the dropout is a dropout because of a low IQ. As it was found that low income is familiar to the dropout but not a determinant that a youth will drop out, likewise with a low IQ. A low IQ is the intellectual milieu of the dropout but is by no means a determinant that a youth will drop out. United States government dropout statistics are based only upon those children who have reached fifth grade and the 15 percent of the population who are constitutionally incapable of a minimum academic career are thereby excluded from the dropout calculations.

Various national studies indicate that there is a vast overlapping of basic intellectual capacities between the dropouts and the graduates. The United States Department of Labor's study of 22,000 school leavers found that the majority (54%) of dropouts had average intelligence (90–110 IQ) or better. Youth who had an IQ below this level were twice as prone to drop out as their more highly endowed teen-age peers but at every level there was heavy overlapping.[19]

An even more intensive research into the question of IQ and academic achievement than this Department of Labor's study was the longitudinal investigation of the National Science Foundation. In March of 1955 an academic aptitude test was given to a sample of 9,700 high school sophomores. In the fall of 1959 the Educational Testing Service of Princeton, New Jersey, succeeded in determining which of these 9,700 youth had graduated and which had dropped out of high school. Nine out of ten of the most able third had graduated; eight out of ten of the middle third graduated; seven out of ten of the lowest third graduated.[20] Once again it was clear that though a high IQ favored graduation there was a notable overlapping of intellectual capacities and that IQ was by no means the decisive factor in whether or not a teen-ager continued his high school education to graduation.

READING FAILURE AND RETARDATION

Of much greater importance from an analytic viewpoint than the question of finances or IQ was the inability of the dropout to read accurately, to communicate freely, and the frequency of school retardation. Our questionnaire was readily understandable by a youth who was seventeen or eighteen; the dropouts regularly needed assistance in answering it. It was obvious that their reading ability was extremely poor. In responding to the TAT's, the stories and themes invented by the dropouts were less than half as long as those of the graduates. Their ability to express themselves was clearly inferior. Almost one-third of our graduates were retarded in school by one year or more but a startling four out of five of our dropouts were one or more years behind the normal grade for their age. Other national studies indicate the same general patterns.[21]

Time and again the dropouts stated that they felt "goofy" with those "little kids"—their age mates had already graduated and they felt out of place. Their inability to read indicated two things to us: (1) teen-agers who do not read well enough for the work of their grade are likely to fail, feel frustrated, and discouraged; (2) the lack of verbal skills and communication abilities pointed to the deficiencies of their home environment.

We can summarize our observations on the financial and intelligence deficiencies of our dropouts in the words of Bowman and Matthews:

> The above findings are not new or surprising. Dropouts have been found by many studies to be of lower intelligence and lower socioeconomic status. It is true that 90% of the dropouts come from the lower class. However, the fact is often overlooked that there are still 50% of the lower class who stay in school and graduate. The important question therefore arises, why do some lower class children stay in school and others drop out? [22]

"DEFICIENCY ORIENTATION" OF THE DROPOUT

If we have not discovered up to this point a positive difference in the school experiences of the youth who continue their education and those who do not, a series of negative symptoms—"a dropout syndrome"—is beginning to emerge.

The dropout feels that he does not belong. He does not belong because he is retarded in school and thus separated from his age mates; he does not belong because his communication aptitudes—verbal and social—seem truncated. He does not belong because he is not participating in any of the activities of the school. Not one of our dropouts mentioned that he was participating in any activity at the time he withdrew from school though participation in school activities is prominent among the school experiences of the graduates. The dropout girls seem acutely aware of not being "in" because of failure to obtain the right grades, the right dates, the acceptance by the right cliques.

One note that comes through loud and clear when listening to the life stories of the dropouts is that he did not feel identified with the school. It is characteristic of the lower class not to participate in school activities to the same extent as do the upper classes [23] but the dropout seemed to have been utterly without ties of identity at the time he dropped out. In another study it was found that "not one person who dropped out of high school before the third year had engaged in even one activity. Of those who had finished the third year, 89 percent had engaged in extracurricular activities." [24]

Participation in school activities gives the youth a role, a conversation piece, an identification, a comradeship, a support for his academic orientation, a feeling of kinship with the administration and their goals, a sense of accomplishment, a chance for self-development and recognition. Insofar as a youth becomes a participant rather than a detached observer he becomes emotionally committed and feels he "belongs." That is just the feeling that the dropout does not have.

Reconfirming the deficiency orientation that characterized the replies of the dropouts was their response to our questions concerning occupational aspirations. "What type of work are you now doing?" and "Is this the general area in which you hope to continue or did you have something else in mind?" were the interview questions which enabled the youth to disclose their plans for the future. It came as no surprise that the typical dropout had a blue collar position as his goal whereas his matched counterpart had a white collar or professional executive position as his lifetime occupational ideal. Even with their limited goals the dropouts had made few practical plans or positive steps toward realizing their verbalized aspirations whereas one out of two graduates had taken positive steps to realize his aspirations by contacting a potential employer, taking a related course in a specific area, working during the summer at a hospital, or summer camp, or business office according to the direction of his interest. As the dropout seemed more a fugitive from frustration the graduate seemed to have a strong grip on reality.[25]

QUESTION REVISITED

We are now in a better position to consider our original question: If it is not the objective obstacles which precipitate dropping out of high school, what is it? Granted that poverty is the milieu but not the cause of dropping out; granted that a low IQ is the milieu but not the determinant of dropping out; granted that the dropout has a depressive "deficiency orientation"; these inadequacies taken singly or together did not seem to provide an adequate basis for distinguishing radically the school experiences of the dropout from those of the graduate.

A third very common analysis of differential academic achievement is that attributed to differential motivation. It has long been a staple of sociological literature that the middle class places a high value upon education and the lower class does not. Middle-class models, in contradistinction to lower-class models, inevitably point to the different value placed upon education by those who continue in their education in contrast to those who do not.[26]

Talcott Parsons, in pointing out that social mobility rests increasingly upon our educational system and that access is not as blocked by economic barriers as is commonly supposed, goes on to suggest that "an unexpectedly heavy emphasis falls on the factor of *motivation* to mobility, on the part both of the boy himself, and of his parents on his behalf, as distinguished from objective opportunity. This is a conclusion which runs contrary to much 'liberal' opinion, but is at least well enough validated by evidence to warrant further sociological investigation." [27]

MOTIVATION AND THE DROPOUTS

If in the existential situation of their school experiences neither economic nor intelligence deficiencies can account for youths' continuation or withdrawal, the hypothesis of motivational deficiency seems highly attractive. If we could ascertain that the youth who drop out do not really value a high school education and are without motivation to continue and that the youth who continue their education do value a high school education and are highly motivated to continue education, the study would be greatly simplified.

Although the measuring of values and motivations is an extremely hazardous enterprise, the prize is worth the risk.

DO DROPOUTS DESIRE TO GRADUATE?

We cannot presume that dropouts share the host culture's expectancy of high school graduation. This must be empirically proved. So much has been written and stated, as by Mr. Colwell whose interview introduced this chapter, about the independent youth culture that has as one of the characteristics of its subculture an antischolastic bias that bids youth to leave school as soon as is legally or illegally possible that it was with a great deal of uncertainty we approached the framing of a suitable question that would enable us to ascertain whether or not dropouts really did desire to finish high school.

THE INTERVIEW QUESTION

To ask the dropout directly: "Did you really ever want to graduate from high school?" seemed too brutal a question with which to confront any dropout. It would be a question that would inevitably induce deeper frustrations and self-incriminations in the psychic life of the respondent. Furthermore it would put the dropout on the defensive and his responses would become so entrammeled with the conflicts of his academic and family and peer and instinct history that the replies would be dubious or useless as criteria of whether the dropout really did desire to graduate from high school.

The indirect approach that would avoid any of his own obvious experiences was settled upon. Instead of asking the dropout about his own value judgment of a high school diploma we asked him what type of advice would he give to a good friend who intended to drop out of school. If the dropout would ask for details of the problems that his "best friend" was having with school that prompted him to drop out we would take the substance of the dropout's situation—whether lack of money, poor grades, boredom, trouble at home, etc., etc.—mask it somewhat and tell him that this was the situation of his best friend who was seeking advice. We asked the identical question of the graduate. The question was worded "If your best friend came to you and told you that he was going to drop out of high school, what would you tell him?"

RESPONDENTS' REPLIES

It would be profitable to quote at length the replies of the respondents to this question were they not all practically identical. Both dropout and graduate reply in absolute terms: "He'd be a fool to quit"; "A jerk"; "He'd be nuts"; "I'd say, 'Listen, Edsel...'"; "I'd tell her she was silly"; "I'd tell her she was crazy"; "Stupid"; "He's cracked, you have to have at least a high school diploma"; "To me it is just committing suicide to quit school."

The only difference in the replies is that the graduate more frequently includes broader values than does the dropout. Whether

it is because the dropout has already faced the problem of unemployment that his answers are invariably in terms of jobs and
unemployment is difficult to ascertain. That he does answer only in
terms of jobs and that the graduate answers in terms that include
more than jobs is not difficult to ascertain. This is the pattern that
our research found.

Both dropout and graduate would advise friends who might be
potential dropouts to stay in school. No graduate would tell his
friend to drop out; the eight percent of the dropouts who would
tell their best friends to withdraw from school were girls who put
the question into a romatic framework—a high school girl meeting
the "one and only," and being forced to choose between academics
and romance. For these girls there was only one choice and that
choice did not favor the academic value.

Slightly more than 50 percent of the dropouts replied only in
terms of the noncurricular advantages (such as job, income,
friends, status, sports, dances, and "fun morality") and slightly more
than 50 percent of the graduates replied in terms of curricular or
developmental advantages ("You need it to *be* something"; "You
don't know anything unless . . ."; "You need it to get a job"—but
the "job" argument had the connotation that the knowledge, skills,
and attitudes acquired at high school are a value in themselves).

Though the verbatim replies seem pat enough to be their parents' replies, let us cite a few to give interview substance to theory
shadow:

Dropouts
"[My dad] told me if I stayed in high school and got my diploma
he could get me a pretty good paying job where he works. I didn't
listen to him and now he can't help me." (Dropout Pat M., # 224,
Omaha)

"It's hard to find a job when you haven't finished high school. No!"
(Dropout Louise R., # 312, Denver)

"I'd tell her she was silly. I'm not sorry I dropped out of school to
get married but if she wasn't going to get married you can't find a
good job without an education." (Dropout Mrs. Mary J., # 314,
Denver)

"To stay in because you can't find a job if you quit school. You
have to be a bus-boy or wash dishes or something like that."
(Dropout Eddie S., # 334, Denver)

Graduates

"I'd tell him he was crazy. I'd tell him not to because I wouldn't want my best friend to drop out of school now. He wouldn't have nothing." (Graduate Russell R., # 101, New Orleans)

"I'd tell her she was crazy. If she told me she wanted to get married, I'd tell her she was too young and she doesn't know really what life is, while she is in high school. That's why we go to high school. Not just to learn the subjects but to learn about life. I'd tell her that I don't think she is mature enough. I think that she is mature physically but not mentally." (Graduate Geraldine B., # 129, New Orleans)

The dropout's horizon is limited to the instrumentality of the diploma as a ticket to obtain a job. The graduate's horizon more characteristically includes the developmental content that the diploma implies.

THE "COMMON MAN" BOYS

To give broader validation to our own conclusion that the blue collar youth, especially the dropout, consider education in the nonhumanistic and nonliberal terms of assistance in obtaining a job we can quote a more extensive study than our own. The "Mobility Project" of Harvard's Parsons, Stouffer, Kluckhohn, and Kahl canvassed 3,971 high school youth. Kahl reported the results in the article " 'Common Man' Boys." By "Common Man" Kahl means the working or blue collar or lower class:

> School and possibility of college were viewed by all the (lower class) boys solely as steps to jobs. None was interested in learning for the subtle pleasures it can offer; none craved intellectual understanding for its own sake. The most common phrase in the entire body of interviews was "Nowadays you need a high school diploma (or college degree) to get a good job." Often a distinction was drawn between the diploma and the education it symbolized; the boys wanted the parchment, not the learning. In this pragmatic approach toward schooling, the boys reflected the views of their parents (and of most of their teachers). . . . The boys who were not aiming toward college occasionally had a specific common man job as their goal, but more often had no firm goal at all—they would "take anything that comes along." [28]

BOTH EVALUATE THE DIPLOMA POSITIVELY

Our sample revealed no basic difference in the value judgments of dropouts and graduates regarding the desirability of graduation from high school. Both graduates and dropouts would tell close friends to continue education until graduation. The fact that the graduates frequently cited more comprehensive reasons than did the dropouts may have arisen from the graduates' greater verbal abilities and the dropouts' proximity to the unemployment situation. But whatever the reason it in no way voids the fact that both dropout and graduate placed a positive value upon a dipoma. Within the limits of their capacities and circumstances both manifested a positive motivation toward the completion of at least high school education.[29]

PARENTS' EDUCATIONAL ASPIRATIONS FOR THEIR CHILDREN

According to the "value and motivation" hypothesis, the parents of the dropouts would not place high value upon and would not strive to implant the motivation in their children for high school graduation.

The questions posed to the teen-age respondents were: "How much schooling did your father want you to complete?" and "How much schooling did your mother want you to complete?"

As was to be expected not one of the graduates perceived his parents as desirous of his terminating his education before high school graduation. Much less expected was the fact that four out of five of the dropouts likewise judged that both their fathers and their mothers wanted them to finish at least high school and a solid percentage (22%) perceived their parents as wanting them to continue into college or graduate school.

INAPPLICABILITY OF THE "VALUE AND MOTIVATION" HYPOTHESIS

As the deficiency of finances and deficiency of intelligence hypotheses were not applicable to our sample, neither was the deficiency of value-motivation hypothesis. Both segments of our population valued graduation from high school, both saw their parents as wanting it, and, except in the nontypical cases of teen-age girls who made exceptions for the romantic theme, both saw the diploma as a necessary part of youth's equipage.

These findings make us question the "motivation" approach when applied to the dropout problem. This basic theme is that "where there's a will there's a way"; "if the youth really wanted to graduate from high school they would"; "if we can just convince the youth of the United States that it is advantageous for them to graduate they will graduate."

It well may be, as our findings suggest, that the vast majority of the youth of the United States do value a high school education and are to no small degree motivated to complete it. It may be that the situational factors of their day-to-day living channel their energies and motivational powers in other directions and so obstruct the fulfillment of their academic ideals. Unemployment is not such a covert occurrence in the life of the lower class that its members do not recognize that lack of employment and lack of a high school diploma go together. Graduation from high school may now be so much of the general American ethos, and the "success" drive so deeply imbedded in our network of omnipresent "rags to riches" communication channels that even the poorest youth have a culturally, if not familialy, implanted desire to graduate from high school.

The orientation of our analysis will be channeled less toward the "value-and-motivation" cognitive emphasis and more toward the adjustment and social system emphasis. The problem seems more that of means than goals, more of instrumentality than finality.

5 . THE TEACHER

At the hub of the teenager's school experiences is the teacher. The inability of the family to produce civilization-adequate offspring without extended recourse to the teaching profession, the minimization of biological and economic inheritance as *a priori* certificates of ascriptive high status placement, the focalizing of education as the prerequisite for social, economic, and occupational mobility, the contemporary prolongation of the formal educational process, the mushrooming dependence of society upon the educational system as the institutionalized primary socialization agency for youth, have catapulted the teacher to the center of the adolescent's dramatic life. The actualization of the young student's life's chances has come to depend upon the success of his relationships with his teacher.

The ineluctable logic of glacial historical evolution footnoted by the jottings of knowledgeable social analysts underlines the growing influence of the teacher in the life development of modern youth. In sharp contrast, youth themselves testify to the insignificant and minimal influence that teachers have exerted upon them. Before we qualify, dichotomize, and validate this last statement with the pertinent statistical summary we can rehearse some of the specific references and accounts of student-teacher relationships as taken from the taped interviews.

QUESTION

"If we said that a close friend was one who really accepts you as a person, and one that you like to confide in, and that you enjoy being with under many circumstances, would you say that you were friendly with any one of the teachers or staff members at school? How many?"

Dropouts

"There was one counselor who tried to talk me into staying in school and not get married. If I had stopped to think about it then, she was right. But I was always shy and never could talk to teachers." (Dropout Doris C., divorcee, 18 years old, mother of two children, # 208, Omaha)

In high school it's hard to say because you never got to know your teachers too well." (Dropout Ronald C., # 210, Omaha)

"Yes. Mr. Stuart, my counselor in my senior year. I talked to him a lot but I didn't take any of my personal problems to him." (Dropout Patrick M., # 224, Omaha)

"I didn't like some of the teachers and I didn't like my counselor. General Bookkeeping was hard for me because I didn't like my teacher. I think it makes quite a difference whether you like your teacher or not. If you don't you don't feel as if you owe them anything and you don't owe yourself anything.... I tried to get my counselor changed but they wouldn't let me. It seems like the whole two and one-half years I was there she was always fighting with me.... I think she was glad I was dropping out and she didn't try to discourage me one bit." (Dropout Sherry W., # 236, Omaha)

"I talked with them when I quit school and they wanted me to stay. Before I quit school I wanted to go just half days but they wouldn't work that. They wanted you to go to school all the time. I think a school is there to sort of please the public because it is a public service and they should work along with all the kids because the kids are going to run the schools of tomorrow and if they don't go to school to learn there won't be any schools of tomorrow.... I used to know a lot of teachers in junior high. You could talk with them and joke around with them—just like a person, not like a mechanical walking teacher. The most I ever learned was in eighth grade and we had a teacher that got down to business. But he sort of made a game out of it. But you didn't wise off or anything because he would put you right where you belonged." (Dropout John C., # 404, Los Angeles)

"Teachers, there were real squares ... you know what I mean." (Dropout Al. C., # 408, Los Angeles)

Graduates

"Sure, there are. I'm nineteen now. I go to night school at Warren Eastern. In night school in my class I'm considered an adult, which I think I am. But if I were going to day school you find that most teachers are nice but some teachers seem to put teen-agers in a category. If maybe one would be bad they would category all of them as bad. That's not the way to do it." (Graduate Anna F., # 149, New Orleans)

"I suppose so. Maybe I would confide in them but I never have." (Graduate Ronald F., # 225, Omaha)

"Yes. Mr. Sharpe and my chemistry teacher.... In the past years I have confided all my problems in Mr. Sharpe." (Graduate Roger B., # 227, Omaha)

"Yes, there is a coach I feel at ease with. I don't confide in him but I do feel at ease with him." (Graduate Mike M., # 233, Omaha)

"They have helped a little." (Graduate Bob M., # 241, Omaha)

"Not really. It's just a teacher-student relationship.... There was one last year who taught chemistry. He isn't here any more because they didn't like the way he taught. He used to tell stories in class and we would laugh and have fun. Half of the time in class we would listen to stories but we would learn something. He taught us well by making everything big fun." (Graduate Frank K., # 317, Denver)

"Yes, one that I had for three classes. As far as the other teachers, anyone that wants to be a friend is a friend to me." (Graduate Gary M., # 327, Denver)

"No. Not one teacher ever." (Graduate Patsy K., # 543, Boston)

"After going to high school for four years it's just something like going to the dentist. You have to do it, and that's it." (Graduate Jackie R., # 561, Boston)

TEACHER-STUDENT FRIENDSHIP

Since premature withdrawal from high school is so frequently the culmination of disintegrate teacher-student relationships it comes as no surprise that two out of three dropouts testify that they were never really friends with any teacher and one out of three maintains that teachers were not even friendly. Only one out of sixteen dropouts feels that he had a number of close friends among the faculty and only six out of sixteen graduates judged that this was the case in their own academic histories.

That more than two-thirds of the youth interviewed denied to interviewers whom they knew were identified with the teaching profession that they had good friends in the teaching profession is rather startling. It is especially remarkable when so many of the teaching profession bask in such theories as the following:

> [The school] induces basically the same kind of identification as was induced by the family in the child's pre-oedipal stage. This is to say that the learning of achievement-motivation is, psychologically speaking, a process of identification with the teacher, of doing well in school in order to please the teacher (often backed by the parents) in the same sense in which a pre-oedipal child learns new skills in order to please his mother. . . . This bifurcation of the [school] class on the basis of identification with teacher or with peer group so strikingly corresponds with the bifurcation into college-goers and noncollege-goers that it would be hard to avoid the hypothesis that this structural dichotomization in the school system is the primary source of the selective dichotomization.[30]

Does the school induce "basically the same kind of identification as was induced by the family in the child's pre-oedipal stage"? The evidence of this study would indicate negatively to such a query. Neither the questionnaire, the interview, nor the thematic apperception tests indicate any such depth of influence and identification. It would seem that the slight influence of the teacher as a person (in contradistinction to the obvious great influence of the

complex of teachers as formal educators) is that the relationship
between the teacher and student is a *secondary* relationship while
the maternal relationship is that of a *primary* relationship in the
sense of the Broom-Selznick formulation used throughout this work.
The teacher as teacher does not accept the student as a total person
nor does the student accept the teacher as such. The teacher accepts
the student insofar as he is educable, not insofar as he is a person.
The teacher is the representative of a compulsory and determined
societal educational system which is bent upon making sure that
knowledge makes an entrance—be it bloody or otherwise. The
teacher is a taskmaster with objective standards that devastate any
personal acceptance based upon mutual regard and affection alone.
At a time when the youth is striving to establish his adult identity,
when he is striving to free himself of adult domination, he en-
counters the teacher who is a sterling representative of this exacting
adult society; unlike his parents, this parental surrogate can readily
be rejected and, perhaps, even scapegoated. When the respondents
speak of a teacher as a "real square" or as a "walking mechanical
teacher" or, in more favorable terms, of being a "real person" or
"she's really human" they are amplifying the general recognition of
the youth that their relationship with their teachers is a relationship of role, of inferiority, of limited mutual access. Teen-agers do
not use the language of friendship, much less of parent-child sym-
bolism, in speaking of teachers.

DELUSIONS OF GRANDEUR

Educators seem to be suffering from delusions of grandeur when
they infer that a great number of students are "identified" with the
teachers. We fail to find compelling evidence of this psychic affiliation, mass acceptance, sympathy, and internalizing of the teachers'
attitudes that would be characteristic of such "identification." It is
true that the graduate must come to terms with the teacher in order
to graduate, that in general those who are more favorably disposed
toward teachers and the goals for which the teachers stand will
more probably graduate. But the term "identification" is more
properly used of mutuality within a primary relationship. Such a
relationship does not ordinarily exist between teacher and student
on the American scene. Every day, every year, every change of
schools, the student sees multiple teacher figures. Their limited role
relationship is further fragmented by the constantly changing
kaleidoscope of teacher-substitutes and various and sundry educa-

tional functionaries. There is little opportunity for a cumulative emotional build-up and feed-back. Most telling, as we shall see in the next chapter, is the group pressure of other teen-agers. If the youth would go beyond the limited role relationship with any one teacher he must cope and counter the peer group system with its very pointed and potent sanctions.

THE TEACHER: ENEMY OR ALLY?

The American system of education which makes the teacher both instructor and judge in effect pits the students against the teacher. In the English system, the teacher teaches the subject matter but someone else judges whether the student has passed the examination. When teacher and student join forces to beat the examinations of common enemies in the central office a quite different *esprit de corps* develops than when the judge is in the midst of the classroom—in fact at the head of it. There is no avoiding him—except by doing your best to ignore him. This the American student seems to do quite effectively.

6. "INFLUENTIAL OTHERS" AS SEEN BY TEEN-AGERS

Considering the built-in student-teacher tensions that exist within the American school system it is understandable that superficial role relations are the mode rather than encompassing friendship relations. More revealing than the lack of friendly relationships that exist between youth and teacher is the lack of influence that the teacher has upon the youth of America.

The teacher is a professional. He is the parents' and society's embodiment of the wisdom of the ages and the bridge to all our bright futures. That such a public figure would be in continual structured contact with youth and yet elicit little confidence in his ability to assist the student solve his problems—even though those problems be specifically academic—is difficult to comprehend.

As direct proof that the teacher does not elicit the confidence of the youth who come under his tutelage even in matters relating to school we have the fact that only one out of sixteen youth conferred with any one of their teachers on the critical issue of leaving school. Such was the tally of the answers to this question, "At the point of leaving school, from whom did you seek help?" The dropouts did consult their age mates, especially their heterosexual confidants, on whether or not they should leave school but not their teachers!

THE PATTERN OF NONINFLUENCE

That this pattern of nonconsultation and noninfluence is not confined to the relationships between the teacher and the dropout is apparent from the answers to the following series of questions:

34. (To both dropout and graduate) Which person do you judge to have been most influential in your choice of an occupation?

35. Which person do you judge to have been the most influential in your life?

36. And whom do you judge to be the second most influential person in your life?

37. Is there any person whom you have not mentioned who influenced you greatly?

38. If you needed help and advice to make a big decision, to whom would you go for that advice?

This series of questions gives us an indirect method of gauging the depth of impact made by the teacher upon the teen-ager. Since the youth were forced to compare the relative influence of each of the reference groups the resulting placement of the teachers in his life provides a reliable index of where the teacher fits on the teen-ager's totem pole of his life's influentials.

Judging by the responses of our limited sample the teacher is the low man on the student's social totem pole. Despite the fact that the teacher is with the teen-ager more than anyone else, his influence is accredited by the youth as being the least of all their friends and acquaintances.

". . . TO WHOM WOULD YOU GO FOR THAT ADVICE?"

In the Harvard "Mobility Study" Kahl reports that:

> There were no cases in which the boy found in schoolwork sufficient intellectual satisfactions to supply its own motivation. And there were no cases where a sympathetic and encouraging teacher had successfully stimulated a boy to high aspirations.[31]

In our own study it is just as incredible that not one youth replied that if he needed help and advice to make a big decision he would go to a teacher.

A social analyst from another country would say that one of the

most objective and knowledgeable resource persons for the teen-
agers would be a teacher. The teacher is a professional who would
not charge any fee. He is thoroughly conversant with the youth's
problems. He has dealt more with youth than anyone else in the
community. He is dedicated to the youth's welfare. Who would be
in a better position to help and advise a youth who is faced with a
big decision than a teacher?

Who would be?

According to the perceptions of the dropout everyone else
would be. The dropout of our sample implicitly and effectively
states:

> If I needed advice to make a big decision I would not go to any
> teacher ... past, present, or future. I would go to members of
> my family who may not know community resources. I would go
> to a relative who may not have gotten beyond eighth grade. I
> would go to my pony-tailed and torreador-panted girl friend
> who has never read a serious book or a complete editorial in
> her life. But I would not go for any advice to any teacher!

Not one dropout of our sample in any one of the six major
metropolitan areas would have recourse to a teacher for advice in
time of major decision. Yet one out of six of these identical dropouts would go to their teen-age contemporaries for such assistance.

Not one youth in our sample—dropout or graduate—judged a
teacher to have been the most influential person in his life. One out
of eleven youth (dropouts, 11%; graduates, 8%) judged a companion
of his own age to be such.

Though the graduates nominate a teacher as some type of influence in their lives twice as often as do the dropouts, this influence is still minimal—an afterthought—in the judgment of youth.
Our interviews were apparently perfectly frank and open, carried
out in the case of the graduates within the teachers' bailiwicks and
by interviewers who were connected with the teaching profession.
Yet even with all these cues pointing in the direction of the teacher,
the teacher is the great unchosen, the rejected sociometric star.

A SUMMARY

We can summarize the sociometric choices of the youth in a composite "index of influence." It is a weighted composite score. Each
time a particular person was made a first choice he was given one
more point than if he received a second choice and a second choice

was worth one more point than a third choice. The total composite is the sum of the frequencies reduced to a percentage of the total weighted scores.

Table 7.—The "influentials" in the lives of teen-agers *
(by percentages of total weighted scores)

	Father and/or Mother	Relatives & Family Friends	Peers	Teacher	Clergy	Other	No Significant Other
Dropouts	45	16	15	1	2	5	16
Graduates	52	18	8	3	4	2	13

* Significant beyond the .01 level.

Both dropout and graduate nominate their parents as the greatest influences in their lives. The more frequent nomination by the graduate is due to his more frequent citing of his father. Relatives and family friends play a greater role in the lives of the graduates as do clergy and teachers. The greater influence of peers in the lives of the dropouts will have to be analyzed more carefully in the following chapter. Here we shall merely note that the dropout cites friends who are approved by his parents as influencing him less often than does the graduate and the dropouts' greater index of influence from peers stems completely from his being influenced by peers who are not approved by his parents. The teen-age pattern of influences upon their lives then seems to be: The graduate derives his characteristic influence from sources that originate in the home or emanate therefrom (relatives, approved family or personal friends, teacher, clergy) whereas the dropout derives his characteristic influence from sources that originate outside the home or are not controlled therefrom (nonapproved companions, "other"— strangers, individuals met at work, casual acquaintances, etc., "self alone," "no one").

The key point from Table 7 is that it clearly shows the relative position of the teacher in the mind of the youth. The central figure on the academic stage—the teacher—is all but a nonentity when viewed through youths' brutal binoculars.

CHAPTER FOUR
The Dropout Youth Culture

1. AMERICAN YOUTH CULTURE: INDEPENDENT OR DEPENDENT?

Is the American youth culture dependent on or independent of parental control? Is the youth culture in harmony or in conflict with the adult culture? More specifically, in the cross-currents of parent and peer pressures do youth choose parent or age-mate influences? Such is the question posed by this chapter on the influence of peers in the lives of our teen-age respondents.

When a youth is caught in a conflict of interests between his peers and his parents, the majority academic opinion would have us believe that the youth opts with his peers; the minority academic opinion would have us believe that he opts with his parents. Reductively, the former are saying that the youth culture is independent of parental control and the latter are saying that the American youth culture is dependent upon adult control. The procedure in this chapter is to present the thought of these opposing viewpoints as presented by some of their leading exponents and then present the testimony of our youthful respondents as to whether in circumstances of conflict between parent and peer they choose the cues and directives furnished by parent or peer.

School #1: The American Youth Culture Is Independent of the Adult Culture

James S. Coleman's analysis of American youth continues the dominant theme of the past generation of social analysts—the American youth culture is independent of the adult culture.

> What our society has done is to set apart, in an institution of their own, adolescents for whom home is little more than a dormitory and whose world is made up of activities peculiar to their fellows. They have been given as well many of the instru-

ments which can make them a functioning community: cars, freedom in dating, continual contact with the other sex, money, and entertainment, like popular music and movies, designed especially for them. The international spread of "rock-and-roll" and of so-called American pattern of adolescent behavior is a consequence, I would suggest, of these economic changes which have set adolescents off in a world of their own. . . .[1]

This setting-apart of our children in schools—which take on ever more functions, ever more "extracurricular activities" —for an ever longer period of training has a singular impact on the child of high-school age. He is "cut off" from the rest of society, forced inward toward his own age group, made to carry out his whole social life with others his own age. With his fellows, he comes to constitute a small society, one that has most of its important interactions *within* itself, and maintain only a few threads of connection with the outside adult society. In our modern world of mass communication and rapid diffusion of ideas and knowledge, it is hard to realize that separate subcultures can exist right under the very noses of adults— subcultures with languages all their own, with special symbols, and, most importantly, with value systems that may differ from adults. Any parent who has tried to talk to his adolescent son or daughter recently knows this, as does anyone who has recently visited a high school for the first time since his own adolescence. To put it simply, these young people speak a different language. What is more relevant to the present point, the language they speak is becoming more and more different.[2]

Standard texts in the social sciences verbalize their belief in the independence of the contemporary American youth culture in such words as these:

With the accent on youth in our culture, there is for many a reluctance to doff "young" clothing, to leave romance behind, and to accept adult responsibility. At the same time, there *are* striking discontinuities in culture sharing according to age. The so-called youth subculture, for example, is a world of irresponsibility, specialized lingo, dating, athleticism, and the like, which rather sharply cuts off adolescent experience from that of the child and from that of an adult, however reluctantly the latter status may be accepted in many cases.[3]

Ernest A. Smith came to the same conclusion from summarizing the various research studies on American youth. At the end of his work, *American Youth Culture: Group Life in Teen-age Society,* he states:

> The autonomy of youth culture has been verified by the setting up of norms which, although they change from institution to institution, in all cases dominate and pattern youth behavior. These norms pre-empt the loyalty of youth, the degree of their conflict or competition with adult norms varying (inversely) with youth's approximation to adult status.[4]

Talcott Parsons has presented to a generation of academicians what he considers to be the three characteristics of the American youth culture:

> In general, the most conspicuous feature of the youth peer group is a duality of orientation. On the one hand, there tends to be a compulsive independence in relation to certain adult expectations, a touchy sensitivity to control, which in certain cases is expressed in overt defiance. On the other hand, within the group, there tends to be a fiercely compulsive conformity, a sharp loyalty to the group, an insistence on the literal observance of its norms, and punishment of deviance. Along with this goes a strong romantic streak.[5]

Fifteen years earlier, at a meeting of the American Psychoanalytic Association, he had developed the same points more forcefully:

> The essential facts (of the American youth culture) are matters of common observation. Starting at about high school age young Americans, especially in the urban middle classes, embark on patterns of behavior and attitudes which do not constitute a stage in a continuous transition from childhood to adulthood but deviate from such a line of continuity....
>
> This pattern of attitudes and behavior is sufficiently general and pronounced to be singled out as a distinctively structured complex conveniently called the youth culture. Its principal characteristics may be summarized:
>
> (1) Compulsive independence of and antagonism to adult expectations and authority. This involves recalcitrance to adult standards of responsibility and, in extreme instances,

treating the conformist—who, for instance, takes school work seriously—as a "sissy" who should be excluded from peer-group participation.

(2) Compulsive conformity within the peer group of age mates. It is intolerable to be "different"; not, for example, to use lipstick as soon as the other girls do. Related to this is an intense fear of being excluded, a corresponding competitiveness for acceptance by the "right" groups, and a ruthless rejection of those who "don't make the grade."

(3) Romanticism: an unrealistic idealization of emotionally significant objects. There is a general tendency to see the world in sharply black and white terms; identifications with one's gang, or team, or school tends to be very intense and involve highly immature disparagements of other groups.[6]

The first group of social analysts—whom we have heuristically termed "School # 1"—seems to have no doubt as to whether the American youth culture is independent of or dependent upon parental control. In the cross-currents of parent and peer pressures they see the youth as choosing age-mate influences, cues, suggestions, and commands. This more prevalent academic opinion maintains that the youth culture is in conflict rather than in harmony with the adult culture.

School #2: The American Youth Culture Is Subject to Parental Control

It may seem strange that another group of highly competent social observers, studying the identical universe of American youth, could come to just the opposite conclusion. Rather than concluding that the American youth culture is independent of adult control, this second "school" maintains that it is subject to parental control. Rather than irresponsible, it is responsible; rather than hostile to parental values and control it is accepting of them, etc.

Jessie Bernard acted as Special Editor of a volume of *The Annals* entitled "Teen-Age Culture." In her foreword to the volume she summarized the work by stating:

Some twenty years ago, Kingsley Davis described the sociological or structural factors which made for youth-adult conflict. But even 19 million individual rebellious adolescents do not add up to an army or even a resistance movement. They add

up—as so many of the articles in this volume indicate—to
bearers of a conservative, traditional culture which, far from rejecting adult values, pays them the supreme compliment of
imitating or borrowing them and adapting them to its own
needs. Teen-age culture, even in its contrapuntal forms, is an
adaptation or prototype or caricature of adult culture. This
volume might well be viewed, therefore, as a picture of adult
culture today as reflected in the teenage culture which it
fosters.[7]

"THE MYTH OF ADOLESCENT CULTURE"

A study that more vigorously attacked the predominant academic
analysis of the "independent" American youth culture was a study
that was not completed in the United States but in Canada. Its
sample was extremely limited: twenty youth of fourteen and fifteen
years of age were interviewed as were their parents; twenty other
youth were included in the sample but through "life history materials." The total sample was taken from the upper middle class of
Montreal. However, since Elkin and Westley included a great deal
of corroboratory evidence from the pertinent research available in
the sociological literature their case assumed substantial proportions. Their article is entitled "The Myth of Adolescent Culture":

> In the current sociological literature, adolescence is often de-
> scribed as a unique period in development, distinct from child-
> hood and adulthood. . . . The writers (Kingsley Davis, R. Wil-
> liams, N. D. Humphrey, M. Mead, R. Benedict, T. Parsons,
> etc.) tend to ignore deferred gratification patterns, the inter-
> nalization of adult modes of thought and behavior, positive
> relationship with authority figures, instances of family soli-
> darity, or "inner directed" interests which may set an adoles-
> cent apart from his age mates.
>
> The statements in the literature about adolescence or-
> dinarily purport to describe a modal adolescent pattern. As
> such, the descriptions should not be inapplicable to upper
> middle-class urban groups. With this problem in mind, the
> authors have been engaged in a study of adolescent socializa-
> tion. . . .
>
> *Suburban Town*
>
> One dominant pattern in Suburban Town is that of adult
> directed and approved activity. The activities of the adoles-

cent take place almost completely within the suburban community and in view of adult figures. The adolescent, in effect, has little unstructured time. Typically, on school days, he spends his time out-of-school doing two hours of homework; helping in household activities; and participating in school organizations, directed sports, or church and "Y" activities. On weekends, with more free time, he participates in some family projects, has certain allotted household tasks, and often attends gatherings at which adults are present. In summers, he either works, attends camp, or vacations with his family at a summer cottage.

Family ties are close and the degree of basic family consensus is high. The parents are interested in all the activities of their children, and the adolescents, except for the area of sex, frankly discuss their own behavior and problems with them. In many areas of life, there is joint participation between parents and children—the boys may help their fathers build patios, the members of the family (female) may curl together, and the parents may attend the school's athletic competitions. In independent discussions by parents and adolescents of the latter's marriage and occupational goals, there was a remarkable level of agreement. The adolescents also acknowledged the right of their parents to guide them, for example, accepting, at least manifestly, the prerogative of the parents to set rules for the number of dates, hours of return from dates, and types of parties. The parents express relatively little concern about the socialization problems or peer group activities of their children.

In many respects, for this given sample of adolescents, the continuity of socialization is far more striking than the discontinuity. With future education and career possibilities in mind the adolescents discuss their choice of school courses with their parents. The parents encourage their children to play host to their friends. Also, since the parents themselves engage in entertaining, dancing, and community sports, the adolescents observe that in many respects their own pattern of social life is not very different from that of the older generation. The continuity of socialization is especially well exemplified in the organization of parties and the concern with social proprieties. Typically, when a girl gives a party, she sends out formal invitations, and her guest list includes those she *should* invite as well as those she wants to invite. The girls take great pains to play their hostess roles properly, and the boys so strongly recognize their escort responsibilities that they may privately draw straws to decide who walks home with the less popular girls.

The adolescents themselves demonstrate a high level of sophistication about their own activities, in many respects having internalized "responsible" and "adult" perspectives. For example, they took their homework very seriously; they tended to view their household tasks as their contribution to family maintenance; some suggested that the clubs to which they belonged gave them valuable social or organizational experience; and the boys, after telling of their practical jokes in school, spoke of this behavior as "silly" or "kid stuff." Furthermore, the youth culture elements in which they participated were recognized as transitory and "appropriate for their age." Thus the "steady date" was likely to be viewed as a pleasant temporary association, not directly related to marriage, which gave a certain immediate security and taught them about heterosexual feelings and relationships. Some spoke of the dating pattern as "the kind of stuff kids do at our age."

The description of adolescence in a suburban town is not an isolated portrait; it is supported in various aspects by other discussions of upper middle-class and upwardly mobile groups. Most noteworthy is the study of Elmtown (or Jonesville) by Hollingshead, Warner, et al. Although Elmtown is an isolated community of 10,000 population, we find many similar patterns of behavior. In Elmtown, likewise, the upper middle-class adolescent spends much of his time in supervised extracurricular activities; the parents know the families of their children's associates and bring pressure to bear on their children to drop "undesirable" friends; the children are taught to be polite and refined in their speech and behavior and to repress aggressive tendencies. The children of the middle and upper classes, concludes Hollingshead, "are guided by the class cultures with remarkable success." [8]

Similar descriptions are given in other studies which discuss the deferred gratification pattern among upper middle and mobile lower-class adolescents. The child learns to forego immediate indulgences for the sake of future gains and thus inhibits his aggressive and sexual impulses, strives for success in school, and selects his associates with care.[9] This pattern is in direct contradiction to the implications of a strong and pervasive youth culture. The individual who internalizes a

deferred gratification pattern does not act solely in terms of
irresponsible pleasure seeking and conforming peer group
pressures and, much as he may apparently be absorbed in
dances, gang activity, and sports, he does not lose sight of his
long-run aspirations.

It is to be stressed here that we have been focusing
throughout on the overt and behavioral, and not the psy-
chiatric, aspects of adolescent development. No implications of
any kind are intended about the psychological health or ill
health of the adolescents concerned.

Conclusion

The data from Suburban Town and other empirical studies
suggest that the characterization of adolescent culture advanced in the sociological literature needs to be questioned.
The empirical data do not deny that there are psychological
tensions and distinctive interests among adolescents; however,
the data do suggest—at least among these middle-class groups
studied—that the current model of adolescent culture represents
an erroneous conception. And if so, the theories which employ
such a culture to analyze the social structure are without adequate foundation.

. . . In Suburban Town and other communities studied the
youth culture elements exist, but they are less dominant than
are accepted family and authority guidance patterns. The
adolescents in their peer groups are not compulsively independent, rejecting adult values; they are not concerned solely
with immediate pleasurable gratifications. Furthermore, in regard to those aspects of their lives which might be regarded as
youth culture, they are remarkably sophisticated, they themselves pointing out that their dating patterns and their "kid-
ding around" are passing temporary phenomena. . . .

It was likewise assumed, in this characterization of adolescence, that the youth culture was both etiologically and func-
tionally linked to the psychological needs of the individual. . . .
There is reason, as we have noted, to question this characterization of youth culture; but even to the extent that it is valid, the
theory leaves no place for empirical data which evidence continuity of socialization. Such a theory neither explains the correlation between adolescent class position, choice of school
courses, and subsequent occupational goals, or the acceptance

by adolescents of adult guidance of many of their activities, nor does it make allowance for deferred gratification patterns, the internalization of adult values, solidary family relationships, or positive relationships with authority figures, all of which are found in studies of middle-class groups.

This contradiction between the current sociological characterization of adolescence and the reported data for middle-class groups suggests that "adolescent culture" has a somewhat mythical character.[10]

CONTRARY CHARACTERIZATIONS

The contrary characterizations of the American youth culture by opposing schools of thought set the background for the findings of our own study. What will become immediately evident is that our research does not allow the absolutist, homogeneous, all-black interpretation of a Parsons in which every youth is allegedly psychopathically ridden by antiadult compulsions, nor the all-white interpretation of the idyllic, Rousseauvian "Suburban Town" where every youth is seemingly saccharinely submerged in a comfortable upper middle class parental honey-pit.

To give empirical contours and descriptive validity to our conclusions concerning the American youth culture as found in our sample, we can transcribe a field interview with a New Orleans principal from whose school not a few dropouts and graduating respondents originated. The previous interview (pages 68 ff.) accented the car-orientation, employment problems, and varied delinquencies of the dropout youth culture; the present interview takes the delinquencies as a part of the lower class environment (the neighborhood bar girls must be willing to accommodate the customers both at the bar and in the bed; every year several of the former students "graduate" from penal institutions) and concentrates on the day-to-day family, school, and peer relationships of the blue collar or working class youth.

2 .   A HIGH-SCHOOL PRINCIPAL REPORTS

The dropout can be counted on to be negativistic about his school experiences. At least that is what we thought until we interviewed the dropouts from a school in New Orleans that we shall call Xavier High. The dropouts from this school were unanimously enthusiastic about the principal, even if they had been expelled. To investigate this unique phenomenon the principal, Sister Mary Jacqueline, was

interviewed. It was soon obvious why this spontaneous, knowledgeable, and warmly human woman enlisted such enthusiasm
among the student body and the staff. The interview serves as a
realistic appraisal of the school-family-peer patterns of youth enmeshed within the mores of a lower class section of a municipal area
where "social dynamite" is a standard part of the environment.

Interviewer: "Would you give us some general ideas about the
  background of your students here at Xavier High?"
Principal: "In the first place, our children come from about fifty-
  two parishes throughout the city of New Orleans and it covers the
  entire city, all the way out to the lake and all the way beyond the
  industrial canal. To the people in the city, that means strictly
  suburban. They come from all the way across the river. Some
  leave as early as five thirty in the morning in order to get to
  school on time. That's what a Catholic education means to many
  of them. But again, a lot of them live here in the neighborhood
  and we have to force them to get here in the morning, because we
  have to do the training to teach them what has to be done and
  what time to do it, and what the time element means in their life
  later on because they have no concept of punctuality, that is one
  sure thing...."
Interviewer: "You have twenty-five teachers. How many students do
  you have?"
Principal: "We have seven hundred and thirty."
Interviewer: "You draw chiefly from this area, which is a poor area,
  is that correct?"
Principal: "Very, very poor. Economically a family might be taking
  in anywhere from $110 from Social Security per month, up to
  about $350 a month. That is about the maximum salary. A man
  who might be making more than that is probably a seaman who
  never gets the money home...."
Interviewer: "You were mentioning the other day about home economics. What do you find in home economics?"
Principal: "I maintain that, if it weren't for the school, the children
  would have no education in this, and when I say no education, I
  mean that in every phase of life. At home they just vegetate and
  grow. They are not trained and they are not taught the niceties
  of life. The simple niceties, not the elegant niceties. The simple
  niceties of life they do not know. Take for example in a home
  economics department. Instead of sister teaching them about a

knife and a smaller knife, and three or four spoons on the side,
and three or four forks on the other side, they don't even think of
that, they only think of a knife, a fork, a spoon, and a napkin.
These are things that many, many of our children have never had
the pleasure of indulging in—seeing the table set with a table-
cloth and a plate, knife, fork, and spoon. Many of our children, a
very large number of them, eat right out of the pot on the stove.
The families are large and they are confined to a small area in
the project, maybe two rooms with possibly eleven children, and
in that small area there is definitely no room for a table with
settings for eleven people. I know of instances where, even our
better children, have never sat at a table as a family. They
get it right out of the pot and put it on their dish and they go
over and sit on the bed, on the floor, or on an orange crate to eat.
Therefore, the setting of the table is an unique experience.
Learning how to eat properly, not choosing what type of a knife,
but using a knife, makes a lot of difference. Propriety is the thing
that they have to be taught. I'll give you an idea of what I mean.
There is one boy who can't get to school on time because he is
one of ten or eleven children and they sign up for the bathroom.
By the time it is his turn, it is quite late. He will come and he
will say, 'I had to go and that was all there was to it. I had to wait
my turn. My turn was number eight today and my sister still has
to come. She is not here yet. She is next and she will be coming in
a little while.' You cannot go along with the children and say,
'Son, I understand that, it's too bad.' You tell him that the first
time, but the second time you can't tell them that. Our children
are quick, very, very quick, to take advantage of the sympathy
that is due them but you cannot go on with that because the
minute you agree to accept that excuse, they will take advantage
of you. They are little politicians of the first order and whenever
you give them a loophole, they grab it like that, and they will
play on your sympathies.

"Just to give you an example, this little Louis S., that you
interviewed yesterday—I let him be one that was chosen by you
and he came in a little while ago and he said, 'Tonight is ring
night and I'm kind of short a little money. Could you lend me a
dollar for tonight for my girl? I need it.' So I said, 'Louie!' And
he said, 'Aw, please, come on now, please.' His friend Randy was
also interviewed. They are special. They are a little bit different
from the other kinds, so they are allowed little privileges; so they

both borrowed a dollar. Then one of the sisters came in a few minutes afterward and said, 'Do you know where they went?' And I said, 'No.' And she said, 'They went and played the pinball machine.' So I'll shoot them when I see them.

"But that is what I mean. They will take you for a ride every-time they have a chance, but there is no malicious intent. There is no maliciousness whatsoever in it. But the second time he comes late like that, you have to tell him that is the end of it and that he will just have to sign up earlier for the bathroom. You have to pressure, pressure, pressure to get them to do the little simple things. Otherwise, he would delay every day. He would line up for number eleven just because it was an easy way out.

"There are a thousand little ways that show how uninhibited our children are. Just yesterday, one of the boys came up to sister and said, 'Please tell me that I passed my course.' And she said, 'Go away.' And he said, 'Come on, tell me. I know I'm not sup-posed to know until tomorrow, but you will tell me secretly.' And she told him to go on. He thinks very much of her and he kept tormenting her and finally she said, 'Go ahead. You can sleep tonight. There is nothing to worry about.' So he grabs her hand and kisses her! A great big boy—he must be six feet-four, and it was just absolutely nothing to him."

Interviewer: "In conducting interviews in their homes, we noticed how little privacy any of them have. And how members of one family walk into another's home without knocking. Does this lack of privacy lead to their spontaneity?"

Principal: "Yes, I would say that is very true. They just aren't trained that way from babyhood on. They are just not trained concerning the proprieties of life. . . ."

Interviewer: "About parental control, why is there so little parental control of the children in general?"

Principal: "For one thing, let's take a look at the education of the parents. Many of our parents are foreigners and have had no education of any kind. They can neither read nor write in their own native tongue and, if they do know a little English, they cannot respond properly. Those who have gone to school and are native Americans—we have never really done it statistically, but I have looked through records and just gotten a general picture— might have gotten as far as the third or fourth grade. That makes the parents feel inferior to their children, because no one in the history of their family has ever had a high school education. Out of a number of children in a family, not all of them will get this high school education, so the child who does get it, or does succeed in coming through with a high school education and graduates, he is the hero of the family and of the neighborhood. As you mentioned the other day about this one particular boy that looked like he was going to graduate, he is the hero of his other buddies because he is graduating. I think that is one point, that the parents feel so inferior to their own children, educationwise, that they are afraid to tell them what to do because the children know so much more about life. By life I mean the things around them like social order and how to make a living and this, that and the other thing, that their parents have no concept of whatsoever. The parents cannot seem to rise to the level of their children."

Interviewer: "But this seems to be true of the dropouts as well as the stayins. It seems from our investigation, that, if a child will go along with the peer groups that his parents approve of, he will graduate. But if he gets off in a group that is independent of the family, he will not."

Principal: "Our parents depend on that, and they will come around here and say to me, 'Sister, will you get him to stop going with so and so and go with so and so, so he can stay in school, because so and so doesn't believe in staying in school.' He is earning money, about $250 a month, and then he will probably drop back to $150 and then quit working completely because there is no future in what he is doing. But the parents will beg us. They can't do it. They can't make their children do that. They want help."

Interviewer: "So they use the friends as a sort of support for their own ideals?"

Principal: "That's right, and for their authority. They are afraid to use authority. I don't know whether it is just lack of education, I wouldn't say that. Of course, in any family where there is a low economic status, most of that is a deliberate action on the part of the parents. People will help them rise from such a situation, economically, but they do not support the help they get. Therefore, they don't come out of it. Many of the parents are there of their own free will. They can't rise from it. They don't want to really. They are just as contented. They figure they tried once and they didn't succeed, so they might as well stay that way."

Interviewer: "Why does that militate against their attending

graduation? How many people will be in attendance at one of
your school's graduation ceremonies?"

Principal: "Any kind of a function where we honor our graduating
group, like tonight we are having this little ring ceremony, we
don't have to worry about ushers because there will be ample
room, but graduation night is the night that everybody comes
just to take pictures. They don't care what happened at the ceremony, just to take pictures. To these people a picture is a testi-
monial. They can show this to someone. It is something that is
tangible and they can say, 'See, he graduated. He has a cap and
gown on.' They don't care a thing about what it means to him
educationally, it is just that he has a cap and gown on. This is the
only reason they are interested, they are great for external things.
Like on class night. That is the night that the children get
honors. We have had children that we gave distinct honors to,
maybe for four years of service of some kind. We have different
awards that we give them, and this child has to receive this on his
own and nobody is there to celebrate with him. I have been here
four years now and I've made it a practice, while we are listening
to these long, drawn-out speeches, to look around and count the
adults that are there and we get, roughly, about the same number
of people at the ceremony as there are graduates. But then I look
around and try to single them out and then I see one family and
there is the grandmother, an uncle, an aunt and at least seven
or eight of a clan, or twelve or more of one clan, which automatically eliminates twelve other students who have no one there
to see them. If it weren't for the girls' boy friends or a couple of
the girl friends in school that come to be their fan club, they
would have no one there to celebrate with them. Why that is, is a
hard thing to say. In many instances the parents are embarrassed
to come to something like that because it is too educational. They
think it is too high for them and they would never be able to sit
through it or understand it. Even if they understand English, it is
still too lofty for them. A number of them are exempt because
they work, but they could get off to go to a wedding or something
like that, but they won't take off to come to this because it is not
important enough. Why it is not important enough, we have not
been able to figure out. The parents won't tell you why, 'We just
had to work. That's all.' They will never give you a good excuse
why they don't do something. Again, some of them are very proud

of their children and they will sit there in all their rumpled messiness—they just don't know how to dress and they have some horrible looking clothes on, but they will sit there and they will clap loudly when their child gets something. But there are dozens of others who have no one. I'll say to one of them, 'Where is your mother? Isn't she here tonight?' And they say, 'No, she had another engagement.' Just as indifferent as the parents can be and we wonder why our children become indifferent about certain things, and we wonder how they will ever turn out because that indifference is certainly ingrained in them. It is bound to come out and they will probably reproduce their own kind."

Interviewer: "We were appalled at the number of broken families. For a whole day we didn't have one integral family. What would you say of that of both the stayins and the dropouts?"

Principal: "When I gave you those names, I deliberately ignored those that had broken homes because I didn't want to just cater to the problem that you were trying to prove. I just indiscriminately took those children because they are a very good sampling of, I would say, a good 75 to 80 percent of our children. As I told you before, we could never get statistics on our children—how many of them do come from broken homes or separations or family problems or anything like that—because if there is a mental disorder among the parental folks at home the children will never tell you that. You have to get that by trackings. Sometimes the child gets fed up and can't take it any more and they break down and come and tell you or something will happen by which you find it out. They just won't tell you that. I suppose they are embarrassed. I don't know what it is. In other schools where we had this sort of thing, the child's father will come and tell you that the mother is here or there or the other place, or the mother will come and explain to you, but these children won't tell you at all. It is another skeleton in the closet and they want to keep it there because maybe daddy got there because he was an alcoholic, and many of them are war victims too, and they are alcoholics and they are in veterans hospitals and things like that.

"Why are these families broken? I can say in every one that I have met, because it is the promiscuous living of both members, or, if one of them happens to be loyal for a long time, the circumstances in which they are thrown constantly from the type of work they are doing. Our children's fathers do not do any kind of

stable work at all, we might have ten or twelve or maybe fifteen
in the whole school who have fathers that are white collar men,
and they are not big men, they just happen to have simple jobs as
a clerk in an office. The others are stevedores, merchant marines,
pipe fitters, taxicab drivers, bartenders—that is a common thing
—or the very, very small grocery store that at first serves soft
drinks and then alcoholic drinks on the sideline, bus drivers,
truck drivers, nothing with a definite future, because they don't
want anything with a future. They don't have the sticktivity to
stay with the job. The type of work they do, leads to a broken
home. If a father is a seaman, he is home maybe twenty-four
hours or perhaps three days. If a baby comes from the intercourse,
he is back to sea again. He doesn't see the baby. Maybe he will
see it when it is born, maybe he won't. Maybe he won't see it for
a year. Some of them are gone to sea as high as twelve to eighteen
months. They are not big enough seamen to get a certain routine
run where they can say, 'I'll be home in three or four weeks.'
Some of our boys haven't seen their dad in so long that they have
forgotten what he looks like. There was one seaman that was
home six times and had six children. He died in Hong Kong and
no money ever came from him, because he was an alcoholic on
the ship. Naturally a family like that can easily be broken up.
The mother gets awfully tired of going out to work and support-
ing what he produces when he is home, so she looks for companionship and that renders more promiscuity there.

"Then you have the bartender. In this neighborhood, you
can't be a barmaid unless you promise to lie at night. That is one
of the requirements of a barmaid in this neighborhood. My girls
tell me that all the time. But if he is the father of the family ... if
he is a cabdriver, it is an off and on job. He doesn't have enough
to support the family and most of the cab drivers in this area
spend three-fourths of their time in a barroom, between Magazine
Street and Chocatulus down here. They are constantly commuting
back and forth between their runs. There are very few families
where the father has a job that he has been at for any time. The
lack of sincere interest in what they are doing and the desire to get
ahead is completely lacking in these people and we couldn't begin
to keep up our records on them. This week dad will be a truck
driver and you talk to the kid and he says, 'Oh no, he has had a
couple of jobs since then.' This leads to a broken-up setup in the
home. It is bound to tear the families apart.

"Another thing around here is that you must be married by the time you are seventeen or eighteen. I have found only a precious few where there was real stardust in the girl's eyes. I always tell them that it is only puppy love and it's going to lead to a dog's life and that's all it is for them. I can give you many examples of this same pattern—a girl seventeen or sixteen marries a boy seventeen or eighteen. They have now set aside $150 to $200. There they go. It's time to get married. He is paying off a car. He has a wonderful job and she has a wonderful job. Her job is about $180 a month and his job is $250 a month. They get married. They have got to buy a refrigerator and they move right into the project because it is cheap."

Interviewer: "I believe I saw a sign—$16.75."

Principal: "Yes. It is federal housing. So that is the way they start out. Our children are very fertile. I haven't found any of them that aren't thoroughly fertile. The child gets here. It's quick action, anywhere from three to four months after they are "married." I put married in quotes. I used to think that babies took nine months, but it doesn't any more. They come like mad, so that means that the girl has to stop work, either shortly after she is married because her pregnancy begins to show, or within the nine months she is definitely pregnant. She has to quit work, so that is one salary gone. Meanwhile they have bought a car, a TV, a refrigerator, and they are paying for everything with maybe a dollar down and a dollar a month for the rest of your life for this item and that item until they have so much and then they will go out and borrow because the baby is coming. They don't have any kind of insurance. It is impossible to sell insurance, school insurance or anything to these children around here. Even at three dollars a year, they won't take insurance because it has no meaning to them. That is planning for the future and you don't ever plan for the future. You only live today. That is something we try like mad to teach our children. That there is a tomorrow and a next day. They wouldn't think of putting aside some money for a rainy day. The rainy day comes and it storms. If they had a whole lot on Monday and they lose it on Tuesday, well—if you just don't have it you start over again. You never think of Wednesday and Thursday and Friday—that is ridiculous. It is simply ridiculous. So that makes for a lot of trouble in the home."

Interviewer: "I would like to give you our hypothesis. We have been working on primary groups, meaning by that, that if anybody has a relationship where they accent the other person as a person and not what they can get out of them, and they have reached a communication level where they can confide with them and have pleasure with them, that this person is going right. As long as he has a primary relationship with the family, more probably he will continue school. Do you think this is correct?"

Principal: "I think it definitely proves out in our area here. Those of our children who do continue school on their own definitely have good relations with their parents. They tell their parents everything and their parents talk it over with them and that is the normal homelife of a number of our children. Then we have a number of our children who might have one member of the family, one parent or an older sister or brother with whom they can talk over their matters and in whom they can confide. Now with that member of the family the work is half done. Someone is there working along with them and helping them. Then there is this god-forsaken group. They stayed in school not because of parental interest and following through with the children, but because somebody in school, some teacher in school here is acting as his or her parent. That is the answer. That is the group you interviewed where they were in school, but had very bad home lives. They are in school because Sister X or Mr. B is deeply interested in that child and that child constantly tells them everything that is going on in his life. They tell the teacher every little thing that they would tell a mother or father, or an older sister or brother, whoever may be bringing them up at home. That is the reason those children are here. Take Louie S. for example. He is here for no other reason. His uncle said he had to graduate, but that wouldn't keep him from dropping out of school at all. There are two or three people that watch Louie and help Louie along. Teaching is incidental and accidental to us here at school. We are doing nothing else but running a place for boys and girls to stay for six or seven hours a day and we are acting as parents toward them. They tell us everything that is personal in their lives. We have sat down time and time again and discussed this matter and teaching is purely the reason why they come here. To be taught. But we don't do that much teaching out of the books."

Interviewer: "How do the kids here with such serious economic problems—how do they manage to surmount them? A kid, I don't care if he has an IQ of 150, if he sees that his mother needs money and if he goes to school . . ."

Principal: "Mother will stay home and work in a cigar factory ten hours a day if she thinks that her son is going to bring honor and glory to her. Take this boy that went to West Point. They lived in a Negro neighborhood and if you live in a Negro neighborhood in New Orleans you are the lowest of the low. You are just not low, you are really low. That mother spent hours in a cigar factory and she had nothing else but an old calico dress on for his graduation night. Of course, she didn't furnish the finances for him to go. I started on politicians down the line and got money together to get him up there. It took about five hundred dollars to get him up there, but we did it. We gave dances over here to get some money to get him up there; and other children that want to go to college, their parents tell them, 'If you think you can do it, then go ahead.' They don't get that much support from home, practically none. Meanwhile the rest of the family will keep on struggling day after day, eating bread, beans, and rice on their own. Again, not too many of our parents really depend upon the children to graduate and to bring in money, because either after graduation you get married right away and you are independent of the family, and you earn money with your diploma for either your husband or your wife, or the child walks away from the circumstances at home and doesn't send anything home. They are glad to get away from the situation. Even if they sent money home, it wouldn't do any good, because dad would drink it or mother would consume it one way or another for some foolishness, or the child goes on to higher education and supports himself or herself. We have boys that go on to Loyola. They want a good education. They don't want to go out to the Lakefront, because it is really nothing more than a glorified high school. It doesn't have ivy on the wall as yet, and they have a bunch of teachers that are just brought in. It is an overnight situation. They don't want to go out there. They want something better, so they will go to Loyola and they will stay up all night working in a drug store and study while they work to get enough money. I know many of our boys that get three and four hours of sleep and I don't know how they can keep it up. But they seem to have some kind of resistance that we don't have. Whether they take these old goof balls or not to keep them going is a debatable point; but they see a good thing and nothing is going to stop them from getting it. But the parents do not seem to demand the money from the children. That is another odd situation. You would think that they couldn't wait until they graduated so they would give them so much. They don't even have that much determination in the upbringing of their children to say, 'You have got to give me so much from your paycheck. We have educated you.' Many of our parents can't say this, because their children have educated themselves. We must have a good 65 to 70 percent of our children that go right from school at night to work. That's why we find it very difficult to participate in any events of any sort and all our games have to be at night because our children can't stay after school."

Interviewer: "Would you say that if the father did have steady work they wouldn't be in this neighborhood?"

Principal: "They shouldn't. They could get out of it like that. We had a couple of our children who did live in this project area. They were young married couples and some disease hit them or the mother might have had too many children in a row or they just couldn't get their heads above water. Then all of a sudden with constant hard work, they get ahead and the first thing they do, if they have any self-respect, they get out of the project as soon as they can, as fast as they can. They might not move to anything that is elaborate, but it is their own. They begin to buy their own home."

Interviewer: "Would you say that the father's inadequacies is why you have a high maternal domination among the families?"

Principal: "Dad is not home half of the time. There are many families where there is no dad. You just can't find him. He has been a playboy all his life. He is what our children would be without education. They wouldn't fail to be a duplicate of their father; and their father has no education, and they just don't have any intestinal fortitude. They just don't have anything that makes them stand up and say, 'I'm a man and I'm going to show that I can do something for my family and lift them out of this status.' This just doesn't exist. They are hand-to-mouth people. They get paid on Saturday and by Wednesday it is gone and Thursday and Friday they do without food. Saturday they get paid again. That is the way the week goes. By the middle of the week it is gone and Saturday night they blow most of it. It is rare when you meet a real good genuine father. They just don't care

and even if mother did care, she just couldn't pressure him that
much. If she cares, all she can do is hold the children together,
but apparently she doesn't have enough pressure. In these early
marriages, as I have said, the girl is nothing else but a thing to
the boy. It is not genuine love and if it is not genuine love, then
he doesn't care. He really doesn't care for her. He doesn't love
her, therefore, she is only there to do what she should do. The
cleaning and that kind of stuff, that is what she is there for. That
is marriage to them. It takes two people to get married; but they
don't have the same idea in mind when we say it takes two people
to get married. It is just that you've got to have a girl. You've got
to have a wife, and 'she is as good as the next one, so I'll take her.'
Many of our children get married because they don't want to
hurt the girl. The girl proposes around here. The boy doesn't
propose. She says, 'Let's get married.' When she says that, then it
is time. If he says, 'No,' it is the end of it. Therefore, it can't be
love. I've had some boys that say, 'What should I do? How do you
tell a girl no?' I tell them to tell her that they have no intentions
of getting married. They say, 'Aw Sister, she is such a nice kid
and her mother treats her so bad.' Then you try to show them
that they have to live together the rest of their life. But there isn't
that real sincere genuine love. But in many cases love does develop later on. But they are so frustrated that they couldn't love.
They couldn't genuinely love each other, because love means give
and they aren't ready to give. They have had to give all their life
for what they ever had and therefore they don't want to give.
Their marriages are so often very bad. They have never loved in
the beginning and when he goes off she really has no right to
complain."

Interviewer: "Why are the young couples not emotionally ready for
marriage?"

Principal: "They have been stifled. Their emotions have been
stifled. They have never been able to go up and say, 'Mom' and
have Mom hold them to her. She either is in a bar, or she is an
addict, or she is indifferent, or she is hard against the husband
who has deserted her and she feels very hard and very mean
toward society. I have seldom seen mothers show affection. You
seldom ever see real genuine sincere motherhood showing the
maternal instinct of caressing their child. Our children long for
that. They long for that little touch that makes them feel that
somebody cares. That keeps them childish, very childish. They

remain childlike for a long time, because they still want something they have missed when they were little kids. They just don't grow out of it and our girls are not ready to give it to the boys. That is why I think those marriages break up. Our girls have never gotten it either. But in a woman the instinct can rise above it. It does something to her. It definitely takes the tenderness, maternal, from her, but she can lavish it upon her child. But the father still hungers for it, but we can't get our girls to give it to the father, because they never saw it in their homes. . . ."

INTERGENERATIONAL CONFLICT

From the New Orleans principal's and the Hollywood youth counselor's interviews, as well as from the various case histories—such as Robert Rawlinson's—the daily life and environment of the "Common Man Boy" has emerged. From the viewpoint of the middle class observer the youth culture of the lower class seems unroutinized, undisciplined, and unsocialized. They seem unlettered, unambitious, and uncommitted. The lads and lasses on the wrong side of the track may seem characteristically impulsive, carnal, childish, stifled, frustrated, permissive, and promiscuous. Theirs is a hand-to-mouth, make-shift, quasi-communal existence in a government project, rented flat, and second-hand dilapidated home. Theirs is a castrate existence of fade-away fathers and frustrated mothers—of bars and barmaids, of lechery and alcoholism interlaced with a slight odor of marijuana or morphine. Here is a world of muscular immature sons and initiated aggressive daughters; it is a culture marked by the influential presence of the hot-rod buff and unmarked by the absent egg-head intellectual. Here is an adult world of fragmented familial, unstable marital, desultory occupational, truncated educational, and nonexistent social service histories. Here is an adolescent world which by polar tendency considers hard work an imprisonment only for the conned and the stupid; studies, a pastime for the "fruits" and "pansies"; male chastity, a negation of manhood; female virginity, something for one's own sister and future wife; monogamy in any strict sense, an unintelligible and unattainable ideal; policemen and other guardians of the law or pensioners of the state are "flatfeet" and congenital enemies. These are youth who have heard their parents say, "I'll knock your teeth down your throat" and "I'll bang you up against the wall" and found more succorance and security in these less-than-affectionate situations than the girl next door has found in her situation of not having seen her father for ten years or her mother for one.

But what has not emerged in any specific form is wherein the value system of the youth culture differs from that of the adult culture. Are the parents responsible and the children characteristically irresponsible? Is the adult culture altruistic and the youth culture egocentric? Are the oldsters teetotalers and the youngsters bibbers? Could we say that the lower class youth are in revolt against their parents' adamant pattern of deferred gratification? These questions are merely oratorical, they are expected to be self-answering. The data that we have seen seems to indicate that the apples have not fallen far from the tree—the youth are impulsive, unroutinized, and undeferred in their gratification patterns as their parents are. What, then, is the basis of parent-youth conflict as ascertained from our research?

3. THE SOCIOLOGY OF PARENT-YOUTH CONFLICT

Kingsley Davis remarked that "In other cultures, the outstanding fact is generally not the rebelliousness of youth, but its docility." He then addressed himself to the question: "Why does contemporary western civilization manifest an extraordinary amount of parent-adolescent conflict?" [11] Though our conclusions will come to modify his suppositions as regard the incidence of parent-youth conflict among that segment of the youth who continue their education, we can distinguish with him between those universals of the parent-child relation and certain variables which are peculiar to modern culture and which tend to heighten the parent-youth conflict. The universals are (1) the basic age difference between parent and child; (2) the decelerating rate of socialization with advancing age; and (3) the resulting intrinsic differences between old and young on the physiological, psychosocial, and sociological planes. The specifics of our modern culture that appear from our study to encourage this intergenerational alienation are (1) *the rate of social change* which, from the viewpoint of the teen-agers, seems to divide the universe into two worlds—those who grew up in the pre-atomic age with Dad, Mom, Moses, and Methuselah, and those who as modern youth have grown up in the postatomic age; (2) *the adolescent peer group* which, from the viewpoint of the parents, is liable

to lead their child into trouble with the law, the school, with sex;
(3) *parental authority* which, in trying to guide the youth's tomor-
rows with the maps of yesterday, brings restiveness and resentment;
(4) *smaller families with intensified emotional burdens* which
heighten oedipal antagonism, feelings of rejection, sibling rivalry,
alleged parental favoritism, and generalized hostility; (5) *conflict
of parental and commercialized youth cultures;* (6) *parental delinquency* (divorce, desertion, alcoholism, etc.).

These six categories were derived from our teen-age respondents' replies and in descending order (most of the complaints in the
first category and the fewest in the sixth) contain the point of
emphasis of most of the youths' complaints and disagreements with
the values, norms, and mores of adult society. It is interesting to
note that in not one in ten cases was there a major discrepancy
between the judgment of the youth concerning his own parental
relationships and his judgment of all American parent-youth relationships; if he felt that his parents did not understand him then he
was just as sure that the total "older generation" does not understand the "younger generation." The whole world is the same color
as the little, little windowpanes of his parents' home on Vine Street.

We can take snippets of the examples of the complaints and
expressed antagonisms of the youth against the adult world and
indicate how they fit into these categories.

1) The Rate of Social Change

"They are much older. My parents don't understand me at all."
(Dropout # 32)

"Everything was different then ... they just don't fit with today."
(Dropout #106)

"We just seem to have different ideas." (Dropout # 116)

"... instead of letting us do [our homework] the way we learned,
he wanted us to do it the way he had learned...." (Dropout # 320)

"They didn't have electricity and stuff...." (Dropout # 508)

"They didn't have ... cars, movies, ... electronics...." (Dropout
518)

"... old fashioned ... doesn't understand." (Dropout # 520)

"My mother says, 'Now when I was a girl...' and I say 'Oh, Ma,
that was in the way, way olden times....'" (Dropout # 524)

"The old generation don't believe in ... drinking, smoking, ... a girl in shorts, ... bikinis. ..." (Graduate # 147)

2)   *The Peer Group*

With the diminishing of authoritarian parental control parents have come to recognize that the social control of their children must be through the juvenile peer group. This is as true in their children's monosexual relationships as in the heterosexual ones. In regard to the latter there is the added difficulty of a sexually permissive society precipitating early mating which would terminate educational commitments:

"They never let me go out" (Dropout # 130).

"When they didn't like the boy ... they didn't let me go." (Dropout # 142)

"The car. ..." (Dropout # 404)

"No friends any more ... Mother scared them away." (Dropout # 502)

"Dating and whether I should wear lipstick. ..." (Dropout # 220)

"They say the cops are right." (Dropout # 510)

"Doesn't usually like my friends." (Dropout # 514)

"We understand each other except on boys." (Graduate # 143)

"I feel I should be able to choose my own friends; ... they choose their own." (Graduate # 215)

"When I come in late they don't understand." (Graduate # 341)

"I used to hang around with a few hoodlums. ..." (Graduate # 513)

3)   *Parental Authority Resented*

Adolescence is the transitional period between the complete dependence of the child upon parental authority and the independence of the adult. Within a society of competing authorities and divergent norms where independence is highly valued by all but where there is little explicit institutionalization of the steps of adolescent manumission from parental saturation authority the transition is inevitably pocketed with hostility and resentment.

"She still thinks I'm a baby and treats me as one." (Dropout # 130)

"Since I'm acting like a man and helping support the family, I should be given the responsibilities and the status of a man. But still my mother considers me a child." (Dropout # 526)

"They just keep on telling you what you should do." (Dropout # 532)

"Teen-agers want to feel free and be on their own." (Graduate # 209)

"My dad thinks what he says is right and everybody should go along with it. My mother thinks you should do what dad wants because he's the head of the family and if you do anything outside of that it's wrong." (Graduate # 315)

4) *Intensified Emotional Burdens of Smaller Families*

"I don't think my mother understands me. She doesn't have time to understand me. She's got to be worried with my brothers and sisters and I can take care of myself.... Even when I was in sixth grade and later I did all my homework and all my lessons myself.... [Everybody is against you?] Yes!" (Dropout # 102)

"They never showed their love toward us.... They never hugged and kissed us...." (Dropout # 548)

"Never let me go out when she would let my brother go out...." (Dropout # 126)

"I was thirteen and my father claimed I was boy crazy." (Dropout # 144)

5) *Conflict of Parental and Commercialized Youth Cultures*

"I don't understand their purpose in life. They don't seem to be doing anything. They just seem to be living in their own world with their own beliefs. They think they are right in everything.... I like Rock and Roll and they say it is 'nigger music' ... I like to watch *The Untouchables* and they say there is nothing but killing in it.... They tell me that I'm a lazy loafer.... Then they bug me about staying in the bathroom. It takes me about an hour to take a bath and everything.... I kept wanting to use his car and a couple of times I stole it on him.... They think they are religious and they think they have high morals. My mother says she has perfect morals and nobody has better morals than she does. She doesn't know the first thing about morals! I disagree with my family's morals on everything!" (Dropout # 324)

6) *Parental Delinquency*

"My father didn't care. He didn't spend many years with us. He deserted us when I was six years old. . . . He is very happily married and has two daughters." (Dropout # 130)

"My father? He was mostly 'laying in the gutter.' " (Dropout # 101)

"I don't think parents are strict enough." (Graduate # 241)

EVALUATION

What, then, can we conclude from the replies of our teen-age respondents concerning their culture? Is it in harmony or in conflict with the adult culture? If we consider only the material traits as clothes, cars, TV, records, films, cosmetics, photographic equipment and recreational paraphernalia these are seen as the product and adjunct of an affluent adult culture. There is no disharmony here. Youth's clothes, youth's cars, youth's TV programs, youth's records, etc. are accepted if not idealized by the adult culture. There are no specific "adolescent" movies; the "adult only" movies are in reality made for the teen-age market. It is difficult to see how the nonmaterial traits of the youth culture as language (this study found minimal differences between the speech habits of adults and youth), songs, and such characteristic values as conformity, beauty, fun, popularity, sports, dating, and romanticism, are not harmonious age-needs of the parent culture. The heavy emphasis upon sports is not radically different in the adolescent society (except that the youth are able to participate more vigorously) than it is in the adult society with its strong emphasis upon spectator sports. Sports assist in the establishment of broad identities, competition, and heroes for the adolescent world. The strong emphasis upon dating, romance, popularity, and grooming is quite in harmony with an adult culture which places high emphasis upon marriage but places the burden of mate choice upon the adolescent. The youth in such a situation have a need for early heterosexual role testing and play acting. The artifacts and values of the youth culture do not seem to be in general conflict with the adult culture. It is a rare youth who rejects the values of the larger society; his complaints are primarily lodged against his parents' attempted deferral of his more complete participation in the adult society with all its values. Peer group problems are primary in the parent-youth conflicts but both parent and youth agree that companionship with members of the same and opposite sex is desirable; the conflicts concern prudential judgments as to whether a particular person is a "good" person or one who would lead the youth astray. The use of lipstick or the car, the time to come in at night or the time to get up in the morning create no noticeable value conflict between parent and child; there is merely a difference of opinion as to when the youth should be considered an adult. Our society does not formalize this time—is it one's sixteenth, eighteenth, or twenty-first birthday? The youth have difficulty in waiting to become adults in the cultural context in which they find themselves. This is not a basic conflict of values but a harmony and acceptance.

When our "School # 1" of youth analysts states, in Talcott Parsons' words, that the "principal characteristics" of the youth culture are: "(1) Compulsive independence of and antagonism to adult expectations and authority.... (2) Compulsive conformity within the peer group of age mates. It is intolerable to be 'different' "; our study finds it impossible to validate the analysis. Neither the criteria of "compulsiveness" nor the empirical source of such sweeping conclusions has been identified. When our "School # 2" of youth analysts minimizes parent-youth conflict under the subsumption of "The Myth of Adolescent Culture" we find that our evidence from the dropout segment of our respondent population indicates that there is a great deal of antagonism between the adults and the youth of our society. Roughly four out of five of our dropout sample voice intergenerational conflict and four out of five of our graduate sample do not. This would mean that, as far as our evidence is concerned and as far as the inadequate formulation of both schools is concerned, the "antagonism" analysis of American parent-youth relationships is true of the dropout youth culture and the "harmony" analysis is typical of the graduate youth culture.

THE CRITICAL CONFRONTATION:
PARENT VERSUS PEER

In trying to evaluate the relative valence of the influence of parent and peer in adolescent choices, in attempting to measure the degree of independence between youth and adult culture, the literature of the social scientists has not produced a clear-cut question that would measure this respective valence. Neither specifying the content of the two cultures nor cataloguing the complaints held by youth against adults is a valid method of proving the independence or degree of antagonism between the two generations; there are too many unknown variables. Just because youth is more interested in dating and athletics, and adults are more interested in business and politics is no indication that their respective interests or cultures are either dependent or independent. A more certain and specific indication of the relative independence or dependence of the two subcultures and of the relative valence of the adult and peer culture is to ask the teen-age respondent what he would do if his parents forbid him to continue his friendship with one of his choice peers. The critical bridge between the world of the adult and the world of the peer is that of the *authority* of the adult. If the parental authority controls the personnel of the teen-ager's peer world then that peer world is subordinate and dependent to the adult world; if the teen-ager refuses to heed the dictate of the parent at this critical bridge then it is likewise obvious that his peer world is independent and that at this particular juncture of his life the attraction of his youth culture is greater than the persuasions of the adult world and its culture.

TEEN-AGE REACTION TO PARENTAL
OPPOSITION TO PEERS

In the belief that by directly questioning the youth as to what they would do, or what they do do when their parents oppose their choice of some friend we would have a new and better way of evaluating the relative influence of parent and peer culture, we asked the following questions:

> Did you think you were being contrary to your family in your choice of friends at any time?

> If your parents oppose your choice of some friend, what usually happens?

The question of friendship is one of extreme sensitivity in the lives of American youth. Their family, their home, their neighborhood, their school, their church—these are all of somebody else's making. But their friends are *their* friends—something of their own making. A close friend is to a sensitive adolescent "another self" and the questions we asked were by no means academic. Every youth recognized that we were asking about a real life situation and one of which he was acutely aware; quite probably just such a choice had been the cause of the most critical decision he had ever made in his life. The question provoked a cascade of replies which were quite readily reducible to five ultimate categories.

In reply to the question, then, of "If your parents oppose your choice of some friend, what usually happens?" these categories emerged: (1) *I pay no attention* to my parents' opposition; (2) *retain friend secretly;* (3) I *evaluate parental objections* and decide as I see fit; (4) *gradually reject friend* because of parental opposition; (5) *immediately reject the friendship* or have so internalized the values of the parents that I always choose the type of friends they would choose.

1)   Rejection of Parental Objections to Friend (Ignore Parents; Retain Friend)

Dropouts

"I choose my own friends.... They say they don't like them but so what?" (Dropout Larry W., # 44, St. Louis)

"She used to tell me who I should hang around with. She told me not to run around with this Benny because he was a troublemaker. But I slipped out of the house with him and that's how I ended up in jail.... Some of them used to call for me at three or four o'clock in the morning. She'd get out there and call them down." (Dropout Ron M., # 340, Denver)

"I keep going with them." (Dropout Mike H., # 504, Denver)

"They would tell me to leave them alone. Forget about them. What I would do? It would be like going in one ear and out the other ear. I would still hang around with them until something would happen. And then I would get in trouble causing my father to get the blame... and my mother." (Dropout Ronny R., # 522, Boston)

2)   Retain Friend Secretly

Dropouts

"If she didn't approve of one, if I liked the guy I'd keep hanging around with him on the side anyway. I figured I knew the guy better than my mother did and I could judge him better than my mother." (Dropout Marshall M., # 100, New Orleans)

"Oh, I'd let them jaw for awhile and then things would cool down. I guess I went with the ones I thought right... some way or other." (Dropout Ed T., # 234, Omaha)

"Most of my friends were at school but I did travel with a rough crowd on the sly . . . I did go around with a wilder crowd on the side but when I got pregnant, nobody so much as looked at me. I am completely alone now. (Dropout Eva T. S., # 244, Omaha)

Graduate

"If they opposed them they probably wouldn't be the kind of friends I should have but if I really thought them to be friends I don't think it would make any difference. I'd have to sort of see them quietly." (Graduate Margaret D., # 221, Omaha)

3)   *Evaluate Parental Objections*
And then Act as See Fit

Dropout

"She would give me advice not to go with them. It would depend . . . if I saw the wrong I wouldn't go out with them any more. But I would go out with him if I seen that he done good, but if I seen that he done bad I would quit. Since I've been fourteen or fifteen I've been deciding for myself. She said since I was old enough to work I was old enough to decide for myself." (Dropout Charlene T., # 128, New Orleans)

Graduates

"If it was someone that she didn't like, I would bring her over to the house and ask her why she didn't like her. She'd say, 'I just don't like her; she doesn't appeal to me; I just don't like her.' I bring them over once in a while for my mother to get to know them—to find out what kind of a person she is . . . boy or girl. If it was a person that got into trouble a lot I wouldn't stay with them." (Graduate Mary W., # 525, Boston)

"If he was completely bad throughout, I probably would drop him; if I knew the kid and I knew my ideas of him were more accurate I probably would stay with him but not too much." (Graduate Mike K., # 547, Boston)

4)   *Gradually Reject Friend*

Dropouts

"I still saw them once in a while but I didn't run around with them anymore." (Dropout Sherry W., # 236, Omaha)

"I would gradually break off with them." (Dropout Vivian M., # 248, Omaha)

"I would see them once in a while but not very much." (Dropout Marie L., # 308, Denver)

Graduates

"I wouldn't exactly drop them like a hot blanket but I would gradually estrange from them. I usually make it a point to accept their decisions on certain things." (Graduate Thomas L., # 413, Los Angeles)

"They just told me quietly not to go around with the person and gradually drop the relationship. That's what I did though I then thought it was a little harsh." (Graduate Allen P., # 427, Los Angeles)

5) *Immediate Rejection of Friend or Internalization of Parental Values so Never Would Choose Disapproved Friend*

Dropouts

"They wouldn't let me hang around with them and before they would let me go out with them they would keep me inside. If they didn't approve of somebody that person was just gone as far as I was concerned." (Dropout Kathleen M., # 136, New Orleans)

"I'd have to stop going around with them and just keep completely out of their life." (Dropout Ramona A., # 306, Denver)

Graduates

"First of all I don't think I would choose a friend that she wouldn't approve of." (Graduate John O., # 117, New Orleans)

"I guess I wouldn't go around with them anymore if they thought I shouldn't." (Graduate Elaine D., # 135, New Orleans)

"They usually tell me not to run around with them and I don't." (Graduate Roger B., # 227, Omaha)

"I guess I'd go with my parents because they know better then I do. They have gone through the years." (Graduate Tom L., # 507, Boston)

These revealing facets of the American youth culture can be reduced to the categories and percentages seen in Table 8.

Table 8.—Teen-agers' reactions to parental opposition
to their friends (in percentages) *

	Ignore Parents; Retain Friends	Retain Friend Secretly	Evaluate Objections; Act as See Fit	Gradually Reject Friend	Reject Friend or Prevenient Internalization of Parental Values
Dropouts	53	5	19	12	11
Graduates	7	2	18	30	43

* The hypothesis that dropouts will more frequently reject parental direction is sustained at the .001 level. $D = .484$; $X^2 = 68.87$; $p < .001$.

RESOLUTION OF CONFLICTING PROFESSIONAL INTERPRETATIONS OF AMERICAN YOUTH CULTURE

The typical (53%) dropout of our sample completely ignores parental wishes, directives, and commands in his choice of his peer group. He is independent of parental control in the establishing and maintaining of the personnel of his adolescent society. The *dropout* youth culture *is*, in Parsons' words, characterized by an "independence of and antagonism to adult expectations and authority" and by a "compulsive conformity within the peer group of age mates." [12] When Smith in the summary of his *American Youth Culture* states, "The autonomy of youth culture has been verified by the setting up of norms which, although they change from institution to institution, in all cases dominate and pattern youth behavior. These norms pre-empt the loyalty of youth ..." [13] he is summarizing what we have found to be true of the dropout youth culture. When Coleman in his *Adolescent Society* states that the American youth is " 'cut off' from the rest of society, forced inward toward his own age group ... and maintains only a few threads of connection with the outside adult society," [14] our data substantiate this conclusion of the dropouts. This conclusion also agrees with those of such social analysts as Kingsley Davis,[15] Margaret Mead,[16] Ruth Benedict,[17] Erik Erikson,[18] Herbert Bloch,[19] and in general the psychoanalytically oriented theorists who stress the rebelliousness and antagonism of youth culture. These interpretations and analyses are in accord with our findings on the dropout youth culture.

But if our data indicate that independence, antagonism, and rebelliousness are characteristics of the dropout youth culture, they likewise indicate that harmony and continuity with the adult culture are characteristics of the graduate youth culture. Despite the fact that our youthful graduating respondents were usually interviewed in an academic environment where they were very much aware of their friends, 73 percent of these graduates indicated that they would either give up these friends immediately or gradually if their parents told them they should. Only 2 percent (1 out of 50) of the respondents who were to graduate stated that they would secretly retain an undesirable friend and a small core of 7 percent affirmed that they would ignore their parents' wishes in the matter of friendship choices. And all of these graduates are predominantly lower class youth where presumably lies the molten lava of smouldering antagonism and erupting rebellion of American youth culture. Our conclusions concerning the American youth culture—only when applied to the graduate segment thereof—are in harmony with the adult-youth continuity-of-culture analyses of Kahl, Halsey, Martin, Bordua, Simpson; [20] Bernard; [21] Bealer, Willits; [22] Elkin, Westley; [23] Havighurst, Hollingshead, Whyte; [24] Zimmerman; [25] etc. Our study indicates that independence, antagonism, and rebellion are more characteristic of the lower class youth who have dropped out of school and do not opt to go along with "the system"; it likewise indicates that youth-parent mutuality, concurrence, and harmony are more characteristic of the lower class youth who are "going along with the system." Since "the system" primarily is the product of the middle and upper class culture, and since the youth who are continuing their education are making their way up into these classes we may state that their actions are no longer characteristic of the uneducated lower proletariat from which they are emerging but are imbued by an "anticipatory socialization" element. Since practically all the research of the authorities who incline to the "harmony" thesis of adult-youth cultures has been conducted among the middle class (Elkin and Westley's "The Myth of Adolescent Culture" in "a well-to-do-suburb in which, according to the 1951 census, 69 percent of the male labor force were executive, managerial, or professional"; [26] Whyte's "Organization Man" and "The Transients" have lost sight of the other side of the tracks;

Brittain's adolescent girls were representative of a middle class, not a lower class youth culture; [27] Zimmerman's data from graduate seniors who by definition were "civilization adequate," etc.), it is quite understandable that they would reach the "harmony" conclusion. Since Parsons' thesis of the "compulsive independence and antagonism" and "compulsive conformity within the peer group of age mates" was first delivered to psychoanalysts who specialize in themes of oedipal compulsions; since most of the other authorities were striving to explain the growing delinquency which is a lower class characteristic, it is quite understandable that they would conclude that "rebellion" and "antagonism" are the characteristics of the whole of American youth culture. Our conclusions of the two divergent youth cultures may point the way to the resolution of the conflicting professional interpretations of American youth culture.

4. DROPOUT HETEROSEXUAL PATTERNS
a) Sexual Behavior in the Human Male and Academic Achievement

Kinsey was surprised at his own findings. Academic achievement could be predicted from adolescent heterosexual patterns.

Though Kinsey's studies were highly vulnerable when judged on the criteria of representativeness and responsibility this was no inconsequential finding. Frequency and type of teen-age "sexual outlets," just as IQ or class membership, could serve as an index of future school success. One half of the male youth who continue their education to college report coitus in their teens; three-quarters of high school dropouts have coitus in their teens; four out of five of youth who are dropouts before entering high school report premarital intercourse during their teens.[28]

Our study corroborates the conclusion that dropouts tend to have a different heterosexual pattern than do the graduates. It has been apparent throughout our case histories and the reports from our resource contacts that the dropouts retain the general more promiscuous pattern of the lower class and that the graduates have been presocialized into middle class "deferred gratification" patterns of chastity and monogamy.

The nonupwardly mobile segment of the male lower class learn the intimate details of sexual relations at an earlier age—or at least report them more meticulously than do the upwardly mobile segment; often, too, they know of the sexual affairs of their brothers and sisters, of the extramarital relations of their parents; and some hold suspect their own legitimacy. Their sexual attitudes and practices are not divorced from their general personality structure. They are not expected to assume responsibilities, are not held to careful time schedules, home tasks, school assignments, work requirements. They stay up later, roam the streets more often, travel in gangs more, participate in family leisure activities less, are subject to paternal influence less. They have fewer restrictions placed upon them as regards time, space, and sex.

The males of our sample who originate in the lower class but are being presocialized for upward mobility through completion of at least high school education tend to be different. They seem more influenced by the middle-class taboos on freer sex expression and freer direct outlets for aggression. Their heterosexual contacts are less likely to stray outside the control pattern established by their parents. Hollywood Youth Counselor Colwell highlighted this difference of heterosexual attitudes of dropouts and graduates when he remarked:

> Concerning dating we find that the girls get involved when they are young. Junior high girls get involved when they are twelve or thirteen; the dropout boys will be sixteen or older.... It is part of the game to get around parental control. With my other boys who are still in school, the parents will pick up the girl and the boy, take them to a movie, and after the movie pick them up. But with the dropouts, this would be the lowest of the low to have your parents or anyone else pick you up in a car and come and get you because you're not a "stud" then.[29]

b) The Pregnant Dropout

Illegitimacy is not a new problem. But what is new is its heavy incidence among high school teen-agers. It is not known with any certainty what percentage of girls drop out of high school because they are pregnant. A rough estimate is that 5 percent of high school girls will drop out of school because of pregnancy in any one year.[30] In four years this would mean that almost one out of five girls have dropped out of high school while pregnant. This in turn would mean that almost one out of two girls, who leave school before graduation, leave while pregnant.

Kinsey's findings are considered conservative for our own decade. Eighty percent of his 5,293 female sample (white, middle class,

Protestant, collegians—all to an unrepresentative degree) had not
participated in pre- or extra-marital coitus. Using twenty years of
age as his cut-off point, only 3 percent of the college group became
extra-maritally pregnant; double that percentage of high school
graduate girls did; and double again that percentage for those who
did not finish high school.[31] More recent data indicate that the
pregnant dropouts begin their dating, kissing, and petting behavior
earlier than those who continue their education and marry later.
Steady dating is the setting for petting to orgasm and premarital
intercourse.[32] When upper class females become pregnant outside
marriage the pregnancy is more likely to be the result of a love
affair; when lower class females become illegitimately pregnant, the
pregnancy is more likely to be a result of a casual affair.[33]

HETEROSEXUALITY: THE GENERAL PATTERN

The general pattern of sexual behavior of the teen-ager seems clear
—heterosexual relationships are not isolated phenomena in the life
histories of either the dropout or the graduate. The impulsive,
independent, undisciplined, unsupervised, short-term, rebellious,
peer-oriented style of life which characterizes our dropout sample's
general behavior is likewise characteristic of his sexual behavior.
The teen-age youth who sensitizes, indulges, and habituates himself
to permissive and irresponsible heterosexual relations will more
probably not continue his education. Young Lotharios, Bluebeards,
and Cleopatras in contemporary America do not signalize themselves by their academic aspirations or achievements. The skills,
values, attitudes, interests, discipline, academic motivation, cor-
roborative friendships—all of the personal and social constellation
that is needed to continue one's education in face of the tremendous difficulties that confront especially the lower class are lacking. The sexually alerted and indulgent youth has need of more
and more money for a car, entertainment, or matrimony, if he is to
pursue his heterosexual forays. Contrariwise, the youth who is
conditioned and motivated to long-range academic aspirations will
tend, within the context of his personality structure, to take a more
disciplined and responsible attitude to sexual stimuli. He shows a
greater detachment and long-range appreciation of heterosexual
commitments. His deferred gratification pattern in matters of sex, if
he originates in the lower class as our respondents do, marks him as
presocialized for upward mobility on the social transmission belt of
academic achievement.

TWO EXAMPLES

To illustrate more specifically the different life patterns that characterize our dropout and graduate samples in matters of heterosexual relationships we can take the case histories of Gayle L. and José L. Both of these youth originate in the lower class and both are talented artistically. The dropout, Gayle, is the more advanced economically and intellectually (she has an IQ of 120); she is an only child. The graduate is one of eight children; his father is a Mexican "wetback" in extremely precarious economic circumstances. Their heterosexual relations are seen as integral with their respectively undisciplined and disciplined styles of life.

THE CASE OF GAYLE L.: "FOURTEENTH SUMMER"

"How many children in the family? One—me; and I'm so spoiled! ... My dad usually doesn't ever have any free time. He is a seaman and he is always out. And when he does come home the first thing he does is go to this barroom over on State.... He is mean, I'll tell you that. He is awfully mean. He has a bad temper and I take after him. He is on the ship and he thinks when he comes home he can boss us.... That's what my daddy did to me: he would whip me and five minutes later he would come crying to me asking me to forgive him. Of course that is going to open the road for you and you start thinking: 'Look! What can I get out of it?'

"My mother didn't want me to work because my daddy made enough money to support us and he didn't want my mother to work either. In school my mother would do anything for me—she was brilliant in school; she graduated from school when she was sixteen years old and business school also. She was really brilliant. I wanted to be a chemist; I always wanted to be a chemist. I used to always like to draw posters; I'm pretty good at drawing; and when I had to draw posters she would sit right down and help me. She would get all the paint and stuff and she would give me ideas—she was great for that—she is great anyway; pretty special....

"[My best girl friend] got married when she was sixteen also. That was two years ago. She is eighteen now. And Priscilla and I were this close but she had to get married. Everybody tried to keep it a secret but it wasn't....

"I met Jim when I was fourteen—it was the summer after I had graduated from eighth grade. It was when I ran away from home. I was disgusted. I was always getting picked on. I guess because I was wild. I'll admit I was wild. I think all the things I did before were foolish. I was going out every night. I had all the money I wanted. When I wanted money I would go to my mother and she would give it to me. I think that's what was wrong. When I get mad I just lose my mind. I go crazy. And one night I was going out with Buster and I called him and told him to come up and get me and if he didn't come up to the house I was going to break up with him just to show him that he better come up. But he came up to get me and I started crying. I was crying my heart out to him. My mother had punished me and I wasn't used to it. I think if my mother had told me 'No' a couple of times when I wanted money and if I had been punished . . . but anyway, I just got disgusted and I ran away from home and I went to this friend's house. She wasn't exactly a friend. I didn't like her but it was the only place I could go. I ran away and I went to this girl's house, and she is not really the kind of girl you should go to see—if you want the truth she and her mother are prostitutes—and Jim was there. I didn't believe it about Dolorine, my sorta girl friend, but I knew it about her mother. But her mother didn't make much difference to me. So then Jim took this girl and her mother and I to a cocktail lounge. Well, I don't drink and I had a coke but I saw Dolorine—she kept inching around Jim and she kept saying, 'Come on, Jim; come on, Jim!' So then they left and when Dolorine's mother and I got home they were there. Jim was in the Marines and the office was right across the street from where they live, so when he would stay overnight he just got up and went to work.

"So the next day was his birthday so we all went swimming at the lake. Oh, yes, I forgot to tell you . . . the night that I met him, he was at her house and he brought another Marine friend along and it was supposed to be for me, I imagine, but he didn't get too far. In fact he is married now and he lives right across the street. But we started playing kissing games and that was just that—it was just a kissing game to me and that was all. The next day it was his birthday and I knew a couple of Marines already, not from him, but I already knew them. But this guy Larry wanted me to go out that night and Jim told him 'No,' that I wouldn't go out with him. So then we all went swimming at the lake and Jim told me he loved me. But I knew he was lying because he only knew me half a day, I was going to stay with Buster anyway. But after that he just got to me; I just thought he was real cute and I liked his ways. He could dance real good. That night he told me he loved me; it just kind of hit me in the wrong place and made me feel kind of funny, but I told him I loved him but I didn't really—I just liked him because he danced well. So I broke up with Buster and I went steady with Jim. We was going steady five days and I went back home—Jim made me go back home. He said that my mother was probably worried and he wanted me to go back home. He wanted me to get away from Dolorine and her mother. But I didn't want to go back home, but when I went in, Jim had already gotten in touch with my mother—I don't know how. She liked him right away. Maybe it was because he was bringing me home. But she liked him right away and they got along just swell. We went out a year and a half. . . . She told me not to get married and to go to school. But I told her I was going to get married and I did." (Dropout Mrs. Gayle L., # 146, New Orleans).

The Case of José L.: "A Dumb Mexican? Not This One!"

"We hardly have any time for ourselves. We have eight children and my father works. You might say work is his hobby. Right after work he comes home and eats and then goes back to work at his shop. He takes me and my brother with him and we upholster. . . .

"No, I have never thought of leaving home. If I left home that would give the impression that I know everything. But I wouldn't leave home because I don't know everything yet. I don't know how it is to suffer. I don't know anything right now. In Mexico when the kids were twelve years old they were men because they suffered and they know what it is to suffer. Over here in the United States your father gives you money. They say, 'Oh, I'll get ten bucks from my old man or my old lady—it's nothing.' They never suffer. Maybe some people over here suffer but the majority don't. But in Mexico it's just hard. . . .

"My older brother goes to college and one of my other brothers is a sophomore. When this sophomore brother was in grade school yet, the parish father offered him a scholarship but he refused it because he wanted to stay with us. He would have had to stay at school all week and then just come home on weekends. But he didn't want to do that. He gets all 'A' and 'B' grades. . . .

"We learn from other people's mistakes of not getting the knowledge they strive for. I mean . . . well, I don't want to be dumb. I want to advance myself. Other people when they look at the Mexican they say, 'He's dumb—a dumb Mexican!' But do all of

them have to be dumb? No! I want to advance myself and I can say,
'Not this one!'

"My father didn't graduate from high school. My father you
might say has a low job...maybe you wouldn't call it a low job
but he has to work at the upholstery shop after work because there
isn't enough money. And he says, 'See what happened to me. I
might have achieved a better job if I had finished high school and
gone to college, and I want you to finish high school because you
learn about things and you will be qualified for the things that are
thrust at you in daily life and maybe you can even go to college and
learn a few more things about life.' And I think I have learned a lot
of things in high school but maybe there are even a lot more things
to learn in college that even our father didn't know. . . .

"I'm studying to become an artist. I want to expand my character so that other persons know me but not in a way like 'I'm a big
deal; watch me' . . . I want to become a big person. . . . Friends—
that's what I'm trying to gain. . . . I can draw reasonably well. I sell
my drawings. I started drawing in the fourth grade and it has just
gotten into my blood, you might say. When I was in the fourth
grade, my brother started drawing and I always followed my
brother and one time he sent in a drawing to a television station
and he got acknowledged by his friends when they saw this on
television. And I thought to myself that he was popular because he
got his picture on television and I can do the same thing. So that
started me and I just kept on drawing and got more friends, and I
thought if I drew a little better maybe I could advance myself and
become bigger.

"I have tried hard to advance myself to a point where I could
easily get into a Walt Disney studio. But there is a lot of red tape
and you have to have certain qualifications. But a lot of people
think if they quit school they would have more time to develop
their talent and if they should make it the others look at him and
say, 'Wow, look at him—a big car, a good house, and lots of money.
If he could do it, I can too.' Then they want to drop out too. But
nowadays that's not that way. So I think I'll wait until I graduate
and then try to improve myself.

"Yes, I like the girls—the good ones. Very much. I'll marry one.
But that's a long way off. I have to grow up first. I have to get
established. Then it's time for marriage.

"I think it is necessary to go to school to advance yourself
because at home you don't have the facilities that you do at school

and I'm going to try to go. I have a friend who can copy real good but he can't create and we plan to go to Warner Brothers during the Easter vacation and see if we can get a job. But I won't be satisfied with this because I know I can draw, but the question is: Can I draw everything? I have an idea but I don't know if it will work out. My mother has a friend at Warner Brothers who is the animation supervisor, and I thought I might be able to get a job just sweeping. But you can make a lot of friends just sweeping. You say 'Hello, Mr. Jones,' and he might ask you some questions about art. He may tell you the things they do—how many slides they use and how many pigments they use . . . and I would be advancing myself just sweeping. Then when I think I have comprehended the many facts of this art business, then I will go in and say 'Mr. So-and-so, I would like to work as an artist or a copy boy and I will try to advance myself.' And he will say, 'We know you around here, Joe. And we will give you a chance.' But if I had just gone in they wouldn't know nothing about me but I can get to know them and I can learn while I'm sweeping. . . .

"After all this preparation, it will be time enough to talk marriage. That comes easier." (Graduate José L., # 425, Los Angeles)

ANALYSIS OF THE TWO INTERVIEWS

Our interviews of the dropout Gale and the graduate José illustrate the point that the typical heterosexual orientations are integral parts of a broader lifepattern of the lower class's "immediate gratification" and the middle class's "deferred gratification" pattern. The interviews likewise demonstrate that though lower class ethnic and economic backgrounds no longer present an insuperable barrier between the lower class and higher education, premature heterosexual commitments do.

However, our interviews of Gayle and José are capable of sustaining a greater heuristic load than this. We can footnote any number of statements—especially those of Gayle's—and indicate how they illustrate other characteristics of the youth culture and the divergencies of the dropout and graduate segments of his teen-age way of life.

"FOURTEENTH SUMMER" REVISITED

"I had all the money I wanted"—The fact that American youth have at their disposal more than ten billion dollars unencumbered by income taxes or responsibilities has precipitated the concerted commercial appeal to an independent youth culture. The purchase of the paraphernalia of this separate youth culture—clothes, sports equipment, music, cars, appliances, cosmetics, films, books, magazines, tobacco, and several hundred million admissions to various amusement centers catering to gilded youth—is largely independent of adult control and styling.

Whereas Gayle stated that she had all the money she wanted, José pointed out that in his family "there isn't enough money."

"My mother had punished me and I wasn't used to it.... I think if my mother had told me 'No' a couple of times"—As a matter of reportorial account, Gayle had been whipped by both her father and her mother and slapped in the face on occasion by her mother. In no graduate account were such vicious measures recorded. What Gayle seemed to be revolting against was the erratic permissive-repressive techniques of her parents which are typical of our dropout sample. The youth are left without reasonable norms of expectations and internalized standards of behavior. Gayle's mother would follow up her explosions of temper and pique with exorbitant gifts of money and Gayle's father would follow up his whippings of his daughter, with all their sexual psychopathic overtones, by "five minutes later ... crying and begging me to forgive him. Of course that is going to open the road for you and you start thinking, 'Look, what I can get out of it!' "

José's parents, as typical of graduates' parents, manifest no signs of control of teen-agers through physical repression. The control is an internalized way of life supported by parental love, direction, and authority. Such indirect control has its base in the youth's childhood training.

"I was disgusted.... When I get mad I lose my mind. I go crazy. ... I called (Buster) and told him to come up and get me and if he didn't come up to the house I was going to break up with him—just to show him that he better come up.... He came up.... I was crying my heart out to him."—In a dropout's relatively isolated small nuclear family there is no emotional succorance available in times of parent-child infantile conflict except extradomestic agents. Whereas José could have recourse to his grandmother who lived with his family or to any of his seven brothers and sisters who would have smoothed things over within family framework, Gayle had emotional recourse to "Buster"—an extrafamilial agent. Noteworthy is her threat-and-bribe technique in dealing with her young boy friend: If he did not come, he would no longer be her "one and only"; if he did, as subsequent events proved, she would cry her "heart out to him."

"I just got disgusted and I ran away from home"—We have already found that the dropout's leaving school is a question of "deficiency orientation" that is tantamount to "running away" from school. Here we find in a dramatic manner that a dropout's leaving home is likewise a "running away" from home. The antagonistic terms in which she dealt with her heterosexual agemate are now being acted out in her relations with her parents.

"And I went to this friend's house"—Here is a quasi-communal housing pattern among the lower class that appears time and again in the dropout interviews and less frequently in the case histories of the graduates. The youth take it for granted, as their parents seemingly do likewise, that without further ado or explicit permissions from the adult world, they can sleep here, there, or any other place that strikes them as suitable or available. In time of parent-child conflict this seems to be taken for granted by all concerned even as it is in the case of Gayle. It is to be noted that for the next five days there was no communication between Gayle and her parents. When another "extrafamilial agent" prevailed upon her to return home one of the lesser reasons presented was that "he said that my mother was *probably* worried."

"She and her mother were prostitutes"—This case, of course, is an extreme example of dropout indecorous and unconventional acquaintanceship. That prostitution is a fairly common phenomenon in at least the psychic awareness of the lower class youth has been seen in the interviews with the Los Angeles youth counselor and the New Orleans principal. The increase of teen-age premarital intercourse, pregnancies, abortions, venereal disease, rape, and general permissiveness has acquainted modern youth, especially dropouts, with a demimonde argot with which schoolgirls of a generation ago would have little practical acquaintance. It would be interesting and instructive to inquire how many middle-class mothers today understand such very ordinary terms that are discussed in high school English classes today when taking the works of, say, Joyce or Salinger—"fruit," "fairy," "queer," "punks," "third sexers," "Margery," "collar-and-tie," etc. Be that as it may, this particular dropout—at this time only fourteen years old—saw little that was unseemly in her staying at the home of a woman she knew to be a prostitute. In contradistinction to the centrifugal dynamism of the dropout family of Gayle's, we have the centripetal dynamism of the graduate José's family. When one of José's brothers was offered a scholarship which implied his living away from home midweeks, "he refused it because he wanted to stay with us" (*Supra,* page 157).

"And Jim was there"—Prescinding from the unusual circumstances of this couple's first meeting, we might ask what percentage of youth do date before they enter high school; Gayle has not as yet entered ninth grade. This is only her fourteenth summer though it is Jim's twentieth. In *Elmtown's Youth* it is reported that 58 percent of the girls and 43 percent of the boys have already dated before entering high school.[34] Those who continue their education do not date as early or as consistently as do those who discontinue their education. The age differential of early dating is likewise more marked. The folkways of courtship in the United States counsel that the boy be older than his female partner. There are many reasons for this. The biological reason that could be submitted is that the girl reaches full maturity at eighteen years of age and the boy not until he is twenty-four. A fourteen-year-old girl is a young woman; a fourteen-year-old boy is a young boy. (As a biological contraindication to the custom of an older male marrying a younger female is the fact that in the United States the female outlives the male by seven years; this would argue for a woman's marrying a man younger than herself if they wanted to live out their lives together.) Psychologically speaking the girl is much more mature than the boy. Especially is this true in the lower classes where the boy is disadvantaged because the father-figure is so frequently absent or extremely weak. The fairly constant presence of the mother assures the daughter of someone with whom she can identify. Again, girls have concentrated on social skills and graces; whereas, boys in their early adolescence have concentrated on sports and, later, on occupational orientations. A common complaint of the girls, especially among the dropouts, is that their age mates of the male of the species are "so immature." In first year of high school it seems that the taller girls tower about a head higher than the more "runty" boys. As is more common with the graduate interviews, there is no reference in José's tape-recorded responses to any dating practices. He was eighteen years of age at the time of the interview; he would graduate from high school within several months.

"He brought another marine friend along, and it was supposed to be for me, I suppose"—Typically enough, the social contacts of the dropout are made in places independent of parental approbation such as school, home, at approved friends' and relatives' homes, church functions, etc. Graduates' friends are more regularly brought into the parents' homes for inspection, evaluation, and approbation.

"But we started playing kissing games"—The tempo of the heterosexual meeting has suddenly accelerated. Elementary school children frequently play such kissing games as "spin the bottle," "post office," "flashlight," "artist and model," etc. But for servicemen to be playing kissing games with precocious elementary school girls seems to be a socializer of a somewhat different genre.

"And it was just that to me and that was all"—And here we come to a theme of the dropout heterosexual culture—permissive heterosexual interchange without affection. We can use this dichotomy of "with affection" and "without affection" as a basic variable of heterosexual relations. Gayle stated that she went through a social ritual without any emotional commitment. We can place the sequence of heterosexual interaction on our usual five-point continuum: (1) holding hands; (2) kissing; (3) "necking" (this term is more from mother's and grandmother's day and it is described as "marathon kissing"; the term is used by a minority of female respondents. It would more commonly be called by the youth "light petting" in contradistinction to "heavy petting" or "petting" without qualifications); (4) petting—meaning prolonged and passionate kissing plus "territorial concessions"; (5) coitus. With Gayle's distinction of courtship practice "with" and "without" affection we can subdivide each of the steps of the sexual sequence for a better understanding of the youth culture's heterosexual mores. As shall be seen, the "without affection" sequence is outside of the romantic love syndrome; the "with affection" or at least " with emotion" is of its essence.

Theme #1:   The Game of Sexual Exploitation

"But he didn't get too far"—By this laconic sentence Gayle presumably meant that "he" did not reach the level of "heavy petting" but only the level of "light-petting-without-affection." But more important for the understanding of youth's heterosexual relation is to perceive the structure of the situation: the "game" is so set up that it pits a male against a female in sexual combat. The courtship or dating process is so organized that it is a competitive game involving high stakes and a conflict of interests. The object of the game is for the male, in the words of a number of our respondents, to see "how much he can get" in the line of sexual intimacies from the girl, and the girl is to see "how little she can give" and yet retain his interest. How to be a "virgin temptrix" is the schizoid structuring that the adolescent girl must cope with. This lower-class theme of extreme permissiveness for both boys and girls does not block out the contra-theme that the girl dare not get "caught" with either a pregnancy or an unsavory reputation. In the "game" the male "scores" or "makes out" according to the class of the participants. With the older and lower class, "making out" means that the male has succeeded in his attempt to have intercourse with the girl; in the middle class environment it more frequently means the sexual intimacies of petting. The female is victor if she keeps the male interested and relatively content but without yielding (according to class) at petting or coitus levels. The female is vanquished if she loses the male's interest, if she loses her good name, if she becomes pregnant.

The ritual, then, that our dropout takes completely for granted as a part of the heterosexual mores is that she should engage in a combat; it is a duel in which a young girl, according to her inclinations or manipulative ability, parries the male's thrust. This pattern seems to be one more application of the interactional hostility which is characteristic of the lower-lower class.

MONOGAMY AND THE GRADUATES' DATING

There is a quite different emphasis in the dating habits as found among our graduate respondents. Marriage is taken to be the obvious terminal point and orientation of courtship and heterosexual interactions. It is understood, even by such traditionalists as José, that marriage requires preparation in heterosexual skills, attitudes, and understanding. But the graduates, and more specifically José, emphasize the occupational preparation that is needed—the man must be the breadwinner and the woman primarily the homemaker.

Within the dropout culture, dating is id-oriented. Within the graduate culture it is id-tinged, ego-oriented, and superego-controlled.

Marriage is a sexual community of complementary roles. The

dropouts, as dramatized by Gayle, stress the "sexuality" of the status; the graduates, as dramatized by José, stress the "complementarity."

"Jim took this girl and her mother and I to a cocktail lounge"— Liquor plays a more prominent place in our dropout interviews than in our graduates'. Our present respondent would seem to know more about the ingredients of a whiskey sour or a Tom Collins than she does about the ingredients of a simple declarative sentence which would distinguish the syntax of "I" and "me."

"But this guy Larry wanted me to go out that night and Jim told him 'No,' that I wouldn't go out with him"—Here is a switch in the relationships. Not only a switch of partners but in emotional content. Jim has become possessive of Gayle and assumes the right to say with whom Gayle will or will not go out. Gayle is pleased with the development and according to her norms it is ideal for Jim to assume this possessive, protective, and directive function even though he was an acquaintance of only a few hours.

"So then we all went swimming at the lake and Jim told me he loved me, but I knew he was lying because he only knew me half a day—and I was going to stay with Buster anyway"—Gayle at a rational level realizes that to describe their game with the word "love" is to use a high word in a low masquerade. Jim couldn't *really* love her because he did not know her. And this is the reality principle to which she appeals in her evaluation of the situation to the interviewer. But then she adds what is her own personal reason. It is the teen-age code of the steady: "I was going to stay with Buster anyway." Gayle's new rationale is that she could not accept Jim as a suitor because she is already "monogamously" committed. But as sudden as an infant's whim there is a change in her definition of the situation.

Theme #2: Romance as a Complex

"But after that he just got to me. I just thought he was real cute and I liked his ways. He could dance real good. That night he told me he loved me. It just kind of hit me in the wrong place and made me feel kind of funny. But I told him I loved him but I didn't really. I just liked him because he danced well. So I broke up with Buster and I went steady with Jim"—Gayle now presents us with a second remarkable theme of the youth cultures of the United States—the motif of romantic love.

Romance is defined by Parsons as the "unrealistic idealization of emotionally significant objects [with] a general tendency to see the world in sharply black and white terms." [35] Truxal and Merrill see romantic love as "that complex of attitudes and sentiments which regard the marriage relation as one exclusively of response." [36] We would prefer to distinguish between "romance as a complex" and romance as a standard component of heightened heterosexual relations. The former is a somewhat pathological condition which blocks out and eliminates rationality; the latter builds upon reason, climbs up reason, but then leaps into a broader world beyond.... "The heart has its reasons whereof the mind knows not." Throughout our discussion we are speaking of "romance as a complex" or as a social pathology or as a syndrome of an imbalance. One could similarly speak of food, drink, sex, love, education, politics, religion, or what have you as a "complex" without in any way derogating from the dignity and value of that particular item which serves as the base or focal point of the "complex." We in no way mean to derogate or minimize the importance of romance as a heightened emotional cathexis in everyone's life.

From the context of Gayle's statement that "Jim just got to me," it seems apparent that she is not speaking of genital accession. She is stipulating that from that magic moment on, her relationship with Jim was on a different level than that of "this Larry guy" whose game of sexual exploitation was without affection. The lightning bolt which "kind of hit me in the wrong place and made me feel kind of funny" after Jim said he loved her was, although tinged with eroticism, much more physiological and cultural. Physiologically hers was a highly emotional state; culturally this sudden and majesterial revelation, this "cardiac-respiratory" syndrome of romance, was enough to make Jim her "steady" and her childhood sweetheart, Buster, to whom so few short hours before she had "cried out her heart," a unilaterally rejected pale memory.

We can single out four characteristics of romance as a complex:

(1) It is an *absolute* mystique. "If I love him that's all that matters."

(2) It is *unrealistically* idealistic. "My loved one is all perfect."

(3) It foresees marriage as a continual *hyperemotional* response. "And they lived happily, happily ever after." "What would my parents know about love? They've been married for twenty years!"

(4) Needless to say, within a rational framework, the illusion of romance is destined for inevitable *disillusionment.*

PARENTS AND THE ROMANTIC SYNDROME

Though parents verbally tend to deprecate to their children the idolatrous homage tendered to romance as an absolute, it has been found that unknowingly the parents are the ones who are prime propagators of the myth that romance will "change all." Robert and Helen Lynd, in their *Middletown in Transition,* pointed out that:

> Middletown adults appear to regard romance in marriage as something which, like their religion, must be believed in to hold society together. Girls are assured by their elders that "love" is an unanalyzable mystery that "just happens." "You'll know when the right one comes along," they are told with a knowing smile.[37]

The unrealistic idealization by parents of anything youthful is another contributory stream to the tide of the romantic complex. If parents consider adolescent styles, music, physique, literature, comics, entertainment, and the whole youth culture to be the ideal to which they should subordinate adult society, the youthful penchant for callow romanticism soars skyward without the encumbrance of wisdom or responsibility. In the case of Gayle it would seem that her parents unrealistically idealized the youth culture and romanticism in that they themselves attempted to shed their maturity of years if not of experience and become identified with their daughter's youthful way of life.

"Dad didn't like any of my boy friends but he liked the girls. He got along with all of them and they all called him 'Dad.' They were giving a surprise party for me one day—for my birthday—and he happened to be home and he was cutting up as much as the rest of them. I was at my girl friend's house and I didn't know anything about it and I called my mom and told her I wanted to come home and eat and change my clothes, and she said daddy would be right over. So here he comes walking in. He has my shorts in his back pocket and he had all kinds of sandwiches for me to eat. He didn't want me to go home because they were fixing a surprise party for me. All the girls just loved him. He would do anything for us. If they wanted to go to the lake they would call me up and tell me to get my daddy to drive us. But he didn't like the boys. . . .

"Every boy I went out with my mother welcomed and there wasn't one that I didn't bring home. She would kid around with them and she would cut up with them just like she was a teen-ager. Every Saturday was my day to clean the house and every Saturday all the boys would come to my house and I had to clean and she would dance with them and cut up with them. She approved of all the boys."

With such an "adult" background it is more understandable how Gayle under the highly emotional circumstances of meeting Jim could take the slim evidence of his ability to "dance real good" and build it up in her mind as proof conclusive that he was her eternally predestined "one and only."

Theme #3:   Steady Dating

"So I broke up with Buster and I went steady with Jim"—Why in our culture is there such a close relation between permissiveness, romanticism, and going steady?

"Going steady" is the heterosexual interaction pattern that is presently institutionalized throughout the whole span of the youth culture. From grade school through graduate school it seems to be the dating "ideal." Roughly half the high school students seem to be participants in the practice. Even when our respondents expressed criticism of the system they seemed to accept it as the standard norm of the total youth culture.

A social institution is an answer to some social need. From this viewpoint the institutionalization of steady dating is an answer either to some social need that by hypothesis was not present to such an extent before steady dating became entrenched (since World War II) or an answer to some need that hitherto could not be answered because of a lack of facilities for its institutionalization. It is our viewpoint that steady dating is a characteristic of the heterosexual relations of modern youth culture as a direct outcome of the two general themes developed in the immediately preceding pages. More explicitly, youth is projected into a culture which in heterosexual relationships is *permissive* (Theme # 1) and *romantic* (Theme # 2); youth's adjustment to the discontinuities and contradictions inherent in these themes when they are embedded in a Judaeo-Christian civilization is to institutionalize a dominant pattern of *steady dating* (Theme # 3).

CULTURAL CONTRADICTIONS

It is a contradiction to tell a maiden to be sexually accessible and sexually inaccessible. It is a contradiction to hold up to her the ideal of "the virgin temptrix" or "the chaste call girl." Yet this is the ultimate contradiction and the psychotic strain that a teen-age girl is subjected to when she is released into a culture which is both sexually permissive and sexually puritanical. The sharp edge of the sexual exploitation game in which Gayle participated was that she would be socially damned if she did and socially damned if she didn't; this is mirrored on a broader scale in the American cultural milieu. In many aspects American culture prompts young girls to be sexually accessible, yet at the same time in typical double standard fashion warns, "but if you are caught being accessible, or if it is even rumored that you are accessible, you are ruined."

To be more concrete—from the indoctrination of home, church, and other conservative agencies; from her own observation of the pariah treatment meted out to her agemates who became pregnant without benefit of marriage; from her growing awareness of the sardonic implications of the double standard, the American girl is socialized in the purity-and-virginity theme of our Judaeo-Christian heritage.

Contradicting this ascetic motif is the sensate theme of sexual exploitation. There is scarcely an advertisement for cosmetics, clothes, films, magazines, books, travel, radio, TV, that does not make a young adult woman, attractive of face and figure, its center-piece. Feminine physical charm—alluring or seductive—is the ubiquitous stereotype of our culture. Her standardized smile and gleaming teeth portray the satisfaction that the prospective customer will experience upon purchasing a particular commodity be it an abacus board, or zwieback toast, or just a plain Mack truck. Whether in Maidenform or mink the model's face and figure are seldom concealed. The constant theme is "You, too, can look for, find, see, worship, vicariously enjoy, or actually be a goddess of love."

THE STUDENT LOVER

The second theme—that of the romantic cult—proves to be a cultural contradiction in the life of the teen-ager; it bids him to be overwhelmingly in love with his eternally predestined "one-and-only" or life is not worthwhile and yet at the same time bids him be a full-time, dedicated student under the sanction of depriving him of occupational adequacy, status honoraria, and economic affluence.

It is within the contradictory context of the American culture traits that the steady dating pattern can be seen as youth's attempt to cope with an utterly unlikely situation. Going steady, we suggest, is the youth's adaptive institutionalization to the conflict inherent in the social mores of the presumed sexual abstinence of the single state and the permissive state precipitated by the lack of chaperonage, early age of marriage, recent general availability of cars which free youth from parental and neighborhood control, recent general availability of the telephone which maximizes opportunities for constant adult-free intercommunication with agemates, the affluence of American youth and the consequent specialized youth culture which flows from these facts. Various components of this historical evolution have been developing for centuries. Romanticism has been developing within our Western civilization matrix for six centuries; permissiveness for youth grew with the slackening of the severe academic discipline of the Renaissance and the severe moral disciplines of the Puritans during the past two centuries; industrialism, urbanism, and capitalism have likewise been developing for several centuries. But it is only since World War II that these various factors have converged to such a cultural crescendo that it seemed to make steady dating quite inevitable.

Casual dating, competitive dating, chaperoned dating, group dating—these patterns are not consonant with the themes of permissiveness and romanticism in an affluent society. A youth cannot become highly emotionally and erotically involved with a "one-and-only" if he is dating different partners or if he is hedged in by adult or group chaperonage.

If it is asked whether it has not always been true that chaperonage dampens heterosexual ardor and that consequently our age differs not a whit from previous ages, the answer seems to be this: Granted that chaperonage has a sobering effect, youth of previous generations were captives of space, time, home, neighborhood, and an univocal moral system to a much greater extent than the youth of our car-oriented, phone-communicating, money-happy, mobile moderns.

In order to see the case of Gayle and Jim and their history of steady dating within the complex of the cult of romanticism to its not unpredictable completion let us take up the transcript where we left off:

"We was going steady five days and ... Jim made me go back home. ... But I didn't want to go back home"—Going steady confers whatever rights and duties group standards dictate and the particular couples agree to. Since this young couple had been going steady for five days it presumably gave the male a right over the female's person and dwelling (even though she was unwilling) that neither the law nor feminist writing would validate for a bona fide husband.

"He wanted me to get away from Dolorine and her mother"—Permissiveness and the romantic complex have their limits. It is the limit imposed by the double standard. What is right for the male is not right for the female. Jim was not against what Dolorine and her mother stood for when this was applied to males. From Gayle's account it is apparent that Jim used to stay overnight with Dolorine and her mother. It was at this house of dubious reputation that Jim met Gayle. There was nothing at this house that was not in harmony with Jim's dominant operational morals and ideals. And as he was obviously not opposed to premarital intercourse with prostitutes neither was he opposed to premarital coitus with Gayle as subsequent developments indicate. But with all the logic of the long-entrenched double standard whereby males will insist upon promiscuity for themselves and an unblemished reputation for respectable females, Jim, as Gayle's steady, directs her to absent herself from such tarnished surroundings and to return to her home. Gayle whose head is unbending before the regulations of her parents and her God, recognizes the higher law of romanticism—the word of her steady. He has spoken. She obeys.

"We went steady for a year and a half and got married. ... She told me not to get married and to go to school. But I told her I was going to get married and I did!"—These are brave words of Gayle's. But they mask the critical feature of the romantic-steady-dropout complex—the reason she did not return to school after the following summer—her fifteenth—was that she found herself to be pregnant. She had originally told her principal that she would return for her sophomore year of high school. But suddenly marriage plans had to be made. ("After I got married I asked my girl friend to tell Sister Jacqueline that I got married because I didn't tell her and I didn't write to tell her I wouldn't be coming back. So she sent her congratulations and told me to get my marriage blessed. So I did. We got our marriage blessed.")

INEVITABLE DISILLUSIONMENT

The fourth step in the progression of the romance syndrome is that of inevitable disillusionment. The hyperemotional and unrealistic expectations cannot be realized. As the psychiatrist Theodore Reik observed: "Romance lasting for many years is imaginable only in Utopia. No person can remain in the grip of a strange fascination for a long time. Romance is a nine-day wonder." [38] In Gayle's case, her disillusionment was not long in coming. She was married in August, her child, Virginia, was born the first week of January—the week of Gayle's sixteenth birthday—and by the first of February when the present interview was held, there were any number of areas which had been shaken from their romantic heights by the realities of their married life. It already seemed evident that this teen-age dropout "romantic" marriage would go the way of the majority of them. Whatever the future of the marriage, it is instructive to hear this bride of less than seven months describe their postmarital problems and compare this sketch with more general studies of the disenchantment period of teen-age marriages.

Disillusionment concerning teen-age marriages.—"She is married and I told her 'Don't,' because she will feel it. . . . That diploma means a lot to you. . . . That is just how I feel about it. But this girl friend called me and she came up to the house with her boy friend and they told us they were getting married. This was in November. I told Kathy not to because she would make a fool of herself if she did. She asked me why and I told her that in the first place Paul didn't have a job. . . . I told her if they got married she would miss school and she would kill her mother and father and her daddy hated Paul to begin with. But she said they would try it and I told her I wouldn't if I was her. So Jim talked to Paul and told him the only way they could get by was for him to go into the service and he said he would join after they got married. But they got married in November and he hasn't joined yet. They are living with his grandmother now. But I told them, 'It is hard.' Kathy has a job now but it's only in a little grocery store and she doesn't make much."

Disillusionment concerning the adequacy of a dropout's education.—"That's what I told him when we got married. I told him I wanted to go back to school. But I found out I couldn't go back to a Catholic school and I didn't want to go to a public school. Like when Ginny, our little baby, starts going to school and she would come to me—well, I'd have to send her to Jim. I guess that would give the baby sort of a complex."

Disillusionment with the premarital game of mutual exploitation.—"Also, I want to be able to compete with Jim ... He kind of degrades me when we start talking about things I know nothing about, and I feel funny."

Financial disillusionment: being "cute" and a "good dancer" do not pay the bills.—"Can I tell you some of my problems? Maybe not everybody would have this problem but when I was single I was always going—running here and running there...; and with Jim it's a question of settling down and learning the value of a dollar.... The husband's biggest problem in marriage is just settling down. Jim just has to learn to settle down."

Only a half year of their married life has passed and its multiple disillusionments have approached those of the typical dropout teen-age marriage as outlined by the Hollywood youth counselor, Maurice J. Colwell (cf. *supra,* page 79). "I have followed their marriage careers long enough to see the pattern.... I am referring specifically to the dropouts' marriages. These kids marry at a very early age. They marry a girl who is maybe in the first or second year of high school. The typical dropout is working in a gas station or perhaps by this time he has gone into the service; he gets married; immediate pregnancy; in debt; terrific financial problems; tremendous arguments; the boy going out to be back with his group, with his guys. There is almost the feeling that the girl is marrying this guy for some kind of security. I don't know what kind of security they can get from him.... The basis for marriage is pretty unstable in that the boy can't give himself completely to the home. He simply can't give himself completely to the home."

CONCLUSIONS—HETEROSEXUAL PEER RELATIONS:
DROPOUT VERSUS GRADUATE

A generation ago Ernest W. Burgess in his article "The Romantic Impulse and Family Disorganization" hypothesized that wherever the American romantic ideal took firm root family disorganization would be inevitable.[39] The romantic ideal has taken firm root in the upper echelons of the dropout youth culture (in the lower echelons sexual exploitation and promiscuity seem more prevalent than the romantic theme) and the Burgess prophecy seems fulfilled. More recently Professor Charles W. Hobart took soundings in fifteen areas of disillusionment within marriage in order "to test the hypothesis that it is romanticism or the tendency to build up unrealistic and perhaps unrealizable expectations during engagement which causes disillusionment in marriage." His conclusion was

> The demonstration of such prevalent disillusionment suggests the existence of important unrealism-generating influences in the courtship process. The widespread emphasis on romanticism in the American culture—the so-called romantic cult—which appears to be particularly associated with advanced courtship may in effect be preparing engaged couples for inevitable disillusionment.[40]

The dropouts in their heterosexual peer relationships have concentrated upon the erotic, the romantic, and the sexually exploitative in their preparation for marriage. The resulting disenchantment is tragic. The graduates defer their marriages, embrace the pattern of deferred gratification, discount the excesses of the romantic cult, concentrate upon occupational, maturational, and educational preparation for marriage and from all available evidence emerge from the experience with more disciplined and mature personalities destined for more successful and civilization-adequate family living.

CHAPTER FIVE

Psychological Tendencies of the Dropout

What goes on in the mind of the dropout? What does he think about, dream about, fantasize about? What are his dominant drives, levels of motivation, peculiarities of life style? Are there any moods, sentiments, attitudes, values, and world views whereby his mental and emotional life can be distinguished from that of the graduate? What makes Sammy and Sally Dropout tick?

Previous chapters have relied on the findings of our questionnaire, interview, and related literature. They have indicated that the dropout can be distinguished by types of family background, friends, preschool socialization, school experiences, job expectations, and other situational differences. But what about his "psychological set"? Does he look out upon the world with cumulative sensitivities that would put quite a different interpretation upon classical human situations than would the graduate?

Such is the precarious and intriguing question to which this chapter addresses itself. We depend primarily upon the TAT materials obtained from our teen-age respondents in New Orleans and Boston.

LE STYLE C'EST L'HOMME [1]

In some sense every story is autobiographical. The less sophisticated the story teller the more certainly is the story's hero wearing the psychic clothing of his creator.

Authors are usually thought of as telling us about their heroes: Shakespeare tells us about Hamlet; Cervantes, Don Quixote; Dostoevski, Razaminikin; Dickens, Oliver Twist; Marquand, George Apley; Joyce, The Artist as a Young Man; Hemingway, The Old Man and the Sea; Salinger, Holden Caulfield. But it is no less true that the stories' heroes tell us about their authors. Hamlet tells us much about Shakespeare; Don Quixote, Cervantes; Razaminikin, Dostoevski; Oliver Twist, Dickens, etc. No one would care to deny that Shakespeare was as richly complex as Hamlet; Cervantes as whimsically humorous as Don Quixote; Dickens as sentimentally perceptive as Oliver Twist, etc.

Whether it is the child in first grade telling a story in a "show and tell" session before his entranced moppet audience or an eighteen-year-old youth being interviewed and asked to tell a story about some pictures held before him, every story teller draws upon his own autobiographical interests, attitudes, themes, and values in recounting his tale.

1 . THEMATIC APPERCEPTION TESTS

From an extensive acquaintance with literature, literary criticism, and psychology, Henry A. Murray and his associates of the Harvard Psychological Clinic asked why the same kinds of deductions could not be drawn from an ordered series of stories told by anyone. They hit upon the idea of developing a series of pictures around which stories could be told. With a standardized series centered about basic human experiences they felt that the respondents could be stimulated to react in a personal way that could be scored in a scientific manner relative to the replies of others. The result was the Thematic (in reference to the themes that are elicted) Apperception (in reference to the psychological process of perceiving in terms of previous experience) Test, or TAT for short.

PREVIOUS USE

Along with the Rorschach, the TAT became a prime clinical instrument for the evaluation of personality and its pathologies. In more recent nonclinical developments the TAT has been widely used in anthropological and sociological research as an instrument to obtain cross-cultural data on the respective themes, interests, attitudes, and levels of perception of one group in comparison with another.

Such is our application of the TAT. We are not interested in its clinical use in appraising individual pathologies. As sociologists we are not interested in the individual psychic characteristics. We are interested in the responses of the dropouts and graduates only insofar as these responses give us insight into pyschic differences between their respective subcultures.

The procedure is merely that of presenting a series of pictures to a subject and encouraging him to tell stories about them, invented on the spur of the moment. The fact that stories collected in this way often reveal significant components of personality is dependent on the prevalence of two psychological tendencies: the tendency of people to interpret an ambiguous human situation in conformity with their past experiences and present wants, and the tendency of those who write stories to do likewise—to draw on the fund of their experiences and express their sentiments and needs, whether conscious or unconscious.

If the pictures are presented as a test of imagination, the subject's interest, together with his need for approval, can be so involved in the task that he forgets his sensitive self and the necessity of defending it against the probings of the examiner, and, before he knows it, he has said things about an invented character that apply to himself, things which he would have been reluctant to confess in response to a direct question. As a rule the subject leaves the test happily unaware that he has presented the psychologist with what amounts to an X-ray picture of his inner self.[2]

The genius of the TAT is that it confronts the individual with an ambiguous picture and asks him to fill in the details. The only way he can do this is to draw upon his own pool of experience and reactions. These experiences and reactions are then scored according to an index standardized from the replies of thousands of other respondents. The assumption is, of course, that every story is to a certain extent autobiographical.

2. ALBERT S.: DELINQUENT AND DROPOUT

Before presenting a summary of the TAT data from all of our respondents we can review the case history of one of our delinquent dropouts and then append his protocol or comments on each of the TAT pictures used for the male respondents in our study. The reason we wish to present both case history and TAT protocols of *one* individual as a unit is to illustrate the fact that the history of one's life is mirrored in the manifestation he makes of his life through the TAT stories. Though autobiographical history deals

primarily with observed chronological facts and TAT stories deal
primarily with psychological elaborations and fantasies, both are a
unified part of the identical person. If we did not know the "facts"
of Albert S.'s life, for instance, but only had his TAT protocols we
could fairly well reconstruct the tenor of his life from these protocols. Similarly, if we had only his case history and not the protocols,
we could quite well estimate the nature of the themes, the types of
the conflicts, the vocabulary, the *personae dramatis,* that he would
introduce in response to the TAT.

We use the abbreviated case of the sixteen-year-old delinquent
Albert S. The bitter antagonism and hostility toward all of society's
institutions glare through his words: "My father left when I was
two years old.... I live with my mother and grandmother. But I do
have one younger brother; he's fourteen. He is an epileptic.... I
did live with (my grandfather) but he moved out because I kept
wanting to use his car and a couple of times I stole it on him.... I
don't get along with (my family) too good.... I don't think we
understand each other. They don't like my friends.... My mother
says she has perfect morals.... She doesn't know the first thing
about morals. I disagree with my family's morals on everything....
The way I figure it, everybody is equal; it's just that in capitalism
you don't get the same chances. There is no doubt about it. Some
people are born a Rockefeller but not everybody is, so you can't say
you have equal chances.... I don't understand their purpose in
life. They don't seem to do anything. They just seem to be living in
their own world with their own beliefs. They think they are right
on everything. They don't listen to anything I try to tell them. I
gave up on trying to tell them anything.... They are always bug-
ging me about putting the light out in the bathroom.... I like
Rock and Roll and they say it is 'nigger music' and they don't want
to have any part of it.... Then they bug me about staying in the
bathroom. It takes me about an hour to take a bath and everything.
I just like to take a bath.... They say I'm going to wind up getting
killed or getting the chair or something like that. They say I'll
never amount to nothing and that I'll be a bum because I don't go
out and look for a job any more because it is getting rough. There
is no place to look!... In other words, like I'm free loading on
them ... and I'm going to be a bum and be just like my pa; they
are always telling me that. They say I'll get married and have kids
and walk off and leave them just like pa did. I always tell them my
pa was all right and they get real mad about that.... My mother is

very dependent. . . . That's one reason I'm going to the Navy . . . to get away from home. They want me to go. They keep telling me to go. . . . I always did want to leave home, ever since I can remember. . . . Like one time my little brother found one of my cigarette lighters and he set the bathroom on fire. It burned up the wall. And they blamed me for leaving him get the cigarette lighter. He stole my grandfather's car before I did. He got the keys one morning before we were going to church and he jumped in the car and backed it into a garage and hit a couple of coffins. . . . They never blame him. It was like that all the time.

"They say [my friends] are dirty criminals or something like that. The friends I hang around with now . . . a couple of them have been in trouble with the law . . . just like myself. . . . We used to score in all the stores. We didn't get sent up but we had to go to court. . . . Ever since I got caught the fourth time I've eased up on it pretty good. . . .

"I didn't leave that school; they kicked me out because I was failing. . . .

"The biggest problem guys in New Orleans have is getting in trouble with the law. Then going to school. I myself find it hard to adjust to everything. Like going to school and all like that. There are things I don't see—laws and so on. They have a ten o'clock curfew down here and after twelve it gets pretty rough if you are under eighteen. You could just be walking down the street minding your own business and they will pick you up and bring you in. Even if you are eighteen you have to have money on you and identification or otherwise they will put you in jail. They would bring me down to the juvenile thing and then I would be released. If you are eighteen they put you in jail for maybe a day or until somebody puts up bond for you or until you go to court. . . .

"Another thing is integration. I know a lot of guys that get up gangs and they jump Negroes and they beat them up. They don't jump the Negro girls but they might spit at them and call them vulgar names. The Negroes don't want to start any trouble unless they are in gangs or they are on a bus. I take the bus home and none of them ever hit on me but I hear them talking things in the back, saying different things just to be against me. . . . Some of the students, they don't use their heads sometimes. Like the majority of them hates Negroes. I don't hate Negroes although my parents are against Negroes and most of my friends and about 99 percent of the people I know have been brought up that way. But I still have my own beliefs. A lot of the things they say are true—about them not wanting to integrate, but a lot of them are just stupid ideas and they can't give me a good argument. All they can do is howl that a Negro isn't as good as they are and they haven't the right to go to school. Some of them give me good arguments but the majority of them don't.

"I'm not working now. Most of the jobs that were available were as a messenger boy, news boy, stock boy, delivery boy, and these jobs were all taken. With the other jobs you needed a high school education or you needed to know how to type or something. So I just put applications in all over the place and I just hope that one of them would call me one day."

PROTOCOLS OF ALBERT S.

Ten cards were then shown to Albert S. The directions that he was given by the interviewer were: "This is a test of imagination, one form of intelligence. I am going to show you some pictures, one at a time; and your task will be to make up as dramatic a story as you can for each. Tell what has led up to the event shown in the picture, describe what is happening at the moment, what the characters are feeling and thinking, and then give the outcome. Speak your thoughts as they come to your mind. Do you understand? Here is the first picture."

But the lengthy instructions might well have been omitted. Albert S., as nine out of ten of the other respondents, did not tell a story but merely tried to identify what he saw on the picture. However, since he revealed the basic themes and attitudes of his life fantasy the purpose of the TAT was served.

Picture # 1.—A young boy is contemplating a violin which rests on a table in front of him.

"This kid looks like his old man or his old lady gave him a violin and he has to take up the violin. He's thinking: 'Now I got to learn this thing and I'd rather be playing a guitar or something.' "

Picture # 2.—Country scene: in the foreground is a young woman with books in her hand; in the background a man is working in the fields and an older woman is looking on.

"I see a farm there and the boy looks like he is plowing up the field. I see an old lady in the background and she looks like she is looking at everything. And I see that broad there; she has books in her hands and maybe she is thinking: 'I ain't going to do that kind of work. I can go to the city and make it. I ain't going to hang around here.' She has—not a disgusted look on her face, but not a happy one either, like she is thinking about something."

Picture # 3BM.—On the floor against a couch is the huddled form of a boy with his head bowed on his right arm. Beside him on the floor is a revolver.

"It looks like he had some exasperating experience. He is disgusted, fed up; I feel like that myself sometimes but I don't lay down like that. I just lay down in another way. Maybe he just got some terrible news or something."

Picture # 4.—A woman is clutching the shoulders of a man whose face and body are averted as if he were trying to pull away from her.

"The guy did something or he is going to do something and the broad is telling him not to, or a broad wants him to do something and he don't want to do it. It looks like somebody just came into the room and he is looking at them. The broad looks like she is trying to tell him something. She either wants him to do something or she doesn't want him to do something. I see stuff like this a lot of times on TV. It could be anything. It don't look like they are getting ready to try any loving—I'll tell you that. It looks like they got a paper on the wall in the background with a broad on it. I don't know— It looks like some woman sitting down on a mattress with her night things on, with her legs crossed. It might be his apartment and he has girlee pictures all over the wall."

Picture # 5.—A middle-aged woman is standing on the threshold of a half-opened door looking into a room.

"It looks like some old lady looking for her kid in the room or somebody, maybe her husband. She is looking for the old man or something—making sure he didn't cut out on her."

Picture # 6BM.—A short elderly woman stands with her back turned to a tall young man. The latter is looking downward with a perplexed expression.

"It looks like a guy and his old lady, his mother. He is trying to tell her something, it looks like. And she is just looking out the window. He's trying to tell her something."

Picture # 7BM.—A gray-haired man is looking at a younger man who is sullenly staring into space.

"These two guys look like they are talking over something— maybe a plan." (Interviewer: "What kind of plan?"—No answer.)

Picture # 8BM.—An adolescent boy looks straight out of the picture. The barrel of a rifle is visible at one side, and in the background is the dim scene of a surgical operation, like a reverie-image.

"This is really gore. You got a guy laying down and a guy up there with a knife. He could be cutting him or operating on him. There is a gun over here on the side and there is this joker with a suit on. He is one of these rich-looking guys—the kind that go to military school. This is all mixed up to me."

Picture # 13MF.—A young man is standing with downcast head buried in his arm. Behind him is the figure of a woman lying in bed.

"This guy looks like he just got done killing his wife or something. He has his clothes on. It don't look like he got done doing anything else with her."

Picture # 16 (Blank card).—Directions given to Albert S.: "See what you can see on this blank card. Imagine some picture there and describe it to me in detail."

"I don't know. I guess I'd just draw a stairway and I'm going up. Nobody on it and make it black. Like an old beat-up castle. Something like that."

PRELIMINARY SOCIOLOGICAL COMMENTS

Without anticipating the clinical or statistical analysis of this delinquent's protocols and without benefiting from a comparison of the delinquent dropouts' themes with those of the graduates several preliminary comments can be made. The first is that Albert's TAT material is at one with his autobiographical case history transcript. This is no academic, reality-removed exercise for him. He has clearly identified with the pictures and entered into their situational structuring. For instance his reply to picture 3BM: "... He is disgusted; fed up; I feel like that myself sometimes but I don't lay down like that. I just lay down in another way." Secondly, there is a pattern of murky, black hostility that insinuates a sinister undercurrent into his viewpoint and evaluations. A hard core family or oedipal hostility seems to unfold like an expanding squid or exploding napalm bomb on the impinging and contingent social institutions. Albert is trying to be as cooperative and pleasing as possible within the interview station but the acid venom of his psyche etches in mordant strokes the bitterness and antagonism of his life orientation.

Protocol 1: "Now I got to learn this thing (that 'his old man or old

lady gave him') and I'd rather be playing a guitar or something."
The graduate would more likely see in this picture a youth
dreaming of becoming a great concert violinist or reduce the
conflict in the youth's mind to components of adjustment or
achievement—whether the lad would or would not learn to play
the violin. But not the hostile delinquent. He seems to go to the
root of his own problem: It is his reprehensible parents who have
forced him into this repulsive situation and he will have none of
it. He rejects the violin completely—"I'd rather be playing a
guitar or something."

Protocol 2: "I ain't going to do that kind of work. I can go to the
city and make it. I ain't going to hang around here." We've
already heard these words and their antioccupational and antifamily thematics in Albert's autobiographical materials. There he
went even further in that he vented his spleen against the whole
capitalistic system: "It's just in capitalism you just don't get the
same chances."

Protocol 3: "He is disgusted; fed up; I feel like that myself sometimes"—the word "sometimes" was a mollifying afterthought and
for greater reportorial accuracy, Albert might well have omitted
it.

Protocol 4: "It looks like some woman sitting down on a mattress
with her night things on, with her legs crossed. It might be his
apartment and he has girlee pictures all over the wall." It was a
rare graduate who even noticed the small semihidden cheese-cake
calendar-art background to which Albert is so sensitive and mag-
nifies to rather voluptuous proportions. Two pertinent apothegms
might be: "To the pure all things are pure" and "Beauty is
in the eye of the beholder."

Protocol 5: Objectively, there is nothing in this picture to suggest
what the woman is looking into the room for. Subjectively, there
is a great deal of his own history that makes Albert know what
she is looking for: It is his mother either looking for him or "for
the old man"—"making sure he didn't cut out on her" as Albert's
father did when the child was two years old. We might ask why it
is that graduates typically took this picture as a representation of
a placid and loving home scene?

Protocol 6: "He is trying to tell her something . . . and she is just
looking out the window." A clinician might say that this is the
oedipal situation unresolved. If so, the unresolved conflicts of his
life's pattern would be all of a pattern.

Protocol 7: Albert is quite secretive as to what plan the "two guys" are talking over. He was less secretive in the interview about his and his fellow delinquents' "scoring" plans and techniques.

Protocol 8: "This joker with a suit on. He is one of these rich-looking guys—the kind that go to military school." The withering scorn of the proletarian for the effete capitalist offspring and their educational institutions could hardly be more sardonically and economically expressed. It is a gem of verbal class caricature.

Protocol 13: Murder without remorse and suggested sexual molestation are the themes that spring into Albert's mind when looking at this ambiguous picture. Strangely enough these themes, though less severe in the case of the nondelinquent dropouts and also less frequent in the case of the graduates, were quite common among all of our American respondents. We say "strangely enough" because when we showed this same picture to European and Mid-Eastern respondents (England, France, Germany, Spain, Egypt, Iraq, Israel, Turkey, Lebanon, etc.) the predominant themes elicited were of a nonviolent and even loving marital nature.

Protocol 16: "Nobody on it and make it black"—a black rejection of humanity at large was a motif of Albert's autobiographical manifestations. Whether or not this motif is fantasied here would be for the clinician to assay. But the sociologist can say without fear of contradiction that if society had to build upon such hostile units of society, the social prognosis would be exceedingly black and unpromising.

"HOSTILITY" HYPOTHESIS

Before proceeding to present the dichotomously illustrative protocols of the dropouts and the graduates we can submit a hypothesis of hostility. For the purposes of sorting our data and crystalizing our impressions and integrating our protocols with the general thesis of this book we can submit for consideration a hypothesis of hostility and academic achievement. We have four types of respondents: delinquent dropouts, nondelinquent dropouts, high school graduates, and high school graduates who stated that they intended to go to college. Our hostility hypothesis would be that hostility and academic achievement are negatively correlated. In terms of our study we could draw up an ideal construct for illustrative purposes (see Figure 1).

That Figure 1 is merely an ideal construct with the inharmonious evidence suppressed is obvious from the fact that not all of the delinquents of our sample were dropouts (18% of our dropouts

Degree of Hostility and Academic Achievement

Extreme Hostility	Serious Hostility	Medium Hostility	Slight Hostility
Delinquent Dropouts	Nondelinquent Dropouts	Non-College High School Graduates	College-Oriented High School Graduates

Fig. 1.—A Construct

admitted being arrested by police at some time in their lives and 4% of our graduates did). Nevertheless, the hostility and academic achievement hypothesis is viable. Family variables will be seen as the prime determinants of the hostility component which predisposes toward trouble at school and, when more pronounced, trouble with the police. Illustrations of the validity of the hostility continuum are readily apparent in the following protocols.

ILLUSTRATIVE CONTRASTING PROTOCOLS OF DROPOUTS AND GRADUATES

In presenting these illustrations of the contrasting types of themes, attitudes, and reactions of the dropouts and the graduates we are not trying to be random in our selection of our respondents' protocols. The statistical analysis presented later in the chapter clearly indicates that there is a vast overlapping of the types of responses given by our two classes of respondents. The differences between their responses are frequently minimal and nonstatistically significant. But our selection serves the purpose of heightening the antipolar directions of the contrasting types of replies found in the protocols of the dropouts in contradistinction to those of the graduates. The contrasting attitudes, interests, and norms of the two subsamples are thereby unmasked.

PICTURE # 1 (Violin and boy)

Dropouts

"A boy with a violin here and it looks like maybe his parents want him to take up this—learn the violin—and he looks like he doesn't want to. It seems like he would want to be out with the rest of the kids having fun." (New Orleans Male, # 62; Deficiency orientation and intrafamily antagonism; nondeferred gratification)

"It looks like a little boy and his mother wants him to study the violin and he doesn't want to study. It looks like he comes from a well-to-do family and it doesn't look like he is going to take the lessons." (New Orleans Female, # 69; Class consciousness; individual contrariness as manifested in antifamilial and antischolastic orientation)

Graduates

"I see one of two things. The first thing that struck me is this young boy around eight or nine saying, 'Oh hell, I got to play this thing again.' The second thing is that he is looking at the violin and wishing he could play. In either case he is depressed about it. Being a cellist myself I would prefer, which is natural for me, that he wishes he could play it." (New Orleans Male, # 13; Spontaneity and ability to focus problem. The youth has an alternative dependent upon himself. Positive and altruistic)

PICTURE #2 (Country scene)

Dropouts

"We have in this first picture three symbolic types of individuals. First there is the man; he is plowing and is thinking of nothing beyond the tilling of the soil. Then we have his wife under the tree, bitter and blasted by life's hardships. And then their young bouncing daughter who is determined not to be a peasant throughout her life." (Boston Male, # 54; "Bitter and blasted by life's hardships")

Graduates

"It looks like a family and the girl is going to school and the father is a farmer. He is working in the fields and the mother seems to be expecting a baby. She is waiting for it. The girl looks like she is looking toward the future. She is waiting for her schooling to be over and she is figuring out what she will do in the future. She looks like she will be a teacher or something because she is carrying books." (Boston Female, # 25; Positive attitudes toward school, maternity, marital life, rural life; professionally oriented; provident viewpoint of youth toward future)

PICTURE # 3BM (Huddled form of boy)

Dropouts

"A good one for like a murder picture. It would be like someone committed suicide or something wrong in the family or something happened to one of their loved ones or something. Or a loved person, lovelorn and there would be no way, really, but die. You try to forget those things really. I mean, just like the person . . . the loved one . . . to take the person, really." (Boston Male # 64; A horror fugue with death and suicide the only possible solution)

Graduates

"He must have worked all day and he is tired; he must be day-dreaming or something." (Boston Male, # 5; Positive occupational orientation; absence of internal or external conflict)

PICTURE # 3GF (Young woman with downcast head)

Dropouts

"She looks like she went through I don't know what. She looks like somebody jumped her or something and she doesn't want to show her face. She is disgusted with herself. She looks like she was really running and hurrying to get home. She might have did something herself that she is disgusted about. Or somebody did something to her—maybe beat her or something. She looks like she wants to think by herself; be alone for a while." (Boston Female, # 75; Violence, guilt, masochistic, depressed self-image)

Graduates

"Julie stood there in the door with her face in her hand, because it isn't easy for a girl eighteen to receive the news that her mother had died. It was sort of unexpectedly. Julie had depended a lot on her mother and she never realized just how much she had taken her for granted and she loved her mother very much and now she was gone." (New Orleans Female, # 23. One of the few respondents who followed the TAT directions as given with story including past, present, and future orientations.)

PICTURE # 4 (Woman clutching shoulders of a man . . .)

Dropouts

"He looks like he is mad and he is going to kill somebody. What is this? It looks like a whorehouse! There is a broad back there, half naked and the girl looks like she is trying to stop him. He looks like he has fire in his eyes. He is going to kill somebody or something. The girl would be saying, 'Please, John, don't leave me; take it easy.' And he says, 'I'm going to kill him; I'm going to kill him. He ain't going to do that no more. I'll fix him.' This doesn't fit into the picture back here. It might be her sister or either some boy friend of her's insulted her and the brother-in-law is going to take revenge I guess, or something like that. She just doesn't fit in the picture that much at all. That's all I guess." (New Orleans Male, # 52; A sensate, hateful scene)

Graduates

"They're lovers. They could be thinking about when they're getting married." (Boston Male, # 2)

"This is a nurse and she is trying to comfort this G.I. from battle shock. She is very loving. She has a lot of care in her eyes and this man seems very disturbed. There is something in his eyes and it isn't clear what he is doing. He has no idea of what he is going to do, you can tell by his eyes." (Boston Male, # 6)

"He has lost his job and he can't support his family and she is trying to console him and tell him that everything will work out." (Boston Male, # 8; Sympathetic, loving scenes)

PICTURE # 5 (Middle-aged woman looking into room)

Dropouts

"Maybe she saw a burglar in the house. Evidentally she saw something she wasn't supposed to see. Maybe her child was stealing from her. Maybe her boy friend with her and her mother disapproved of the way they were petting. She may be shocked at the way the girl is walking around the house—the way she is dressed." (Boston Female, # 66; Mother-daughter morality conflict)

Graduates

"It looks like a mother looking into something. She is saying, 'Come on and get to bed, kids,' or 'That's enough TV.' " (New Orleans Female, # 17; Mother as daughter's ego ideal)

PICTURE # 6 (Young woman on sofa looking over her shoulder
            at an older man who seems to be addressing her)

Dropouts

"This looks like a career girl and her playboy. No, I don't know if she is giving in or not. I think she is really quizzed. She really doesn't know what to do, by the expression on her face. I don't know. I don't understand a woman." (Boston Female, # 63; Value system uncertain)

Graduates

"Barbara was shocked at Mr. Stone in the calm way he suggested his plan to embezzle the company's funds. Barbara needed her job and she had always respected Mr. Stone but now here she was with this temptation and what could she do? She knew what was right and what was wrong. Yet somehow the things get mixed up and confused and our imagination runs away with us and we see things in an attractive light. Something that is good we put to bad and something that is bad we put in a favorable light. Now Barbara wondered what should she do. But finally she realized what she had to do and she reported Mr. Stone." (New Orleans Female # 23; Value system certain)

PICTURE # 8BM (Surgical operation)

Dropouts

"This man has been shot by these men. It possibly could have been accidentally. But more probably not. The young man is the lookout." (Boston Male, # 11; It is noteworthy that only in the protocols of the dropouts does the young man of the picture become a "lookout.")

Graduates

"It is some sort of operation or something. Say they were removing a person's appendix. The doctor looks very skilled the way he is cutting the person's stomach. The person on the table has no worries. The boy might be the man's son that is on the table and he is showing a lot of worry and a lot of emotions toward it. He is scared because he doesn't want his father or mother to get hurt. It looks like he might have some confidence in the doctor but he is not sure. He doesn't know what to do. The doctor looks like he knows what he is doing and he is about to start." (New Orleans Male, # 11; Professionalism)

PICTURE # 9GF (Young woman behind tree looking at another girl running)

Dropouts

"This girl has pulled some kind of a trick on her girl friend or her sister, I wouldn't know. The sister has regret in her eyes. To me, this one here I wouldn't trust 'cause maybe she pulled it before and her sister gave in to her." (Boston Female, # 63; Female rejection)

Graduate

"It looks like there is one boy and two girls and this one girl is running off to go with the boy, which this other girl probably likes herself, too. The girl in the tree probably thinks there is something going on between her boy friend and this other girl and she is waiting to see if it is true. So she sees this girl leaving the house to go meet this boy. In conclusion, I don't think that he really comes back to either one." (New Orleans Female, # 15; Romance)

PICTURE # 13 MF (Young man standing, head buried in arm
Woman in bed)

Dropout

"How can he get away after this rape and murder?" (Boston Male, # 54; Rape, murder, no remorse)

Graduates

"He just come home from school and he found his wife just lying there." (Boston Male, # 18; Placid marriage scene)

"This guy just committed a sexual thing and he feels guilty. He shouldn't have done it." (Boston Male, # 24; Extramarital intercourse with feelings of guilt)

PICTURE # 16 (Blank card: optional theme)

Dropouts

"What I'd really like to see is kids having a good time and not quitting school like I did." (Boston Female, # 61)

"Just big piles of money that say: 'It's yours for the asking." (New Orleans Male, # 52; Sensate)

Graduates

I think I would paint a family house and a large family raising the kids to lead a good life. That seems like it is more important than anything." (New Orleans Male, # 7; Family idealism)

"I'd say that was the soul of a girl that had been very pure. Not that she has been very, very good; but she has tried her best and tried to make her life as pure as possible." (New Orleans Female, # 15, Virginal idealism)

"A mother and a father and their children in one group, happily together." (Boston Female, # 11)

3. PSYCHIC POLAR TENDENCIES
OF THE AMERICAN YOUTH CULTURE

Our selected protocols present the delinquent and the dropout as psychic brothers of the nether world and the high school graduates, whether college oriented or not, as psychic siblings of the bright upper world. The children of psychic social darkness in startling contrast to the children of social light and the antisocial elements versus the prosocial elements give the sharply contrasting impression readily grasped from the comments, stories, value judgments, and themes presented by our divergent sample. Our sampling of protocols, however, was highly selective so that the overall polar tendencies would be brought into bolder relief. The more comprehensive statistical evaluation indicates that there is a broad overlapping of the antisocial and prosocial elements within the verbal pool of the protocols. Nevertheless, our evidence indicates that there is a central tendency toward the merging of the dropout and delinquent in a significantly antisocial bias and the tendency of the graduates to share in a significantly prosocial bias. These oppositional tendencies and positions may be termed the polar tendencies of the modern American youth culture.

The convergent image of the dropout and the delinquent suggests a historical exegesis of the hardening mentality of the new minority.

In our society the reported incidence of delinquency is ten times as great among those who are high school dropouts as it is among those who become high school graduates.[3]

When James Conant stated that the existence in our large cities of thousands of youth who are both "out-of-school and out-of-work is an explosive situation—it is social dynamite," [4] he underlined a growing historical trend. Implicit in his reasoning was the argument that under present technological and social conditions the dropout is severely jeopardized in his opportunities for employment and consequently develops a drift toward delinquency. His widely quoted remarks tended to identify in the public mind the typology of the dropout with the typology of the potential delinquent.

THE SENSATE IN THE DELINQUENT AND
DROPOUT PROTOCOLS

Both the TAT and interview material indicate, in dropout and delinquent responses, a greater incidence of sensate vocabulary and theme: violence, hostility, aggression, tragedy, strife, drunkenness, cheating, suicide, unemployment, prostitutes, whorehouses, pimps, bars, rapes, stranglings, the naked and the dead. A woman is more commonly a "broad" or a "hag"; a man, a "guy," a "stud," and a "bad," if approved; and if not approved, a "square," a "fruit," a "jerk," a "scab," a "goodie," and less printable appellations. "Scoring" (in the sense of self-aggrandizement at the expense of another's gullibility), "making out" (in the sense of sexual exploitation), "conning," "girlee pictures," "rumbles"—all of these terms occur with a greater frequency in the speech and thematic references of the dropout youth.

More important than the vocabulary and themes which are more common in the psychic life of the delinquent and dropout are the attitudes and norms implied. The overriding differential attitude is that of hostility. Hostility against authority or adult controls of all types—home authority, civil authority, intellectual authority, occupational authority. The dropout does have his very definite authorities, controls, norms, and values, but they are more characteristically nonparentally approved peer controls and more characteristically in rebellion against the dominant adult Judaeo-Christian capitalistic orientations.

Human relations are more characteristically brittle, haphazard, unpremeditated, affectless, and exploitative in the dropouts' protocols. Gratitude is a superfluous theme. Fun, pleasure, spontaneity, and emotional upheavals of varied types are much in evidence but not as integrated with the superphysical or with life's goals. Our dropout protocols seem more interlaced with the impulse-ridden, the nondeferred gratification, the unconventional (from the host culture's viewpoint), the unrealistically romantic, the loosely structured, the shallow, the predestined, the fateful.

The graduate, however, more characteristically sees heterosexual relations as monogamously oriented, the dropout-delinquent more frequently sees them without value judgment, as outside the monogamic framework. Divorce and desertion are taken as permissively by the dropout as the graduate takes wars and disease—an inescapable part of life, lacking personal responsibility components. The female-dominated home not built around the expectations of stable or adequate income; the male as a "real heel" during the work-a-day week but a swashbuckling "lady's man" (by which is meant a compelling sexual exploiter and not a life's companion) over the bibulous weekend; the "broad" whose value is commensurate with her anatomical measurements, her Kinsey "sex contact" exploitability, and Freudian "sex object" dimensions; the police as "troublemakers" and kill-joys; the teacher as "a real square—you know what I mean," are stereotyped characters and situations on the stage of the dropout delinquent's psyche.

Suicide is a favored theme and solution that hovers, as a vampire and black harpy, over the dark plots of the dropout delinquent's phantasmagoria. The characteristic hostility and death wishes turn inward. The free floating motif of suicide, as the free floating point of an iceberg, alerts the observer that there are hidden depths of destruction beneath the surface. That hidden depth within the mind of the dropout seems to exhale feelings of inadequacy, worthlessness, frustration, and failure. A dropout, by that very fact, is more clearly cast in the role of outcast and pariah. When one's deflated self-image is scarcely registering zero, suicide and desperate violence seem a logical enough response with which to solve one's own and one's troubled reference group's problems. The contemporary social evolutional context has served to further deflate the dropout's self-image. In the twenties the youth with minimal education was surrounded on his cultural island by similar working class youth who were with minimal education and very modest occupational prospects. Alerting the lower classes to the meaning of a "good *white* collar job" has served to denigrate the status of the blue collar job to which the dropout by circumstances of educational deficiency must aspire. Because of his failure at youth's prime job—his school work, because of his dead-end laborer's job which even his own immediate class reference group is coming to devaluate, the dropout in an affluent upwardly mobile society has come to feel like a second-class citizen. The hostility which is the dropout's defense against the outer world's depreciation of his position seems destined to become intensified as the two worlds—the dropout's and the graduate's—become more estranged and alien. That the condition of being "out-of-school and out-of-work" is a status with noticeable components of demoralization is dramatized by our dropout delinquents' TAT's.[5]

PSYCHOLOGICAL CHARACTERISTICS

This study has found psychological trends or tendencies characterizing the two groups. As already emphasized in the discussion of the TAT protocols there is wide overlapping although the underlying trends are evident. The social-psychic variable will fit into the law of polarization as follows. The law of polarization states that per-

Table 9.—Psychological tendencies of the dropout

Dropout	Graduate
Troubled	Calm
Hostile	Friendly
Antagonistic	Cooperative
Instinctoid	Holistic
Pessimistic	Optimistic
Destructive	Constructive
Concrete	Abstract
Radical	Conservative
Dissatisfied	Satisfied
Narcissistic	Alterocentric
Class-bound	Upwardly mobile
Proletarian	Capitalistic
Antisocial	Prosocial
Affectless	Affectionate
Maladjusted	Adjusting
Impulsive	Controlled
Unstable	Stable
Hyperactive	Alert
Sensate	Idealistic
Outer needs	Inner needs
Weak self-image	Strong self-image
Deficiency-oriented	Proficiency-oriented
Immediate gratification	Deferred gratification
Leisure-and-thrill oriented	Occupation-and-goal oriented
Sexually exploiting	Monogamous
Double standard	Single standard
Unconventional	Conventional
Violent solutions	Verbal compositions
Antiauthority	Proauthority
Nonmethodical	Methodical
Nonroutinized	Routinized
Pawn of environment	Master of environment
Nonstructured value system	Structured value system
Attention-getting behavior	Objective-getting behavior
Males: Compensatory hypermasculinity	Males: Blended male-female traits
Females: Unrealistically romantic	Females and males: Romantic

sons who would ordinarily tend to be quite neutral about common issues will, in time of crisis—such as being out-of-school and out-of-work—tend to manifest extreme positions. The listing of polar tendencies derived from our TAT materials serves as a summary of this chapter.

CHAPTER SIX

Summary and Solutions

Gaffney, S.C. (AP)—Four youths appeared in General Sessions Court in connection with a series of break-ins. Judge Frank Epps, learning that they had quit school, gave them the choice of returning to school or going on the chain gang. Without hesitation, all four chose the chain gang.[1]

The names of the dropouts who chose to go on the chain gang rather than return to school were not mentioned in the national press releases. Perhaps their name is legion. If these four youth were statistically typical of the dropout population there are a number of identification marks whereby they may be known.

Our definition of the dropout has been: any youth who for any reason, except death, has left school before graduating from high school and without transferring to another school.

The little band of delinquents who chose the chain gang may be considered the black cloud, no bigger than a man's hand, on the horizon, destined to grow to whirlwind proportions during the coming generation. They are tomorrow's proletariat.

The dropout is no longer a boon to the national economy. He is clumsily dysfunctional in the computer-precise, machine-oriented, communication-saturated society. His muscles are a drug on the market; his truncated education makes him inadequate to qualify for available jobs; he is in no position to bargain for himself and has little chance to develop himself within an expanding socioeconomic universe. The appalling fact is that there are so many of him—7,500,000 during the 1960's. Like most things in our automated world, he appears in quantity.

Conservative unemployment records indicate that there are 750,000 youth who are seeking work but cannot find it. The proportion of youth who are out of school and out of work is greater than it was during the depression of the 1930's. More probably the type of youth who would choose the chain gang (here meant to indicate a delinquency-tinctured, community-burdening, marginal employment) rather than return to school belongs to that group of 350,000 out-of-school and out-of-work youth who have fallen from our misery charts. They aren't even looking for work any more, consequently they are not listed as unemployed. It is this hard core of the rising proletarian class that Labor Secretary Wirtz described as that "outlaw pack" who are "unemployed today and will be for the rest of their lives at a cost to us of $1,000 a head a year for the rest of their lives." It is from this hard core of dropouts that a high proportion of the gangsters, hoodlums, drug addicted, government-dependent-prone, irresponsible and illegitimate parents of tomorrow will be predictably recruited. Many of their submarginal families have been on relief for a second and third generation.

Though the dropout rate among Negroes is twice as high as is that among whites, four out of five dropouts are white. Though the dropout group cuts across all ethnic, social class, and geographic lines the overwhelming percentage originates in the blue and lower-white collar socioeconomic classes. A majority of the dropouts throughout the nation fall within the average IQ range and have more than adequate talent to complete a high school education. Fifteen percent of the total population would seem to have inadequate talent to finish high school profitably. Many dropouts have IQ's between 75 and 90. However, most youth in that IQ range do complete high school. Twenty-five percent of the country's top talent (above 110 IQ) is lost through premature withdrawal from the secondary school process.

The dropout rate nationally is between 30 and 40 percent. The rate is higher in the South than in the North; higher among boys than girls (53% versus 47%); higher in the slums than in the suburbs. Most dropouts withdraw from school during or before their sixteenth year. There is ten times the incidence of delinquency among the dropouts as there is among the stayins. In view of society's educational expectations for modern youth and dropout youth's inability to get a job while "just waiting around for something to happen," the very state of being a dropout has all but become by definition a condition of semidelinquency.

THE DROPOUT STUDY

Against such a social background was the present study planned. The hard core dropouts were proliferating in the poorer areas of the metropolitan centers. The large urban schools of the lower class were the prime target of the study. We wanted to know *why* half of these youth were dropping out.

Until we found out—primarily from the dropouts themselves —why they were dropping out and found out why youth in the identical situation were staying in, we would not be able to understand the situation realistically or make sound proposals for its amendment.

It is obvious that every dropout, as every graduate, is an individual with unique characteristics, problems, and personal history. No single category will pinpoint all dropouts no more than any single solution will be a universal answer. There are, however, certain central and characteristic tendencies of the dropouts that emerge from this and related studies. Findings are summarized in a Dropout Prediction Table.

1 . DROPOUT PREDICTION TABLE

The following twenty characteristics are commonly found among youth who are potential or actual dropouts:

School

1. Two years behind in reading or arithmetic at seventh grade level. Majority of grades are below average.

2. Failure of one or more school years (1st, 2nd, 8th, 9th grades most commonly failed; 85% of dropouts behind one year; 53% two or more years).

3. Irregular attendance and frequent tardiness. Ill-defined sickness given as reason.

4. Performance consistently below potential.

5. No participation in extracurricular activities.

6. Frequent change of schools.

7. Behavior problems requiring disciplinary measures.

8. Feeling of "not belonging" (because of size, speech, personality development, nationality, social class, family disgrace, retardation in school, dress, lack of friends among schoolmates or staff, etc.).

Family

9. More children than parents can readily control (e.g., only child for divorced and working mother; five or more for non-

divorced and working mother of blue and lower white-collar class).

10. Parents inconsistent in affection and discipline.

11. Unhappy family situation (common acceptance, communication, and pleasurable experiences lacking; family solidarity minimal).

12. Father figure weak or absent.

13. Education of parents at eighth grade level.

14. Few family friends; among these few many problem units (divorced, deserted, delinquents, dropouts).

Peers

15. Friends not approved by parents.

16. Friends not school oriented.

17. Friends much older or much younger.

TAT (Psychological orientation)

18. Resentful of all authority (home, school, police, job, church).

19. Deferred gratification pattern weak.

20. Weak self-image.

THE POWER OF PRIMARY RELATIONSHIP

The greater the number of negative factors working to the disadvantage of the pupil, the greater the chance of his dropping out of school. However, if the teen-ager has a primary relationship favorable to his remaining in school, all disadvantages are fairly readily overcome.

2. PROPOSED SOLUTIONS

We are now in a position to entertain proposed solutions. Having adequately identified the sickness we are now in a position to recognize with some degree of certainty what might be valid cures. We do not confine ourselves to solutions that flow from our own research.

a) What the Community Can Do

The rise of a new proletariat is of community concern. The resources of the community must be mobilized and all segments of society alerted to the inherent danger in a situation in which more than a third of the coming generation are not receiving a minimum high school education. It is intolerable that 20 percent of the total population lives in poverty while manpower, educational facilities, machinery, and capital are wasted.

A citizens' body with representation from the schools, employment services, labor and management, social service agencies, "character-building" agencies, churches, civic and fraternal groups, service clubs, foundations, communication and government agencies should be established in every population center.

1) ALERT THE COMMUNITY

Through saturation communications the community must be informed of the fact that there is no longer any room at the bottom. In our highly complex automated society the unskilled dropout is faced with all but impossible odds. The major opportunities of the future lie in professional, technical and white-collar occupations and in special mechanical skills connected with scientific development. The growing occupations demand more highly trained and better educated people to fill them. The setting for progress is youth's feeling of acceptance, development of communication skills, and ability to get along with others, whether in work or leisure situations. A greater portion of taxes is needed for the upgrading of the school systems. Providing better educational programs rather than $1,000 a year unemployment doles is good business and solid philanthropy.

This citizens' youth development and employment committee must stimulate research, promote each community group's acceptance of its role in meeting the problem, update information, cooperate with state and national organizations, coordinate the efforts of all groups on behalf of youth, and eliminate gaps in service. More specifically it must stimulate industry personnel managers to hire more untrained young workers, call on labor unions to take the initiative in expanding their efforts of service for the total community, develop programs of training, placement, and follow-up. This committee should form action committees—especially those that enlist support of parents, establish citizens' committees in neighborhoods, schools, churches, and develop creative plans to take advantage of new programs of the federal government. Charitable and church organizations with their vast resources of manpower and dedication should be encouraged and subsidized in their efforts to assist youth.

EXAMPLE—THE SUMMER DROPOUT CAMPAIGN

One example of a national program that stimulated community-wide efforts is the following. On August 1, 1963, President Kennedy announced that he was making $250,000 available from his emergency funds to promote community activity in fighting the dropout problem. The modest sum was to be allocated on a first-come, first-served basis. Within two weeks after the announcement, the total amount was allocated to sixty-three communities in twenty-three states and the District of Columbia. Community programs shifted into high gear immediately to contact potential dropouts before the September registration. The results of this "quickie" summer program statistically are as follows: 1,375 counselors and other professional workers participated in the campaign; 59,301 young people identified by these workers as dropouts or potential dropouts were contacted during the campaign; 30,361, or 51.5% of the total, returned to school in September; 28,078, or 92.4%, of the youths who returned to school as a result of the summer campaign were still enrolled as of November 1.[2]

No dropout campaign can be summarized completely in statistics. There was much accomplished besides getting 28,000 youths back to high school. "The sense of unity achieved as the community joined with the schools to help the youth of the city was profoundly impressive and no less beneficial to the adult participants than to the youth who were helped," one superintendent noted. Summary after summary stressed the "public relations" value of the campaign—the heightened spirit of school-community cooperation—as being of inestimable value. For the first time, many reports stated, there was community-wide recognition of the dimensions and seriousness of the dropout problem.[3] Such awareness is a necessary preliminary to effective community action on the many-faceted problem of dropout.

2) PRESCHOOL HEALTH AND SOCIALIZATION SERVICES

Once the community has been alerted to the importance and the magnitude of the problem, the nature of the dropout problem must be revealed to them. The high school dropout problem is not basically a question of the high school. It has become abundantly clear throughout the study that the damage has already been done to the child even before he has entered first grade. The typical dropout's problems are those of a weak self-image, weak communication skills and inability to get along pleasurably with others. But this triad of primary relationship components is established before one enters school, rarely after. If the family has not taken care of the child's preschool health and basic socialization needs, then the community must assist the family in its functions of early child care by establishing wherever necessary family clinics, health centers, and nurseries.

Recognizing the imprint plasticity of the infant and child and the deficiencies of the family background prompted NEA's Daniel Schreiber to deduce:

> Over the long haul, programs in the nursery and kindergarten areas will probably be most beneficial in preventing dropouts. The various approaches include summer kindergartens and centers at which four and five year olds get educational experiences they would otherwise miss.[4]

It is true that the child is born to parents who are the prime educators of the child; only with the parents' cooperation is there any reasonable chance of forming a creative personality. It is equally true that when parents are incapable of developing civilization-adequate children, the community must provide for the deficiencies.

It will cost society less to work with parents while the children are still babies than to try to make up the deficiencies later. Providing facilities for prenatal care, inculcating the need for proper diet, rest, play, hygiene, physical examinations, and dental care, and assisting parents to know that parenthood is an educational project means providing a milieu of acceptance, communication, and creative play. Nurseries can assist parents and to a certain extent compensate for parents' inadequacies. Such nurseries will provide cooperative play opportunities, contact with picture books, words, and art objects. Underachievers in verbal tasks are often highly competent in mechanical projects. Lower class homes can hardly provide shop equipment, large blocks and other heavy mechanical devices; these can be provided in the community's preschool projects. Prenatal clinics should include developmental programs for *fathers* and mothers. If every hospital had such a parental enrichment program a new generation would be formed. A.D.C. grants should not be given unless the parents attend vocational and parenthood courses.

PRESCHOOL PARENT-CHILD ORIENTATION-ENRICHMENT
CENTERS

Examples: Baltimore, Philadelphia, New York, Racine

Under its project HELP, Baltimore opened two centers in poor neighborhoods to assist parents in preschool socialization of their children. Each center has a staff of at least four persons including a volunteer mother who serves on a once-a-week rotating basis. The preschool socialization centers are neither day-care centers nor nursery schools. They are designed to assist parents to provide their children with learning experiences. There is special emphasis on the development of language and communication skills, on the reinforcement of stable self concepts, and on habits of pleasant group cooperation.

In Philadelphia special programs are held during the summer for preschool, disadvantaged children. Of special note are the weekly parent workshops at which parents are given the assistance they need to carry on their basic functions as prime socializers of the children. It was found that before the programs were undertaken most of the children were unable to name such simple objects as tree, flag, pitcher, leaf. Within a month's time the average rise on the Stanford-Binet IQ Test was fourteen points.

Martin Deutsch is conducting a research and demonstration experiment in New York in ten city schools and five day-care centers. He is attempting to develop a set of teaching techniques that could be used anywhere in the country so that parents may be taught to teach their children the verbal and perceptual skills they need in order to bolster their sense of self and to learn to read.

Racine's preschool parent-child program has recognized that most of the learning that takes place in school is highly dependent upon the *speech repertoire* that the child brings to school. By the time the normal middle class child enters school he has already learned most of the phonology and grammar of the English language along with substantial vocabulary. The disadvantaged family has not provided its children with this background because of a lack of intellectual stimulation, substandard dialects, retarded mental and psychomotor development because of protein-calorie malnutrition, etc. Racine has developed an all-day kindergarten pilot program. The disadvantaged children follow a typical school program in the morning with the afternoons devoted to hearing stories, looking at pictures, books, slides, watching selected films and TV programs, taking frequent field trips to parks, museums, stores, civic centers, historical spots, farms, factories. Such carefully planned readiness programs help to build a background of experiences which later give meaning and motivation for the regular school tasks. Parental participation is insisted upon and made the basis for hopes of permanent substantial assistance to the child.

Of all the suggestions made for the upgrading of youth, the most promising, next to that of upgrading the family itself, is that of the preschool parent-child socialization centers.

b) What Government Can Do

In the depths of the depression in 1932 it became tragically obvious that the private sector of the economy was incapable of solving the general unemployment problem. Today it is equally obvious that the private sector of the economy is incapable of solving the equally tragic problem of dropout unemployment. The public sector must enter the field.

EXAMPLES OF WHAT LOCAL, STATE, AND NATIONAL
GOVERNMENTS HAVE DONE

Seven cities in New York are participating in the School to Employment Program (STEP) under the aegis of the state department of education. This is primarily a work-study program for fifteen-year olds identified as potential dropouts. In this program students spend two hours a day in school followed by work in public agencies. They are supervised by the school and paid by state funds.

The Economic Opportunity Act of 1964 provided for the creation of a job corps, a work-training program, and a work-study program. The programs enlisted some 100,000 young men whose background, health, and education make them least fit for useful work. Half of them presumably will work in camps and centers around the country on special conservation projects designed to give them some education, to provide useful work experience, and to enrich the natural resources of the country. Other youth would receive a blend of training, basic education, and work experience in job training centers. The Labor Department would likewise provide a national work-training program for 200,000 men and women between the ages of sixteen and twenty-one. State and local governments and nonprofit agencies are to develop this program.

The experience, the income, and the sense of purpose which

useful part-time work brings to disadvantaged or mistaken dropouts may mean the difference between their being or not being integrated with the socioeconomic system.

c) What Business Can Do

Businessmen are coming to realize that it is cheaper to help the dropout through work experience than through taxation. The public, and this financially means business, is taxed roughly $1,000 per year per unemployed youth and no productive work accrues to society. Youth has no access to economic life except through a job. Of the many recommendations made for business and industry we may list the following:

1. Conduct a "dialogue" on youth employment between and within the organization.

2. Re-examine existing policies and take action to achieve equal job opportunities.

3. Establish realistic training programs, making sure they do not compete with programs better offered in the schools.

4. Cooperate with schools and other agencies in school work and upgrading programs.

5. Make resources available to school vocational counselors.

6. Locate and establish protective entry jobs for unskilled, untrained, and unendowed youth.

7. Study next steps toward spread of employment, including present standards of working day and week.

8. Cooperate with the federal government in developing information on technological changes, displacement of workers, and requirements for new skills.

9. Provide realistic job descriptions, overcoming tendency to overstate requirements.

10. Provide many more opportunities for young people to visit plants and offices so they may hear realistic discussions of job requirements.

11. Participate in community service programs at schools and at various meetings as well as on radio, TV, and other channels of information.

12. Offer to speak at student assemblies and gatherings and tell the students why high school *graduates* are wanted for employees.

13. Encourage the students hired for the summer to return to school in the fall by showing them the increased benefits that they could obtain in their job if they graduated.

14. Plan production so youth can work four hours or so a day but yet continue his education in either day or night school.

15. Offer scholarships to fifth graders of blue collar background contingent upon their continued academic achievement. Such scholarships offered at an early age would have a great effect upon the academic and occupational aspirations of the lower class youth.

EXAMPLE: A CHICAGO DEPARTMENT STORE'S DOUBLE E
(EDUCATION AND EMPLOYMENT) PROGRAM

There are hundreds of industries promoting and participating in work-study programs. Junior and senior high school students spend part of their time in school and part on the job under the supervision of trained coordinators. The Double E Program of a Chicago department store may serve as a specific example. The Carson Company, seeing that the new jobs created by industry are getting farther out of the dropouts' reach, decided to try its own dropout upgrading program. They hired thirty-five boys and twenty-four girls between the ages of sixteen and twenty-one as selected by summer school counselors. The plan called for the dropouts to work three days in the store and spend two days in classroom activity—the department store provided the classroom space for the first year. The youth were provided with $2.00 daily lunch and carfare allowance. An informal dinner was given to launch the program and to enlist the parents' support. "The big problem for these kids is insecurity," a store official explains. "Arousing interest at home is half the battle.... Even the briefest encounter with work experience leaves the dropout with a more realistic idea of what society expects of him." [5]

d) What Labor Can Do

Once upon a time labor had to tell capital that jobs in an industrialized society are not any one in-group's property but that everybody needs a job in order to survive as a complete human being.

That was once upon a time. Today labor has the job of selling itself that same message. Exclusion from industry by management is no easier than exclusion from industry by labor—if one is an unemployed dropout.

Labor is in a central position to help the dropout obtain a foothold in the occupational world. Every group must accept its share of the human burden to promote the common welfare. No one is in a better position to appreciate the dropout's straits than is the laboring man and to identify with him and to espouse his occupational training and placement.

Each one of the suggestions for business given above applies to labor and labor unions. More specific ones are the following four:

1. Eliminate arbitrary restrictions in union membership, relating any restrictions to continuously evaluated projections of manpower potentials.

2. Emphasize the elimination of discrimination especially in the building trades.

3. Vigorously promote training and open apprenticeship programs for youth.

4. The fact that Negro youth have almost as little chance to obtain a job with a high school diploma as without one is a serious block to their continuation in the education process.[6] The historical function of labor unionism has been to promote the welfare of the disadvantaged laborer. The historical challenge is incarnate in the Negro dropout.

EXAMPLES: LABOR ASSISTS IN LEBANON AND ROCK COUNTY

An expert in building trades in Lebanon, Tennessee, sparked community interest when he took thirty-two boys, and with no other assistance built a three bedroom house. The house was beautiful and the project received wide attention. The community now drives past on weekends to inspect the house; and community spirit has developed. The schools gave youth credit for this work and the youth who participated were taught fundamental marketable skills. The project contributed greatly to keeping the students vocationally oriented and in school.

In many areas labor union restrictions throw stumbling blocks in the path of those who have been trained in vocational schools.

Some top-flight trade schools give first class training in plumbing for three years but their graduates must go through apprenticeships for four or five years relearning what they had been taught in trade school. But in Rock County, New York, unions have helped with money, work, and teachers. The Carpenters' Union gives two prizes each year to top students and automatically accepts graduates each year into an apprenticeship training program, cuts the union initiation fee from $125 to $20 and gives the graduates credit for one year of apprenticeship.

e)   What the Schools Can Do

1)   CURRICULUM

(a) Multi-type curricula are needed
- (1) Academic—for many college-bound pupils
- (2) Technical—for some college-bound pupils and other oriented directly for industry
- (3) Vocational—for those who will move into skilled crafts
- (4) Commercial—for some college-bound and others going directly into business
- (5) Occupational—for those whose aptitudes suit them for unskilled labor

The last four of these five types are of great import to the potential dropout.

(b) Multi-track systems are needed

Classes must be divided according to ability. The gifted and energetic student must not be condemned to a scholastic prison of tedium because of the background deficiencies of the disadvantaged and less talented. Nor should the disadvantaged and disturbed be condemned to a scholastic prison of the unspeakable tortures of constant discouragement, frustration, and final alienation from school and society.

(c) Multi-approaches are needed
- (1) The book approach is one approach but not the only one.
- (2) For the potential dropout the tactile and aural and personal approach may be better than the book and oral and impersonal one.
- (3) Increased pressures upon students and faculty, the trend toward tougher curricula, heavier work loads, earlier graduation, higher achievement, should not obscure the fact that perhaps one out of three high school students is neither

emotionally nor intellectually prepared to cope even with the present curricular demands.

(d) Multi-purposes of curricula must be accepted

    (1) For the college and university oriented youth the goal of a curriculum may well be the acquisition of facts and the covering of academic areas.

    (2) For the disadvantaged, the noncollege oriented, and the less talented, the goal of a curriculum may well be helping each child to become his best self, a good citizen, and a productive worker.

(e) Greater standardization of curricula for all parts of the country should be sought since potential dropouts more frequently come from highly mobile, semi-employed parents whose wandering ways jeopardize not only their children's social life (in each new school they gravitate toward the social rejects because the elites like the status quo) but their academic life.

(f) Extra courses that are not college preparatory can be offered for the welfare of the withdrawal-prone: baking, barbering, bookkeeping, building, auto-repair, consumer education, commercial cooking, homemaking, mechanics, typing, and various vocational arts.

Example: Minneapolis—"Comprehensive High School Approach"

Minneapolis' "comprehensive high school approach" to the dropout problem is based upon a wide spectrum of curricular offerings in eleven different areas such as art, business, English, foreign language, health and physical education, home economics, industrial arts, etc. Thus it is possible for the student who continues in high school to leave school with either salable skills or the necessary background to continue his education.

The program is supported by many other services for the potential dropouts as the following partial listing indicates:

(a) A flexible curriculum.

(b) The development of new curriculum guides, manuals, and handbooks.

(c) A city-wide testing program.

(d) An increased number of reading centers.

(e) An increased use of programmed learning materials.

(f) A program of pupil personnel services in which a team made up of a special service teacher, counselor, psychologist, and nurse visits the schools to help the students, parents, and teachers to understand themselves and set attainable goals for the students.

(g) A "school excuse" committee to assist the satisfactory placement of students who have not been able to adjust to their home school.

(h) TV lessons.

(i) Professional case conferences to meet the needs of the individual student.

(j) Exploratory courses (grades 7 and 8) in industrial arts, home economics, and art.

(k) Classes for emotionally disturbed.

(l) Vocational evening and summer school.

(m) Overall administrative procedures.

    i) Higher ratio of teachers and pupil personnel workers assigned to schools situated in low socioeconomic areas.

    ii) Increased emphasis on increasing the flexibility of school offerings.

    iii) Principal and counselor may exempt a student from required courses.

(n) Workshop and institute attendance by school personnel.

2)   COUNSELING

Fifty percent of the type of jobs that exist today did not exist one generation ago. How can parents direct their child into the right slot without professional assistance? In a rural society the father could readily guide his son as the father himself had been guided in turn by his father and his father's father. That day is gone. Counseling programs are needed from the first years of elementary school— and before. Junior high school is entirely too late for the guidance of the potential dropout. Fifth grade seems to be the latest at which counseling can be reasonably introduced. By using scales and tests, as well as by astute interviewing methods, the counselor can place a

disadvantaged or retarded child in a special class for remedial measures before he becomes overly discouraged and drops out. Counseling services should be available to the total community even as
medical services are. The school must throw off its ghetto mentality.

(a) Professional testing services should be made available for all
    children at as early an age as reasonably possible. This should
    be made a part of their permanent record in whatever school
    their parents choose to send them. This record would likewise
    provide an inventory of the dropout in follow-up procedures.

(b) The school must take the leadership in the early identification
    of both pupils and parents who need help. Adequate counseling
    services must be made available to both age groups.

(c) The nub of dropout therapy and final cure lies in early identi-
    fication of the school difficulty. Only the school and its coun-
    seling program can handle this critical situation.

(d) An elementary school ratio of 1 counselor to 600 pupils in
    middle-class neighborhoods and 1 to 300 in lower socioeconomic
    situations seems reasonable.

(e) An evaluation of the physical, intellectual, emotional, and
    social qualifications of each child through professional services
    after three years within the school system should be made
    available to the parents of all children. A multidisciplinary and
    multiagency approach is necessary. Both human and physical re-
    sources are available. It is inspiration and organization that are
    needed.

(f) Some youths cannot continue school because their families
    need financial assistance. The school should aid such students
    to find part-time jobs that will not interfere with schooling.

(g) School guidance should emphasize how to get a job, human
    relations, and the rationale of choosing courses.

(h) School counseling with parents should include references to
    standard agencies and resources on prenatal care, proper diet,
    medical assistance, etc. Knowledge of these middle-class institu-
    tions are frequently unknown by potential dropouts' parents.

(i) Parents must be counseled on giving their children sex in-
    struction, assistance in courtship, and providing a sound social
    life.

(j) Continuous training for responsible and full family life should be encouraged from prekindergarten to postgraduate programs.

(k) Many states provide for every type of handicapped child except the emotionally disturbed child. He likewise is a handicapped child and must have specific professional services.

(l) The vicious circle of the disadvantaged hard core of society generating the next generation's disadvantaged hard core cannot be broken unless a new definition of the school is made to include the parents. The deproletarianization of our society will not be accomplished without a massive adult education program. The school is destined to become a day and evening social center on a twelve-month basis. The counselor's action role is strategic.

Examples: High Schools' "Holding Power"

As far as is presently known, Milwaukee has the lowest metropolitan dropout rate (3%). One of the many reasons for this slight educational defection is its counseling program which includes conferring with the parent as well as with the potential dropout. In any serious situation the parents are included in a counseling situation with their child.

Another major factor contributing to the high holding power of Milwaukee's schools is the full set of special services available. The local school system operates the following program of services which support the work of the classroom teacher and contribute to the overall welfare of the child:

(a) Psychological Services
    —includes counseling and city-wide testing program

(b) School Social Work Services
    —welfare counselors assigned to groups of schools

(c) Guidance Services
    —includes guidance programs and counseling staffs in all secondary schools

(d) Special Education Services
    —includes classes for the physically, emotionally, or culturally handicapped

(e) Reading Improvement Services

—reading centers in many elementary and all secondary schools and *all* schools of the central area.

(f) In-Migrant and Transient Pupil Program
—trial program for newcomers and highly mobile pupils.

Finally, a remote but effective cause of the holding power of Milwaukee's schools is its upgraded plan of organization in the early elementary years. The city's "primary school" arrangement enables each child to begin his post-kindergarten education without fear of failure. Each pupil works at his own level of ability and maturity until he is ready for advancement into the fourth grade. Then, with confidence and self-assurance, he moves up through the intermediate grades and beyond. Hopefully, it is expected that the pupil's initial success and his satisfaction with school will create within him a desire to continue his education through high school graduation. Because strong foundations are being laid and good instructional programs are being provided at succeeding levels, most children in Milwaukee never think of leaving school before completing their high school education. And the "dropout" report proves it.[7]

3)   THE TEACHER

(a) One of the reasons for the appalling lack of influence of the teachers is that mass education has minimized personal relationships. A teacher who is contacting 300 students per day has no time to be interested in the individual. There is grave need for recruiting more and higher motivated teachers. Such an increase would allow smaller classes and individual attention.

(b) Special recognition must be given to those teachers who serve the educationally disadvantaged. Rather than serving as penal institutions for recalcitrant teachers, the lower class schools should be made situations of special salary increases and incidental bonuses—for example, choosing as administrators only those who have shown special skill in dealing with the disadvantaged. In medicine the more serious the illness the more skilled the specialist and the more honored the cure; a similar mechanism is needed in the profession of education.

(c) The number of teachers needed should be determined by the needs of the pupils and not based on fixed ratios such as one to thirty. Handicapped, disadvantaged youth may need one-to-ten or even one-to-one teacher-student relationship. Economic and cultural deprivation can be a greater handicap than blindness.

(d) The relationship between teacher and student is particularly important. Teachers should be selected for their ability to make a contribution to students rather than on the basis of their isolated competency in a subject field.

(e) Teachers should be kept up-to-date through seminars, workshops, and consultations with resource persons from various areas. If population is doubling every forty years, and the economic system every twenty years, knowledge is doubling every ten years. Teachers must have in-training enrichment.

(f) Sympathetic understanding, and friendly advice from a teacher can help a child remain in school. Every teacher should try to learn the name of each of his students—and use it occasionally with a certain amount of respect.

(g) The early recognition by teachers of the danger signals of the potential dropout and a referral to the counseling program would be a great help toward correcting the situation. Skilled teachers can frequently recognize the dropout by the third or fourth grade.

(h) Because of the slight presence of the father figure or of any male who would be a worthy ego-image in the lives of the potential dropouts, male teachers are especially necessary in schools whose clientele are primarily youth in the lower socioeconomic brackets. These youths' bias toward the muscular and physical also recommends that the teaching staff be weighted with males.

(i) A teacher must constantly rededicate himself to his profession realizing that there is nothing more noble than the molding of character and the building of personality.

(j) Methods of raising the status of the teacher must be explored and operationalized.

Examples: (1) Teaching "interns"; (2) the "most desperate" school; (3) upgrading veteran teachers

(1) Bennetta B. Washington, Principal of Cardozo High School in Washington, D.C., needed good teachers for the underprivi-

leged children. She signed up ten Peace Corps veterans as "interns"—teaching "interns." On-the-job training helped her to tap the vast reservoir of dedication and idealism among young Americans that the Peace Corps veterans symbolize.

(2) New York's Junior High School 120 in East Harlem was judged to be the "most desperate" school in the system. Hunter College adopted it as a challenge and persuaded 10 percent of its junior year majors in secondary education to volunteer for special training. A master teacher supervised each trainee. Twenty-two of these special volunteers became the backbone of the new and highly successful "desperate" 120 which is now beyond national norms in its achievement. On-the-job training with dedicated volunteer teachers has proved itself.

(3) New Haven, Connecticut, has found that on-the-job training is as important for upgrading older teachers as it is for preparing new ones. School principals in eight slum districts now pick two of their best teachers, relieve them of regular classroom chores and ask them to work helping and building other teachers. Each week a psychiatrist from Yale University's Child Study Center visits the schools to discuss problems and solutions with the "helping teachers."

As yet, such pioneering in on-the-job training is producing only a trickle of qualified teachers for working with potential dropouts. The trickle could, with due pump-priming, become a torrent.

f) *What Volunteer Groups Can Do*

Any group of persons or any person who is willing to assist the potential dropout has a vast untilled field waiting for him.

Examples

In New York City an organization of parents operates a school volunteer program. Each volunteer spends three hours a week during school hours helping non-English speaking children learn English. They coach the children in reading or tutor them in art or music. For most of the lower class children, the sessions with the volunteer who has academically "adopted" them, is the only opportunity they have of reading continuously, under supervision, for forty-five minutes at a stretch.

High school and college students act as volunteers to coach

children. The home-study plan provides that parents turn a part of their home into a classroom where students—preferably from the same social strata—tutor their children.[8]

High school graduates, college-trained parents, widows with adequate education and other knowledgeable laymen are tutoring and helping teachers grade papers. In Chicago it was recognized that the correction of themes in English class presents an all but insuperable job for teachers. English compositions cannot be assigned by the teachers every week because of inability to correct them. Even if an English teacher had only one hundred students this would still mean one hundred themes per week, each taking at least ten minutes to correct. This would mean seventeen hours of work—two and a half hours, seven nights a week. Chicago would need 330 more teachers, adding $2,500,000 to the budget. Solution: hiring part-time "lay readers" who can take over the chore at twenty-five cents a theme. This idea is being used in sixteen cities.

In 1962 a group of college students were organized by Peter Countryman into a group called the Northern Student Movement. Without pay they share their education with the disadvantaged— English, mathematics, science, any subject that the youth are interested in or are willing to accept. For the college students, the program answers their need for reality and altruism; for the slum children it supplies assistance and identification-figures which are not otherwise available.

The "See and Touch" program instituted by Dr. Samuel Shepard in St. Louis is a program of enrichment for the culturally deprived. In his program he arranged to take the children to the zoo, art museum, restaurants, hotels and other places of interest and phantasy stimulation. Assisted by various benefactors, volunteers, and school systems the trips proved of inestimable value to slum children, many of whom had never been more than six blocks away from home.

g)   What the Family Can Do
Conclusion

A Letter to Parents

The following letter of the Director of Elementary Education in a sprawling slum area of St. Louis named the Banneker District serves as a fitting close to what the families of potential dropouts can do. It can likewise serve as a final focalization of a key finding of our study—the central position of the family in the biography of the dropout.

"Board of Education
"City of St. Louis
"Banneker District

"Dear Parents,
"We—teachers, general consultants, principals, and the director—have been working very hard to help your child to do his best in school. We have had some success. But, we want you to know that our best effort will not be good enough if we do not have your full support and cooperation. We realize, as we know you do, that if your child is to prepare himself for a good position in the future, he must do his best job in school every day. We feel sure that you will want to do all you can to make certain that your child achieves as much as he can in all school subjects, especially in reading, arithmetic, and language. May we remind you as parents, that our motto is SUCCESS IN SCHOOL IS MY CHILD'S MOST IMPORTANT BUSI-NESS. Below is a parent's PLEDGE OF COOPERATION. Please read it very carefully and let it serve as a constant reminder and guide.

"With kindest regards,
"Samuel Shepard, Jr.
"Director, Elementary Education"

THE PARENT'S PLEDGE OF COOPERATION

I. I pledge that I will do my level best to help my child put forth his best effort to study and achieve in school.

  1. I *will make sure* that my child attends school every day on time and with sufficient rest to be able to do a good job.

  2. I *will provide* my child with a dictionary and, as far as I am able, a quiet, well-lighted place to study.

  3. I *will insist* that my child spends some time studying at home each day.

  4. I *will visit* my child's teacher at least once during each semester.

  5. I *will discuss* my child's report card with him. I will compare my child's grade level with his level of achievement.

6. I *will join* the P.T.A. and attend meetings as often as I can.

II. I recognize that fact that skill in reading is the key to success in school achievement. Therefore:

1. I *will provide* my child with a library card and insist that he use it regularly.

2. I *will give* him suitable books frequently (birthdays, holidays, and other special occasions).

3. I *will give* him a subscription to one of the weekly school newspapers or magazines (My Weekly Reader, Jr. Scholastic, etc.).

III. I pledge to do my best to impress upon my child the fact that success in school is his most important business.

Interview Schedule for Both Dropouts
and High-School Graduates

SCHOOL EXPERIENCES

1. What did (do) you like in particular about going to school?

2. Was (Is) there anything in particular that you dislike about going to school?

3. Was (Is) there anything else that you can think of that you specifically like or dislike about going to school?

4. (DROPOUT) What reason ranked first in your decision to leave school?

5. (GRADUATE) Did you ever think seriously of dropping out of school? What reason would have ranked first if you had decided to drop out of school? What finally made you decide to continue your education?

6. If your best friend came to you and told you that he was going to drop out of high school, what would you tell him?

7. (DROPOUT) What type of work are you now doing? Is this the general area in which you hope to continue? Or do you have something else in mind?

8. (GRADUATE) Are you specializing in any particular line of studies? How does this fit in with what you hope will be your life's work?

Ego Family

9. Now about your family: Would you say that it is your father or your mother who makes most of the decisions? What type of decisions would your father make and what type of decisions would your mother make?

10. If your *whole* family had some free time, how would they usually spend it?

11. Does your family talk things over with each other very often?

12. To what degree would you say that your *whole* family both understands and accepts each other?

13. And how do you fit into the picture? To what degree would you say that your family both understands and accepts you?

14. And would you say that you both understand and accept them?

15. Did your family encourage and help you in your plans for a good job or in your school plans?

16. Can you remember when you first made plans to leave your parents' home for good?

Friend Family System

17. How many really close friends does your family have?

18. What would your family mean by a close friend?

19. Does your family get together with the relatives on big holidays?

20. Do your family's friends have about the same idea about education as your family did, or what was the situation?

21. [If there is time discuss and probe in your own words the friend family variables.]

22. Can you think of any example of your being influenced by your family's friends or relatives?

Peer Group

23. Did you think you were being contrary to your family in your choice of friends at any time or don't you think they cared who your friends were?

24. If your parents oppose your choice of some friend, what usually happens?

25. How much school will the majority of your friends complete? (TO GRADUATE) And how much do you hope to complete?

26. If we said that a close friend was one who really accepts you as a person, and one that you like to confide in, and that you enjoy being with under many circumstances, would you say that you were *friendly with any one of the teachers* or staff members at school? Was there more than one? How many?

27. And of those close friends who accepted you, that you could confide in, and that you enjoyed being with, were there any of them *among the students* at school? How many?

28. How many close friends did you have that your parents approved of?

29. And how many close friends did you have that your parents did *not* approve of or were indifferent about?

30. And at home, how many were there that you could say accept you, and you like to confide in, and you enjoy being with?

31. And how many of your parents' friends are you friendly with?

Influentials

32. Did you think you were right in leaving school at the time you did?

33. (DROPOUT) From whom did you seek help? At the point of your decision to drop out, with whom did you speak? Did you have any plans for the future? Would you do the same thing, if you were again faced with the decision?

34. Which person do you judge to have been most influential in your choice of an occupation?

35. Which person do you judge to have been the most influential person in your life?

36. And whom do you judge to be the second most influential person in your life?

37. Is there any person whom you have not mentioned who influenced you greatly?

38. If you needed help and advice to make a big decision, to whom would you go for that advice?

The Questionnaire

This is a completely *anonymous* questionnaire. It is part of a national study of family friends. We would like to obtain information about young men and women who left school in order to go to work or get married. First you are asked about the family within which you grew up as that family was *before you left school*. Then you are asked about the five families with whom this family associated most often. (If your family associated closely with fewer than five families, answer only about them.) We are trying to get a picture of the family in which you grew up and their family friends as they all were while you were at school.

INFORMATION ABOUT YOUR FAMILY WHILE YOU WERE GOING TO SCHOOL

1. Region of origin of your father (check one): Pacific Coast_____ Rocky Mountains_____ Southwest_____ Midwest_____ South_____ Southeast_____ Northeast_____ Outside of the U.S._____.

2. Number of years of schooling finished by your father_____.

3. Number of years of schooling finished by your mother_____.

4. Father's occupation_____.

5a. Did mother generally work outside of your home? Yes_____ No_____.

  b. Did either parent live away from home for six months or more? Yes _____ No_____. Was this because of military service or illness? Yes _____ No_____.

6. Family's yearly total income while you were in school was approximately: $_____.

7a. Name of father's religion, if any_____.

  b. Name of mother's religion, if any_____.

8a. First marriage for father: Yes_____ No_____.

  b. First marriage for mother: Yes_____ No_____.

9a. Father or Mother ever divorced or deserted before you left school: Yes_____ No_____.

b. Father or mother ever widowed before you left school: Yes_____ No_____.

10. Approximate present ages of children in this family: _____, _____, _____, _____, _____, _____, _____, _____.

11. How many of these left school before graduating from high school? _____.

12. How many of the children of this family were arrested for delinquency at any time? _____.

13. Which two individuals influenced you most to leave school? (mark "1" for the one who was most influential, "2" for the second): Father_____, Mother_____, Relative_____, Friend_____, Teacher_____, Other (name)_____.

14. Which two individuals were most opposed to your leaving school? (mark "1" for the one who was most opposed, "2" for the second): Father_____, Mother_____, Relative_____, Friend_____, Teacher_____, Other (name)_____.

I. INFORMATION ABOUT THE CLOSEST FAMILY WHOM YOUR FAMILY VISITED, ENTERTAINED AND ASSOCIATED WITH MOST OFTEN AS THAT FAMILY WAS DURING YOUR SCHOOL YEARS

15. Region of origin of husband (check one): Pacific Coast_____, Rocky Mountains_____, Southwest_____, Midwest_____, South_____, Southeast_____, Northeast_____, Outside of the U.S._____.

(Same questions as above for "The Closest Family," "The Second Closest," etc.)

VI. DATA CONCERNING YOURSELF AT PRESENT TIME

70. Your age_____.

71. You are: Male_____, Female_____, Single_____, Married_____.

72. Years of education_____.

73. What has been your approximate yearly income since leaving school? $_____.

74. What type of position do you aim to be holding in ten years or so? _____.

75. Number of friend families described: 0_____, 1_____, 2_____, 3_____, 4_____, 5_____, _____.

76. What circumstance or incident made you decide to stop your formal education? _____
_____

77. Do you now think your decision was wise? _____
_____

(THANK YOU VERY MUCH FOR YOUR COOPERATION)

APPENDIX III
Case History of Robert Rawlinson

HISTORY
INDUSTRIAL SCHOOL, GOLDEN, COLORADO

NAME	BIRTHDATE
Robert Rawlinson	1/12/46

HOME ADDRESS	TELEPHONE
269 St., Denver, Colo.	

FATHER'S NAME	ADDRESS
Thomas Rawlinson	269 St., Denver, Colo.

MOTHER'S NAME	ADDRESS
Eloise Rawlinson	269 St., Denver, Colo.

1st interview 12–7–60

Bob was brought to the State Industrial School from the Denver Juvenile Court on a charge of joy riding and car theft. He had previously been on probation with the Court.

Family Background

Bob comes from a complete home setting but one which has been frequently broken up by separations and at one time an actual divorce and then remarriage of the parents. Both of these parents work outside the home and are rather skilled people but have had a good deal of difficulty in their relationships with each other in the past. The father is currently unemployed and is an airplane mechanic with Frontier Airlines. The mother works at the Finance Center in Denver and receives fairly good income. There are four children in this family, one younger brother and two older sisters. Bob says

225

that he has gotten along equally well with both parents but that he has been frequently disturbed by their quarrels and inability to get along with each other and that the only time he had really felt very happy during the past few years was when he had lived outside the home setting with some relatives in Wyoming. He hoped to be able to return to them when he leaves the institution rather than go back to the home setting because he feels there is so much conflict there and particularly in his relationships in Denver that he would not be able to get along too well. The family is actually in the middle income bracket although the father is currently unemployed and they own their own home out near Westminster in Denver. The relationships between the siblings have always been quite good and Bob feels particularly close to his oldest sister, Diane, and his younger brother, David. In fact, David was involved in the car theft with Bob on this last offense which brought him to the institution. David is presently on probation. The conflict in the family has produced a good many difficulties for the youngster and he feels an acute enough anxiety at this present time to feel that it would be difficult for him to go back into the home situation.

Self-Concept   Bob thinks of himself as a boy who probably has more ability to adjust than he has demonstrated in the past. He seems to think of himself as a boy who has not tried too hard and who becomes easily confused and then does things which appear to him later to be unintelligent and actually very immature. Bob has fairly good feeling about his own intelligence and feels that in school he has been capable of doing very good work although he has never worked up to his capacity. He seems to feel that his parents think that he has been influenced by an older youngster who was quite delinquent and who went with the sister, but Bob tends to feel that he has a mind of his own and that he did not have to follow the path of this older delinquent and that he probably got into difficulty because of other reasons than his dependence upon this stronger and older individual. He seems to have a fairly good insight in this area and has the potential to change and apparently at this time the motivation also. He is a very nice looking, outgoing youngster who appears to be above average in social skills and social development.

School   Bob has always passed his grades in school, although during the last two years he has had difficulty in the academic setting but mainly through his defiance of some of the rules. He says that his favorite subjects are English and math and that he has never worked up to what he could do but that he has felt he has the ability to perform quite well. The school record shows Bob has completed the eighth grade and was attending the ninth grade at Skinner Junior High School prior to his commitment to this institution. He does have an established truancy record in the school during the last two years. While he lived in Wyoming on the state leave from the Court he did not attend school. He seems to have difficulty in adjusting to the rules and regulations and has been in some difficulty in the past. He said that he had been expelled for ten days this year for excessive truancy.

Delinquency   The first charge of delinquency came when he was thirteen years of age when he was involved in a joy riding experience with an older delinquent youngster. He was later charged again with joy riding and was placed on probation at this time. He did fairly well under the strict probation until he got into further difficulty in the family situation and began to act out. At this point he was again charged with joy riding and was sent to live with a relative in Wyoming. While he was in Wyoming he got along quite well and seemed to make a very good adjustment. He came back to the family situation after having been there for four months and did well during the summer until he started back to school. At this point he began to act out again and was involved in truancy and was expelled from school. Then approximately two weeks ago he and his little brother and another boy ditched school and took an automobile and were picked up in Colorado Springs. At this point his probation was revoked and he was sent to the State Industrial School. He appears to be a situational conformist delinquent youth from better than average family. He is acting out some of the difficulties in the family setting and is also very easily influenced by the other youngsters. He also finds himself in a position of identifying very strongly with delinquent youngsters because of his close attachment to this older delinquent youngster in the neighborhood who goes with his sister.

Comments It would appear that due to his very outgoing nature and his very good social skills that Bob will probably be able to get along well in the school situation. He does not seem to have the defiance, hostility, nor the entrenched feelings of cynicism that exist in many of the boys. . . . He is operating with some of the difficulty in the family setting and is reacting to it. Basically, he seems to be above average in intelligence and also in social skills. He wants very much to be in a counseling situation so he can work through some of these difficulties. He finds himself generally very capable in the peer relations although he seems to be somewhat afraid of the older, more hardened delinquent children. He seems to feel he may have some difficulty with them. It would appear that he probably needs a good deal of support at this time and also some counseling to help him through his very difficult confusions and ambivalence toward his parent figures.

W. T. Adams

Notes

Notes for "Introduction and Rationale"

1. Olivia Skinner, *St. Louis Post-Dispatch,* January 30, 1964, p. 1.

2. Quoted in *Studies in Unemployment,* Committee on Unemployment Problems, United States Senate, Washington, D.C., 1960, p. 558.

3. *Manpower Report of the President and a Report on Manpower Requirements, Resources, Utilization, and Training by the United States Department of Labor Transmitted to the Congress, March 1964,* p. 128.

4. Two outstanding bibliographies are *Annotated Bibliography for the Conference on Unemployed, Out-of-School Youth in Urban Areas;* and "Part II—Bibliography" in *Social Dynamite* (Conference Report). Both are obtainable from the National Committee for Children and Youth, Associations Building, 1145 19th Street, N.W., Washington, D.C. The former costs $1.00, the latter, $2.00.

5. "Success" is measured in terms of ability to educate one's children.

6. Carle C. Zimmerman and Lucius F. Cervantes, *Marriage and the Family* (Chicago: Henry Regnery Co., 1956).

7. New York: Pageant Press, 1960.

Notes for Chapter One

1. New York: Scribner's, p. 23.

2. Leonard Broom and Philip Selznick, *Sociology* (3d ed.; New York: Harper and Row Publishers, 1964), pp. 135–70.

3. In the present table the hypothesis that there is a greater degree of intrafamily understanding and acceptance in the families of the graduates than in the dropouts is significant beyond the .001 level indicating that the observed differences could not have occurred by chance in one out of a thousand times. In testing the hypotheses for statistical significance the Kolmogorov-Smirnov two-sample, one-tailed test was used unless otherwise noted (Sidney Siegel, *Nonparametric Statistics* [New York: McGraw-Hill Book Co., 1956], pp. 127 ff.). Because of the uncertainties and discrepancies

in the "matching" of the dropouts and graduates on IQ and socioeconomic backgrounds the nonparametric test for nonrelated data was used rather than the parametric test for related data. The use by different school administrations of different types of IQ tests and the inability to ascertain accurately many items of background counseled this procedure. The resulting conclusions are, therefore, more conservative than would have resulted from the use of a parametric test of significance.

4. Hypothesis: The dropouts perceive themselves as less understood and accepted by their families than do the graduates. $D = .633$; $X^2(2df) = 120.2$; $p < .001$ (significant beyond the .001 level).

5. $D = .614$; $X^2(2df) = 113.09$; $p < .001$ (significant beyond the .001 level).

6. Robert L. Hamblin, "Group Integration During a Crisis," *Human Relations*, XI (November, 1958), 67–76. Cf. Everett M. Rogers and Hans Sebald, "A Distinction between Familism, Family Integration and Kinship Orientation," *Marriage and Family Living*, XXIV (February, 1962), 25–30.

7. $D = .268$; $X^2(2df) = 23.08$; $p < .001$ (significant beyond the .001 level).

8. Replies to Question 11 have been augmented from the respondent's replies to other questions in the same interview where it is pertinent. The addition from another question is indicated by "...."

9. Broom and Selznick, *op. cit.*, p. 125.

10. Paul F. Lazarsfeld and Robert K. Merton, "Friendship as Social Process: A Substantive and Methodological Analysis," in Morroe Berger, Theodore Abel, and Charles H. Page (eds.), *Freedom and Control in Modern Society* (New York: D. Van Nostrand Co., Inc., 1954), pp. 18–66.

11. Testing the hypothesis that our data will manifest more joint leisure activities in the families of the graduate population than in the families of the dropout population we find: $D = .540$; $X^2(2df) = 87.48$; $p < .001$ (significant beyond the .001 level).

12. Luther A. Jansen, "Measuring Family Solidarity," *American Sociological Review*, XVII, No. 6 (1952), 733.

13. Paul W. Tappan, *Juvenile Delinquency* (New York: McGraw-Hill Book Co., Inc., 1949), p. 134.

Notes for Chapter Two

1. The case of Robert Rawlinson as written up in the records of the Colorado Correctional Institution will be found in Appendix III. We were gratified to find that there was practically no discrepancy between this youth's history as reported in the official files and as reported by himself in this interview.

2. Louis Wirth, "Urbanism as a Way of Life," *American Journal of Sociology*, XLIV (July, 1938), 1–24.

3. Ernest W. Burgess and Harvey J. Locke, *The Family: From Institution to Companionship* (3d ed.; New York: American Book Co., 1963), p. 336.

4. Talcott Parsons and Robert F. Bales, *Family, Socialization and Interaction Process* (New York: The Free Press of Glencoe, 1955), p. 10; also Talcott Parsons, "A Revised Analytical Approach to the Theory of Social Stratification," in Reinhard Bendix and Seymour Lipset (eds.), *Class, Status and Power* (New York: The Free Press of Glencoe, 1953), p. 120. Such a careful scholar as Professor Parsons is well aware that the nuclear family is not completely "isolated"; his emphasis, however, seems to help perpetuate the myth of the quite absolute "isolated" nuclear family.

5. Cf. Marvin B. Sussman and Lee Burchinal, "Parental Aid to Married Children: Implications for Family Functioning," *Marriage and Family Living*, XXIV (November, 1962), 320–32.

6. Enrico L. Quarantelli, "A Note on the Protective Function of the Family in Disasters," *Marriage and Family Living*, XXII (August, 1960), 263–64.

7. Marvin B. Sussman and Lee Burchinal, "Kin Family Network: Unheralded Structure in Current Conceptualizations of Family Functioning," *Marriage and Family Living*, XXII (August, 1962), 231. This article is richly documented.

8. *Ibid.*

9. Phillip Fellin, "A Reappraisal of Changes in American Family Patterns," *Social Casework*, XLV (May, 1964), 263–67.

10. Norman W. Bell and Ezra F. Vogel (eds.), *A Modern Introduction to the Family* (New York: The Free Press of Glencoe, 1960), p. 1.

11. Talcott Parsons and Robert F. Bales, *Family: Socialization and Interaction Process* (New York: The Free Press of Glencoe, 1955); Ernest W. Burgess, Harvey J. Locke, *The Family: From Institution to Companionship* (3d ed.; New York: American Book Company, 1963).

12. Fellin, *loc. cit.*

13. W. Lloyd Warner and Paul S. Lunt, *The Social Life in a Modern Community* (New York: Harper and Brothers, 1941).

14. Scott Greer, "Urbanism Reconsidered," *American Sociological Review*, XXI (February, 1956), 22–25.

15. Reuben Hill, *Families Under Stress* (New York: Harper and Brothers, 1949).

16. Fellin, *loc. cit.;* Phillip Fellin and Eugene Litwak, "Neighborhood Cohesion under Conditions of Mobility," *American Sociological Review*, XXVIII (June, 1963), 364–76.

17. Eugene Litwak, "Geographic Mobility and Extended Family Cohesion," *American Sociological Review*, XXV (June, 1960), 385–94; Eugene Litwak, "Voluntary Associations and Neighborhood Cohesion," *American*

Sociological Review, XXVI (April, 1961), 258–71; Eugene Litwak, "Occupational Mobility and Family Cohesion," *American Sociological Review,* XXV (February, 1960), 9–10; Eugene Litwak, "The Use of Extended Family Groups in the Achievement of Social Goals: Some Policy Implications," *Social Problems,* VII (Winter, 1959–60), 177–87.

18. Paul J. Reiss, "The Extended Kinship System: Correlates of Attitudes on Frequency of Interaction," *Marriage and Family Living,* XXIV (November, 1962), 333–39; Paul J. Reiss, "The Extended Kinship System of the Urban Middle Class" (Unpublished Ph.D. Dissertation, Harvard University, 1959).

19. Marvin B. Sussman, "The Help Pattern in the Middle Class Family," *American Sociological Review,* XVIII (February, 1953), 22–28; Marvin B. Sussman, "The Isolated Nuclear Family: Fact or Fiction?", *Social Problems,* VII (Spring, 1959), 333–40; Marvin B. Sussman and S. B. Slater, "Reappraisal of Urban Kin Networks: Empirical Evidence," a paper presented at the 58th annual meeting of the American Sociological Association, Los Angeles, August, 1963.

20. $X^2 = 127.0$; $p < .001$ (significant beyond the .001 level).

21. Wilhelm Flieger, *Differences in the Degree of Homogeneity between White and Negro Friend Family Circles in the Greater St. Louis Area for the Years 1955–1960* (Unpublished Master's Thesis, St. Louis University, 1961), p. 95.

22. Fellin and Litwak find that "the higher the socioeconomic classification, the more likely the individual was to know neighbors . . . with the business-professional category having more friends than the white collar-manual groups." Phillip Fellin and Eugene Litwak, "Neighborhood Cohesion under Conditions of Mobility," *American Sociological Review,* XXVIII (June, 1963), 366.

23. *The Need for Roots* (Boston: The Beacon Press, 1960), pp. 43 ff.

24. Hypothesis: The dropout family reportedly has a lower concept of friendship than does the graduate family. $D = .318$; $X^2(2df) = 8.46$; $p < .02$ (significant beyond the .02 level).

25. Bell and Boat found that almost nine out of ten of their respondents stated that a relative was numbered among their closest friends (Wendell Bell and Marion D. Boat, "Urban Neighborhoods and Informal Social Relations," *The American Journal of Sociology,* XLII [January, 1957] 396). Various independent studies have found that about 50% of middle class individuals in urban centers saw one or more of their relatives at least once a week.

26. $D = .272$; $X^2(2df) = 20.51$; $p < .001$ (significant beyond the .001 level).

27. William F. Ogburn, "The Changing Functions of the Family," in Robert F. Winch, Robert McGinnis, Herbert R. Barringer (eds.), *Selected*

Studies in Marriage and the Family (Rev. ed.; New York: Holt, Rinehart and Winston, 1962), p. 162.

28. *Successful American Families, op. cit.,* Chapter X.

29. Significant at the .001 level. There was no significant difference on the index of "Same Region of Origin."

30. *Amercan Sociological Review,* XXII (October, 1957), 505–10.

31. Edwin H. Sutherland and Donald R. Cressey, *Principles of Criminology* (New York: J. B. Lippincott Company, 1955), p. 78.

32. Significant beyond the .001 level.

33. In Morroe Berger, Theodore Abel, Charles H. Page (eds.), *Freedom and Control in Modern Society* (New York: D. Van Nostrand Company, Inc., 1954), pp. 18–66.

34. George C. Homans, *The Human Group* (New York: Harcourt Brace and Company, 1950), pp. 120, 135.

35. Zimmerman and Cervantes, *Successful American Families,* p. 101.

36. Talcott Parsons, Robert Bales, and Edward Shils, *Working Papers in the Theory of Action* (New York: The Free Press of Glencoe, 1953), pp. 163–269.

37. Burgess and Locke, *op. cit.,* pp. 3, 545.

38. *Ibid.,* pp. 543–45.

39. Daniel R. Miller and Guy E. Swanson, *The Changing American Parent* (New York: John Wiley and Sons, 1958), p. 201.

Notes for Chapter Three

1. Joseph A. Kahl, *The American Class Structure* (New York: Rinehart and Co., Inc., 1959), pp. 130–31.

2. $X^2 = 19.3$; $p < .001$.

3. $X^2 = 30.3$; $p < .001$.

4. Significant at the .001 level.

5. Significant at the .001 level.

6. Significant beyond the .001 level.

7. August B. Hollingshead, *Elmtown's Youth* (New York: John Wiley and Sons, 1949), chap. xiii "Leaving School," pp. 329–59.

8. Cf. Charles M. Allen, *Combating the Dropout Problem* (Chicago: Science Research Associates, Inc., 1956), pp. 10–11.

9. *School and Early Employment Experience of Youth: A Report on Seven Communities 1952–1957,* United States Department of Labor Bulletin No. 1277 (Washington, D.C.: U.S. Government Printing Office, 1960), p. 3.

10. C. V. Matthews and Peter Bowman, *The Motivations of Youth for Leaving School,* Quincy Youth Development Project, Quincy, Illinois (Washington: Office of Education, United States Department of Health, Education, and Welfare, September, 1960), p. 23.

11. *Ibid.,* p. 29.

12. For the years 1960–61, 56.4% of American public school teachers reported that their fathers were either unskilled, semiskilled, skilled workers, or farmers (*NEA Journal,* April, 1963, p. 49).

13. Eli Ginzberg, "Educational and National Efficiency in the U.S.A.," in A. H. Halsey, Jean Floud, and C. Arnold Anderson (eds.), *Education, Economy, and Society* (New York: The Free Press of Glencoe, 1961), p. 74.

14. Cf. Matthews and Bowman, *op. cit.,* p. 29; also Eli Ginzberg, *Values and Ideals of American Youth* (New York: Columbia University Press, 1961), p. 175.

15. Cf. Dael Wolfle, *America's Resources of Specialized Talent* (New York: Harper and Brothers, 1954), pp. 158, 247, and 251 for particulars of this phenomenon.

16. *Ibid.*

17. *Ibid.*

18. Seymour L. Wolfbein, "Transition from School to Work: A Study of the School Leaver," *The Personnel and Guidance Journal,* XXXVIII, (October, 1959), 102.

19. *School and Early Employment Experience of Youth,* p. 13. Cf. Dael Wolfle, "Educational Opportunity, Measured Intelligence, and Social Background," in Halsey, Floud, and Anderson (eds.), *op. cit.,* pp. 216–40.

20. Glen Stice, "Talent Losses before High School. The Number of Tenth Graders in Various Aptitude and Social Categories Who Leave School before Graduation," Research Memorandum, Educational Testing Service, Princeton, N.J., January, 1960, p. 5. (Mimeographed.)

21. *School and Early Employment Experience of Youth,* p. 5.

22. *Op. cit.,* p. 24.

23. J. K. Coster, "Some Characteristics of High School Pupils from Three Income Levels," *Journal of Educational Psychology,* L (April, 1959), 55–62.

24. Robert J. Thomas, "An Empirical Study of High School Dropouts in Regard to Ten Possibly Related Factors," *Journal of Educational Psychology,* XXVIII (1954), 17.

25. The dropout-graduate differences in degrees of upward mobility in occupational aspirations and the extent of realistic and effective planning toward these occupational aspirations were significant beyond the .001 level.

26. Cf. Llewellyn Gross and Orville Gursslin, "Middle-Class and Lower-Class Beliefs and Values: A Heuristic Model," in Alvin W. Gouldner and Helen P. Gouldner, *Modern Sociology* (New York: Harcourt, Brace and World, 1963), pp. 168–76.

27. "A Revised Analytical Approach to the Theory of Social Stratification," in Reinhard Bendix and Seymour Lipset (eds.), *Class, Status and Power* (New York: The Free Press of Glencoe, 1953), p. 127.

28. Joseph A. Kahl, " 'Common Man' Boys," *Harvard Educational Review*, XXIII (Summer, 1953), reprinted in Halsey, Floud, and Anderson (eds.), *op. cit.*, pp. 348–56.

29. Coster found that nine out of ten lower class youth planned to graduate at least from high school (*loc. cit.*).

30. Talcott Parsons, "The School Class as a Social System: Some of Its Functions in American Society," *Harvard Educational Review*, XXIX (Fall, 1959), 297.

31. Kahl, *Harvard Educational Review*, XXIII (Summer, 1953).

Notes for Chapter Four

1. James S. Coleman, "Athletics in High School," *The Annals of the American Academy of Political and Social Science*, CCCXXXVIII (*Teen-Age Culture;* November, 1961), 33–43 for general summary. This specific quotation from "The Adolescent Subculture and Academic Achievement," *American Journal of Sociology*, LXV (January, 1960), 337.

2. James S. Coleman, The Adolescent Society (New York: Free Press, 1962), p. 3.

3. Arnold W. Green, *Sociology* (New York: McGraw-Hill Book Co., 1960), p. 10.

4. Ernest A. Smith, *American Youth Culture: Group Life in Teen-Age Society* (New York: The Free Press of Glencoe, 1962), p. 218.

5. Talcott Parsons, "Youth in the Context of American Society," in Erik H. Erikson (ed.), *Youth: Change and Challenge* (New York: Basic Books, Inc., 1963), p. 111.

6. Talcott Parsons, "Psychoanalysis and the Social Structure," *Essays in Sociological Theory* (Rev. ed.; New York: The Free Press of Glencoe, 1958), pp. 342–43; published in *Psychoanalytic Quarterly*, July, 1950. Cf. *Essays in Sociological Theory*, p. 189. "[This transition] includes emancipation from solidarity with *all* members of the family of orientation about equally, so that there is relatively little continuity with *any* kinship ties established by birth for anyone."

7. *Annals*, November, 1961, p. viii.

8. A. B. Hollingshead, *Elmtown's Youth* (New York: John Wiley and Sons, 1949), p. 443. Elkin and Westley likewise refer to William H. Whyte's series of articles in *Fortune* (May, June, July, August, 1953) under the title of "The Transients." The series deals with the "communes" of the American mobile lower middle class whose self-contained villages are not a mere housing phenomena but close-knit communities where, Whyte concludes, it is "becoming more and more difficult to tell just when adolescence stops and middle age begins" (July, 1953, p. 84).

9. The authors refer to studies by Davis, Havighurst, Dollard, Warner, Whyte, Kinsey, St. Clair Drake, Cayton, Schneider, Lysgaard, and Spinley.

10. Frederick Elkin and William A. Westley, "The Myth of Adolescent Culture," *American Sociological Review*, XX (December, 1955), 680–84.

11. Kingsley Davis, "The Sociology of Parent-Youth Conflict," *American Sociological Review*, IV (August, 1940), 523–35; Winch, McGinnis, Barringer, *op. cit.*, pp. 342–52.

12. Parsons, *Essays in Sociological Theory*, pp. 342–43; but see his somewhat qualified presentation of the same material in Erikson's *Youth: Change and Challenge*, pp. 93–119.

13. *Op. cit.*

14. *Op. cit.*

15. Kingsley Davis, "Sociology of Parent-Youth Conflict," *American Sociological Review*, IV (August, 1940); and "Adolescence and the Social Structure," *The Annals of the American Academy of Political and Social Science*, November, 1944.

16. Margaret Mead, *And Keep Your Powder Dry* (New York: William Morrow and Co., 1942); "The Contemporary American Family as an Anthropologist Sees It," *American Journal of Sociology*, LIII (May, 1948), 453–59.

17. Ruth Benedict, "Continuities and Discontinuities in Cultural Conditioning," *Psychiatry*, May, 1933.

18. *Op. cit.*

19. Herbert Bloch and Arthur Niederhoffer, *The Gang* (New York: New York Philosophical Library, 1958).

20. Richard L. Simpson, "Parental Influence, Anticipatory Socialization, and Social Mobility," *American Sociological Review*, August, 1962, pp. 517–22.

21. Jessie Bernard, *Annals, loc. cit.* Cf. p. 224 of this study.

22. Robert C. Bealer and Fern K. Willits, "Rural Youth: A Case Study in the Rebelliousness of Adolescents," *ibid.*, 63–69.

23. Frederick Elkin and William A. Westley.

24. A. B. Hollingshead and William H. Whyte.

25. Cf. Zimmerman and Cervantes, *Successful American Families,* *passim.*

26. Elkin and Westley, *loc. cit.*

27. Clay V. Brittain, "Adolescent Choices and Parent-Peer Cross Pressures," *American Sociological Review,* XXVIII (June, 1963), 385.

28. Alfred C. Kinsey, Wardell B. Pomeroy, and Clyde E. Martin, *Sexual Behavior in the Human Male* (Philadelphia: W. B. Saunders Co., 1948), p. 550.

29. *Supra,* pp. 68 ff.

30. Lester A. Kirkendall, *Premarital Intercourse and Interpersonal Relationships* (New York: Julian Press, Inc., 1961); Lee Burchinal, *Family Life Coordinator* (Eugene, Oregon: Oregon Coordinating Council on Social Hygiene and Family Life, September–December, 1960), IX, 1–2.

31. Alfred C. Kinsey, Wardell B. Pomeroy, Clyde E. Martin, and Paul H. Gebhard, *Sexual Behavior in the Human Female* (Philadelphia: W. B. Saunders Co., 1948); *Pregnancy, Birth and Abortion* (New York: Harper and Bros., and P. B. Hoeber, 1958).

32. Cf. Ira L. Reiss, "Sexual Codes in Teen-Age Culture," *Annals,* CCCXXXVIII (November, 1961), 58.

33. Clark E. Vincent, "Illegitimacy in the United States," in Evelyn M. Duvall and Sylvanus M. Duvall, *Sexways in Fact and Faith* (New York: Julian Press, 1961), pp. 115–19. Wolfbein prescinds from the contingency of whether the females are pregnant or nonpregnant; pregnant by "love choice" or "chance encounter" when they drop out. He merely states that his nationwide sample indicates that more than half (56%) marry soon after withdrawal from high school (*The Personnel and Guidance Journal,* XXXVIII [–October, 1959–], 102).

34. August B. Hollingshead, "Dating in Elmtown," in Winch, McGinnis, and Barringer, *op. cit.,* p. 503.

35. Parsons, *Essays in Sociological Theory,* p. 343.

36. Truxal and Merrill, *op. cit.,* p. 130.

37. Robert S. Lynd and Helen M. Lynd, *Middletown in Transition* (New York: Harcourt, Brace and Co., 1937), p. 115.

38. Theodore Reik, *A Psychologist Looks at Love* (New York: Holt, Rinehart and Winston, Inc., 1944), p. 295.

39. *Survey,* LVII (December, 1925), 290–95.

40. "Disillusionment in Marriage and Romanticism," *Marriage and Family Living,* XX (May, 1958), 156–62. Burchinal reports that in a sample of sixty girls who withdrew from high school to marry, fifty-five of them expressed disillusionment after six months and regretted their decision to marry before the completion of high school (*Family Life Coordinator,* IX [September–December, 1960], 1–2). "Stability of teenage marriages:

(1) One study—within five years most of these couples are engaged in adulterous relations. (2) U.S. Census Bureau—rate of divorce of teenage marriages is three times as high as for those married between 21–25 (12.6 per 1,000 vs. 4.8). (3) Another study—3 out of 4 teenage marriages terminate in divorce." *Catholic Family Leader,* II (December, 1962), 2.

Notes for Chapter Five

1. Cf. Robert R. Holt, "The Thematic Apperception Test," in Harold H. Anderson and Gladys L. Anderson, *Projective Techniques* (Englewood Cliffs, N.J.: Prentice-Hall, Inc., 1951), chap. vii, pp. 181–229; also Gardner Lindzey, *Projective Techniques and Cross-Cultural Research* (New York: Appleton-Century-Crofts, Inc., 1961).

2. Henry A. Murray, *Thematic Apperception Test Manual* (Cambridge, Mass.: Harvard University Press, n.d.), p. 1.

3. *High-School Dropouts,* Discussion Pamphlet #3 (Washington, D.C.: National Education Association Research Division and Department of Classroom Teachers, 1959), p. 32. Cf. "High-School Dropouts," *National Educational Association Research Bulletin,* February, 1960, p. 11.

4. Conant, *op. cit.,* p. 26.

5. In one sense this is a footnote of failure. It concerns the low level of statistical significance found in the scoring of the TAT protocols of the dropouts in contradistinction to those of the graduates. Numerous systems of scoring results of the TAT have been elaborated. Murray, Stein, Tomkins, Wyatt, Bellak, Aron, and Lindzey have each developed systems. None of these methods are definitive except in the conclusion that reliability and validity of the TAT is not of the same calibre as other more standardized tests. In this study we were not interested in vertical evaluation of one person's protocols. We were interested in an evaluation that would move horizontally to include the protocols of the total group of dropouts in contrast to those of the graduates'. This horizontal comparison could be done in two ways. One way was to compare responses of the two groups to each card; a second way was to compare responses of the two groups on all cards. We pursued both ways. The first way was less satisfying than the second. Neither way produced high levels of statistical significance though in each case the difference was in the direction hypothesized.

In order to utilize the first method—that of comparisons for individual TAT cards—five point scales on a specific continuum were drawn up for the board of judges. Card 1 (A young boy contemplating a violin) was used to measure adjustment-achievement with the continuum ranging from passivity to aggression. Card 2 (A country scene) was used to measure reaction to unstimulating environment with the continuum ranging from very unresponsive to very responsive. Cards 3BM and 3GF measured optimism-pessimism reactions. Card 4 (A woman clutching the shoulders of a man) measured civilized-uncivilized solutions of interpersonal difficulties ranged on a continuum of "antilegal physical solution" to "verbal composition." Card 5 measured reactions toward a middle-aged female. Card 6BM was used to try to measure the degree of successful oedipal resolution ranged on a continuum from "hateful relations developing" to "resolution without recriminations." Card 7BM was used to measure reactions toward a male authority figure. Card 8BM was used to measure destructive-constructive orientation. Card 9GF measured female-female relations. Card 13MF was used to measure male-female relationships ranged on a continuum from "rape and/or murder without remorse" to "nonviolent family scene." In each case it was hypothesized that the dropouts' responses would be on the lower—or less favorable—end of the continua. Only card 8BM (destructive-constructive orientation) yielded a difference that was statistically significant.

In order to utilize the second method of scoring the TAT protocols— that of comparisons not of individual cards but of impressions derived from an analysis of all responses to all the cards we again draw up five point scales. The eight continua are the following: (1) environmental control; (2) Maslow need hierarchy from physiological to self-actualization; (3) sensate-abstract; (4) unstructured-structured value system; (5) inner- and outer-directed needs; (6) attitude toward females; (7) attitude toward males; (8) conformity-originality. In each case it was again hypothesized that the dropouts' responses would be on the lower—less favorable—end of the continua. Numbers 1, 3, 4, and 5 proved statistically significant at the .05 level; numbers 2 and 8, at the .01 level; numbers 6 and 7, not significant. The TAT proved of greater descriptive than statistical assistance. It afforded insight rather than a height of degrees of statistical significance.

Notes for Chapter Six

1. "Four Chose Chain Gang Over Return to School," *New York Times*, August 2, 1962, p. 43M.

2. *The 1963 Dropout Campaign*, U.S. Department of Health, Education, and Welfare Bulletin No. 26 (Washington, D.C.: U.S. Government Printing Office, 1964), p. 5.

3. *Ibid.*

4. "Helping the Potential Dropout," *PTA*, LVIII (November, 1963), 6.

5. *Business Week*, October 13, 1962, p. 112.

6. Conant, *op. cit.;* also James Meredith, "Negro High School Dropouts" (Unpublished Master's Thesis, University of Detroit, 1964).

7. "Factors Which Contribute to the High 'Holding Power' of the Milwaukee Public Schools," Harold S. Vincent, Superintendent of Schools; Eldon A. Bond, Assistant Superintendent, Division of Special Services, Milwaukee Public Schools, 5225 W. Vlist Street, Milwaukee 8, Wisconsin, March 15, 1963.

8. Schreiber, *loc. cit.,* pp. 4–6.

Name Index

Subject Index